100 THINGS DODGERS FANS SHOULD KNOW & DO BEFORE THEY DIE

100 THINGS DODGERS FANS SHOULD KNOW & DO BEFORE THEY DIE

Jon Weisman

Library of Congress Cataloging-in-Publication Data

Weisman, Jon, 1967–
100 things Dodgers fans should know & do before they die / Jon Weisman.
p. cm.
Includes bibliographical references.
ISBN 978-1-60078-166-7
1. Brooklyn Dodgers (Baseball team)—History—Miscellanea.
2. Los Angeles Dodgers (Baseball team)—History—Miscellanea.
I. Title. II. Title: One hundred things Dodgers fans should know & do before they die.

GV875.B7W45 2009
796.357'64—dc22

2009000209

This book is available in quantity at special discounts for your group or organization. For further information, contact:

Triumph Books
542 South Dearborn Street
Suite 750
Chicago, Illinois 60605
(312) 939-3330
Fax (312) 663-3557

Printed in U.S.A.
ISBN: 978–1–60078–166–7
Design by Patricia Frey
All photos courtesy of AP Images unless otherwise noted.

To Dad, who made my childhood jaw drop when he could quote Walter Johnson's strikeout totals from memory; to Mom, who would cut my morning toast into a ballfield if I asked; to Greg, who has brought joy to Mudville my entire life; and to Robyn, who taught me that if you want to play catch, you have to go after it yourself.

To Dashiell, whose sublime babyhood allowed me to work in peace in the wee hours; to Casey, my happy, happy boy; and to Lilah, my sweet, sweet little girl.

And to Dana, my love, my one and only, who is more special to me than words can say.

Contents

Foreword

Several years ago, I was introduced to the website DodgerThoughts.com and writer Jon Weisman. I was immediately impressed with Jon's passion, commitment, and analysis of the Dodger organization. Now he has been given the most challenging assignment to list *100 Things Dodgers Fans Should Know & Do Before They Die*. Even with his selected 100 key items, I suspect that individual Dodgers fans will keep adding more from personal memories.

However, Jon has captured the disappointment of the 1951 and 1962 pennant races while sharing the excitement of Dodger World Series Championships in 1955, 1959, 1963, 1965, 1981, and 1988. From "the Captain" Pee Wee Reese, to the grace and elegance of center-fielder Duke Snider, to the all-out competitiveness of Jackie Robinson; to the courage and indomitable spirit of Roy Campanella; to dominating pitchers Sandy Koufax and Don Drysdale; to the leadership of managers Walter Alston and Tommy Lasorda; to the consistency of Don Sutton, to the famous infield of Garvey, Lopes, Russell, and Cey, to the sheer drama of Kirk Gibson's 1988 Game 1 World Series home run and Orel Hershiser's Cy Young season, to "Fernandomania," "Nomomania" and beyond, Dodger baseball has fascinated us all. This book will be appreciated by baseball fans of all ages.

So, sit back and "pull up a chair" as our friend and Hall-of-Fame broadcaster Vin Scully would say. Happy reading—"It's time for Dodger baseball!"

—Peter O'Malley
President
Los Angeles Dodgers, 1970–1998

Introduction

In my childhood, there was time for everything. The Dodgers were part of that ensemble cast, one of many pastimes I could devote myself to after (or before, or during) my homework. Given that, in many ways, my childhood lasted past my 30th birthday, this meant years and years of unbridled involvement.

Marriage, children, and, after much resistance, a tumble from the freelance, control-your-own-destiny world into the hopeless ranks of the salaried decimated my free time. No longer could I check "all of the above" for hobbies. I had to pick and choose my interests carefully. Of course, ultimately they pick themselves—the things that are most important to you stay with you. And while much left me, the Dodgers stuck around, deep.

In fact, since 2002, I have been spending more time pondering the Dodgers than ever before. At a time most people had still not heard of the word, I started a blog called *Dodger Thoughts* (www.dodgerthoughts.com), where I would pass along notes and essays about the team and express views the mainstream press didn't. You'd think you'd run out of things to say but, on the contrary, no matter how pressing daily life might be, the Dodgers demanded a daily examination and re-examination in every way—from what happens in the games to what happens in the stands, from the present to the past, from the personnel moves to what to do about all those beach balls. The Dodgers aren't the only epic story around, but they're a pretty great one—with fantastic characters, emotions, and plot twists that are nearly impossible to abandon (even if, since 1988, it turned rather Dostoyevskian.) Whenever I wonder why I'm watching a Dodger game instead of doing, I don't know, any of a million other things like going for a hike or doing something constructive for society, I just find there's just too much here to let go of. Why even have a society if we can't use it to follow the Dodgers?

This book, *100 Things Dodgers Fans Should Know & Do Before They Die*, speaks to this tenuously rational but undeniable pull the Dodgers have.

Now, the risk of a book in this format is that the more of a Dodger fan you are, the less you would need to be told what's important about them, and so instead of being all things to everyone, the book ends up being no things to anyone. And that's bad for sales. The task, then, is to reverse that, to give the diehards something new to chew on, while also showing those casual or even antagonistic about the Dodgers what's worth understanding about them. (Attention, San Francisco bookstore patrons: Know thy enemy!) This book is not a laundry list where you're simply told that Jackie Robinson broke baseball's modern-day color barrier or Kirk Gibson hit a big home run. It's an attempt to go wider and deeper, to rethink or re-experience the familiar, and introduce or remind us of the not-so-familiar so that everyone can benefit, from the Dodger fan with all the time in the world to the one who will only read one baseball book a year. I hope this book fulfills that mission.

If nothing else, hidden in these pages are my favorite, underused, avoid-the-traffic routes to Dodger Stadium. The book might be worth keeping handy just for that!

A Word about Statistics

Throughout *100 Things Dodgers Fans Should Know & Do Before They Die,* traditional baseball statistics will be augmented by more recently developed stats, most often Equivalent Average (EQA) and adjusted on-base percentage plus slugging percentage (OPS+). Here's what they mean and why they're being used.

EQA, created by *Baseball Prospectus*, and OPS+, which you'll find at Baseball-Reference.com, are means to measure offensive performance across different years and ballparks. In particular, 20 homers from a batter hitting in Dodger Stadium in the 1960s is a greater accomplishment than 20 homers from a batter hitting in Dodger Stadium in the 1990s, because it simply was harder to hit the ball out of the park in the prior era.

Taking into account these factors, EQA expresses a batter's offensive value in a number designed to resemble batting average—an average EQA is .260, anything at .300 or above is excellent, anything below .200 is awful. OPS+ is similar, though it doesn't take base running into account. An average OPS+ is 100: Anything higher than 100 is above the league average, and anything lower is below.

So, for example, Wes Parker, who batted .238 with eight homers for the '65 Dodgers, had a .276 EQA and 100 OPS+, while Eric Karros, who seemingly had a better season with the 2002 Dodgers by hitting .271 with 13 homers, actually comes in behind Parker with a .260 EQA and 96 OPS+. (It should also be noted that even when citing traditional stats, *100 Things* will lean toward on-base percentage rather than batting average for a truer snapshot of a player's ability to avoid getting out.)

For pitchers, adjusted earned-run average (ERA+) from Baseball-Reference.com works on a similar principle, recalculating traditional ERAs so that they can be compared across time and space more fairly. One reminder: Higher is better. An ERA+ above 100 means that the pitcher was above-average.

These statistics aren't the be-all and end-all, but they do provide a more accurate means of understanding how different Dodgers performed. For those who haven't seen them before, here's hoping you'll give them a try.

100 THINGS DODGERS FANS SHOULD KNOW & DO BEFORE THEY DIE

1 Jackie

From beginning to end, we root for greatness.

We root for our team to do well. We root for our team to create and leave lasting memories, from a dazzling defensive play in a spring training game to the final World Series-clinching out. With every pitch in a baseball game, we're seeking a connection to something special, a fastball right to our nervous system.

In a world that can bring frustrations on a daily basis, we root as an investment toward bragging rights, which are not as mundane as that expression makes them sound. If our team succeeds, if our guys succeed, that's something we can feel good about today, maybe tomorrow, maybe forever.

The pinnacle of what we can root for is Jackie Robinson.

Robinson is a seminal figure—a great player whose importance transcended his team, transcended his sport, transcended all sports. We don't do myths anymore the way the Greeks did—too much reality confronts us in the modern age. But Robinson's story, born in the 20th century and passed on with emphasis into the 21st, is as legendary as any to come from the sports world.

And Robinson was a Dodger. If you're a Dodgers fan, his fable belongs to you. There's really no greater story in sports to share. For many, particularly in 1947 when he made his major league debut, Robinson was a reason to become a Dodger fan. For those who were born or made Dodgers fans independent of Robinson, he is the reward for years of suffering and the epitome of years of success.

Robinson's story, of course, is only pretty when spied from certain directions, focusing from the angle of what he achieved, and

As the first African-American major league ball player, Jackie Robinson proved time and again his talents and integrity were superhuman both on and off the field. Playing nearly every position on the field over 10 seasons, Jackie Robinson was an indispensable contributor to the Dodgers' six pennants and the franchise's first World Series victory.

what that achievement represented, and the beauty and grace and power he displayed along the way. From the reverse viewpoint, the ugliness of what he endured, symbolizing the most reprehensible vein of a culture, is sickening.

Before Robinson even became a major leaguer, he was the defendant in a court martial over his Rosa Parks-like defiance of orders to sit in the back of an Army bus. His promotion to the Dodgers before the '47 season was predicated on his willingness to walk painstakingly along the high road when all others around him were zooming heedlessly on the low.

Even after he gained relative acceptance, even after he secured his place in the major leagues and the history books, even after he could start to talk back with honesty instead of politeness, racial indignities abounded around him. Robinson's ascendance was a blow against discrimination, but far from the final one. He still played ball in a world more successful at achieving equality on paper than in practice. It's important for us to remember, decades

Robinson's Retirement

One of the great myths in Dodgers history is that Jackie Robinson retired rather than play for the team's nemesis, the New York Giants, after the Dodgers traded him there, seven weeks before his 38th birthday. In fact, as numerous sources such as Arnold Rampersad's *Jackie Robinson: A Biography indicate*, Robinson had already made the decision to retire and take a position as vice president of personnel relations with the small but growing Chock Full O' Nuts food and restaurant chain. This happened on December 10, 1957. But Robinson had a preexisting contract to give *Look* magazine exclusive rights to his retirement story, which meant the public couldn't hear about his news until a January 8, 1958, publication date.

The night he signed his Chocktract, on December 11, Dodger general manager Buzzie Bavasi called Robinson to tell him he had been traded to the Giants. Teammates and the public reacted with shock to the news and rallied to his defense, even though Robinson had no intention of reporting. When the truth finally came out, it was Robinson who caught the brunt of the negative reaction at the time. Over the years, however, the story evolved into the fable that Robinson chose retirement because playing for the Giants was a moral impossibility. Robinson left baseball and the Dodgers nursed grievances over how he was treated. The trade to the Giants wasn't the last straw that drove him out, but rather an event that confirmed that the decision he had already made was well chosen.

later, not to use our affinity for Robinson as cover for society's remaining inadequacies.

Does that mean we can't celebrate him? Hardly. For Dodgers fans, there isn't a greater piece of franchise history to rejoice in—and heaven forbid we confine our veneration of Robinson to what he symbolizes. The guy was a ballplayer. Playing nearly every position on the field over 10 seasons, Robinson had an on-base percentage of .409 and slugging percentage of .474 (132+ OPS, .310 EQA). He was an indispensable contributor to the Dodgers' most glorious days in Brooklyn—six pennants and the franchise's first World Series victory.

It also helps to know that some of Robinson's moments on field were better than others, that he didn't play with an impenetrable aura of invincibility. He rode the bench for no less an event than Game 7 of the 1955 World Series. He was human off the field, and he was human on it.

In the end, Robinson's story might just be the greatest in the game. His highlight reel—from steals of home to knocks against racism—is unmatched. In a world that's all too real, Robinson encompasses everything there is to cheer for. If you're a fan of another team and you hate the Dodgers, unless you have no dignity at all, your hate stops at Robinson's feet. If your love of the Dodgers guides you home, Robinson is your North Star.

Vin

He's an artist. Of course he's an artist. You don't need a book to tell you that the man could broadcast paint drying and turn it into something worthy of Michelangelo; to tell you that his voice is a cozy quilt on a cold morning, a cool breeze on a blistering day; that he's more than someone you listen to, that he's someone you feel.

But saying he's an artist is not meant as a cliché or as a convenient way to sum him up. It's meant to stress that spoken words at a baseball game are themselves an art form and, sure, sometimes they're the equivalent of dogs playing poker, but when Vin Scully strings words together (and he's done so at Dodger games—extemporaneously, mind you—for 25,000 hours or more), they'll carry you away on wings.

If it weren't so satisfying, it could make you weep.

But it's not as if Vinny—and at this point, it's hard to resist referring to him by his first name, so vital and personal is the Dodger fan's relationship with him—sets out to construct pieces for the Smithsonian. His principal goal has always been only to simply tell you what's going on. He'll never miss a pitch. He will make a mistake here and there, and in that respect he's like everyone else on the planet. But he never, ever loses sight of his task.

He is prepared with background on the players and the teams he covers. He has a knack for sifting out what's interesting about the men on the field, and has an infectious enthusiasm for what he discovers. Reflecting his desire not to leave any listeners or viewers in the dark, he'll repeat stories on different nights of the same series, but as long as you know that's part of the deal, there's no issue.

"One of the biggest reasons that I prepare is because I don't want to seem like a horse's fanny, as if I'm talking about something I don't know," Scully said in an interview. "So in a sense you could say I prepare out of fear. That's really what you do. I think I've always done that since grammar school."

That may be equal parts humility and truth. Scully's utter genius, however, is the way he reacts when the moment takes him beyond preparation, the way he offers the lyrical when other broadcasters remain stuck in the trite. He offers *bon mots* covering

Vin Scully and Jerry Doggett broadcast the final game played at aging Ebbets Field in Brooklyn on September 24, 1957. Scully started his career with the Dodgers in 1950 and is currently in his 60th season. Doggett worked alongside Scully from 1956–87. Photo courtesy of www.walteromalley.com.

pedestrian occurrences: Who else could deliver baseball play-by-play's timeless philosophical comment: "Andre Dawson has a bruised knee and is listed as day-to-day.... Aren't we all?" His work during Sandy Koufax's perfect game, Hank Aaron's 715th home run, Bill Buckner's error, and everything in between are all unforced majesty.

As far as rising to the occasion, Scully's landmark call of Kirk Gibson's showstopping, history-making homer in Game 1 of the 1988 World Series was practically its equivalent from a broadcasting perspective, minus the gimpiness. "In a year that has been so improbable, the impossible has happened" ranks with Al Michaels'

"Do you believe in miracles? Yes!" among the most memorable lines in sportscasting history for spontaneously summing up a moment. And yet, could anyone have been less surprised that Scully came up with such a wonderful remark? His broadcasts have been dotted with them ever since he joined the Brooklyn Dodger broadcast team in 1950 as a recent Fordham college graduate who had been singularly dreaming of such a job since boyhood.

"When I was 8 years old, I wrote a composition for the nuns saying I wanted to be a sports announcer," Scully said. "That would mean nothing today—everybody watches TV and radio—but in those days, back in New York the only thing we really had was college football on Saturday afternoons on the radio. Where the boys in grammar school wanted to be policemen and firemen and the girls wanted to be ballet dancers and nurses, here's this kid saying, 'I want to be a sports announcer.' I mean it was really out of the blue.

"The big reason was that I was intoxicated by the roar of the crowd coming out of the radio. And after that one thing led to another, and I eventually got the job as third announcer in Brooklyn. And I never thought about anything except, the first year or two, not making some terrible mistake. I worked alongside two wonderful men in Red Barber and Connie Desmond, but I never thought about becoming great... All I wanted to do was do the game as best I could. And to this day that's all I think about."

Lots of people try to do their best, and for that they all deserve praise. But the best of some is better than the best of others, and even though he can't bring himself to say it, we know into which of those categories Scully fits. Regardless of how intense or carefree one's love for the game might be, Scully measures up to and redoubles it. The Dodgers' play-by-play man is an American Master.

Koufax's Perfect Game: The Final Out, by Vin Scully

Audio of the entire ninth inning—which you really need to hear—can be found online at http://www.triumphbooks.com/100ThingsDodgers

"He is one out away from the promised land, and Harvey Kuenn is comin' up.

"So Harvey Kuenn is batting for Bob Hendley. The time on the scoreboard is 9:44. The date, September the 9th, 1965, and Koufax working on veteran Harvey Kuenn. Sandy into his windup and the pitch: A fastball for a strike! He has struck out, by the way, five consecutive batters, and that's gone unnoticed. Sandy ready, and the strike one pitch: very high, and he lost his hat. He really forced that one. That's only the second time tonight where I have had the feeling that Sandy threw instead of pitched, trying to get that little extra, and that time he tried so hard his hat fell off. He took an extremely long stride to the plate, and Torborg had to go up to get it.

"One and one to Harvey Kuenn. Now he's ready: Fastball, high, ball two. You can't blame a man for pushing just a little bit now. Sandy backs off, mops his forehead, runs his left index finger along his forehead, dries it off on his left pants leg. All the while Kuenn just waiting. Now Sandy looks in. Into his windup and the 2–1 pitch to Kuenn: Swung on and missed, strike two!

"It is 9:46 PM

"Two and two to Harvey Kuenn, one strike away. Sandy into his windup, here's the pitch:

"Swung on and missed, a perfect game!"

After 39 seconds of cheering ...

"On the scoreboard in right field it is 9:46 pm in the City of the Angels, Los Angeles, California. And a crowd of 29,139 just sitting in to see the only pitcher in baseball history to hurl four no-hit, no-run games. He has done it four straight years, and now he caps it: On his fourth no-hitter, he made it a perfect game. And Sandy Koufax, whose name will always remind you of strikeouts, did it with a flourish. He struck out the last six consecutive batters. So when he wrote his name in capital letters in the record books, that "K" stands out even more than the O-U-F-A-X."

3

32

Seventy-two-year-old Sandy Koufax came out to Los Angeles in 2008 to throw the ceremonial Opening Day first pitch, and 56,000 fans had the same thought: Get this guy his uniform. He still looked superhuman.

Hitting against Sandy Koufax was like staring into the sun…with the sun coming at you at around 100 miles per hour. Hitting against him was Armageddon. It was as hopeless an experience as any Dodger opponent would ever face on a regular basis.

Three of the five lowest ERAs for starting pitchers in Dodgers history came from Koufax: 1.88 in 1963, 1.74 in 1964, and 1.73 in 1966 (a 190 ERA+ for the latter, second-highest by a starting pitcher in Dodgers history behind Dazzy Vance's 1928 season). In his career, Koufax struck out 2,396 batters in 2,324⅓ innings. One quarter of the batters he faced in the major leagues whiffed.

This lefty, who could have been sold down the river by a wildness that was either the cause or result of sporadic use in his early years, owned Los Angeles. By the early '60s, Koufax's control improved dramatically. After walking 405 batters in 691⅔ innings through 1960, he walked 412 batters in 1,632⅔ innings for the remainder of his career. So the good news was you knew where to look for the ball, even if you couldn't see it.

For a Dodger fan, Koufax provided a kind of nirvana that, for all the excitement that would follow him, would never be repeated. In 86 career games at Dodger Stadium—715⅓ innings—Koufax allowed 109 earned runs (a 1.37 ERA). Some of that, surely, was a product of the stifling environment that Dodger Stadium offered hitters of that era, but there's little need to adjust the emotional ledger. Koufax was indomitable. He was FDIC-guaranteed.

"The team behind him is the ghostliest-scoring team in history," columnist Jim Murray wrote in the *Los Angeles Times.* "This is a little like making Rembrandt paint on the back of cigar boxes, giving Paderewski a piano with only two octaves, Caruso singing with a high school chorus. With the Babe Ruth Yankees, Sandy Koufax would probably have been the first undefeated pitcher in history."

Following his retirement in 1966, a mystique was added to Koufax's persona as he eventually retreated from public view, and the full weight of what he had endured to succeed crystalized among the Dodger faithful. It's not that it was any secret that Koufax's pitching arm should have been protected from baseball by a restraining order, but while he was still active, the consoling thought was, "Who are we to argue if he can bear it?" After all, that's what men were supposed to do, right? Koufax, the soft-spoken Jew from Brooklyn, was the Marlboro Man and John Wayne when it came to steely bravery on the ballfield.

But with time to reflect on the torture of his left elbow, Koufax became something even greater, something more than just a man. Whatever ego Koufax does have, it's hard to imagine a more selfless and talented performer for this team. If God ever put on a Dodger uniform, he wore No. 32 and threw left-handed.

4 Next Year

Putting the 1955 season near the start of a book misses the point, doesn't it? Nineteen fifty-five was the culmination of an agonizing endurance test. This was the end of "Wait 'Til Next Year," but you readers hardly had to wait at all.

When did the wait begin? Baseball in Brooklyn can be dated back to the mid–19th century. National League play began in the city in 1890. The team won the NL pennant in 1890, 1899, and 1900 (three years before the World Series began). Over the next four decades, Brooklyn finished in first place twice.

That was the long, slow dreariness. The so-close-yet-so-far agony commenced in 1941 when the Dodgers might have written an entire other history if they had gotten one more strike in Game 4. Starting in 1946 and with the coming of Jackie Robinson in 1947, Brooklyn played past the scheduled regular season five times in eight years, falling short again and again and raising a fundamental question of sports—is it better to lose big and early or bitterly at the end?

Brooklyn invested a lot of energy in that question—the city was a regular Petri dish for baseball's psychological torture by the time the '55 season began. And then, it set itself up for its biggest delight or disappointment ever. The team won its first 10 games and 22 of its first 24. A four-game losing streak from May 15–20 was all the vulnerability the Dodgers showed to the National League that year. By early June, Brooklyn's lead in the NL surpassed 10 games and would never dip below that number. The Dodgers clinched the pennant September 8, the earliest date in league history.

Though Robinson was 36 by this time and struggling through the worst season of his major league career, several Dodgers were having tremendous campaigns. Centerfielder Duke Snider slugged .628 with 42 home runs (.332 EQA). Catcher Roy Campanella hit 32 homers (.318 EQA), first baseman Gil Hodges 27 (.297 EQA), and rightfielder Carl Furillo added 26 (.295 EQA). Don Newcombe, who not only cruised to a 20-win season (128 ERA+) but also batted .359 with seven homers, led the pitching staff. Brooklyn topped the NL in runs scored and ERA, and basically had half the season to worry about winning four games in October.

Rest assured, no one in Brooklyn could have thought the Dodgers were a lock to win the Series. They certainly kept an eye on their longtime nemesis, the New York Yankees, and had to have taken a collective deep breath when the Bronx Bombers survived a much closer pennant race—edging out Cleveland after being tied with nine games to go.

In Game 1, before 63,869 at Yankee Stadium, the Yankees fed Brooklyn's anxiety like short-order cooks. The Dodgers scored two in the top of the second; the Yankees answered back with the same. The Dodgers scored one in the third; so did New York. And when the Yankees pushed in front on home runs by Joe Collins off Newcombe—a solo shot in the fourth and a two-run clout in the sixth—they didn't let Brooklyn off the hook. Not even a Robinson steal of home in the eighth could catapult the Dodgers to victory. They lost 6–5.

Game 2 was almost as frustrating and equally as damaging. The Yankees combined four singles, a walk, and a hit-by-pitch with two out in the fourth inning for four runs, and made it stand up for a 4–2 victory. Next year already had folks waiting in line.

When the teams reunited at Ebbets Field for Game 3, an 8–3 victory behind Johnny Podres forestalled the potential indignity of a sweep. But that seemed to be all. The Yankees took a 3–1 lead in the fourth inning of Game 4.

Then, the Dodgers burst to life. Campanella, Furillo, and Hodges went homer-single-homer to kick off the bottom of the fourth and put the Dodgers back in front. In the next inning, Snider blasted a three-run shot. The Dodgers had an 8–5 victory, and the Series was down to a best-of-three.

When Snider hit two more homers the next day to lead Brooklyn to a 5–3 victory, the Dodgers had a 3–2 Series advantage over the Yankees for only the second time in their history. The other time, in 1952, the Dodgers had suffered narrow losses in the final two games. And indeed, Brooklyn would score only three more runs in their final two contests of 1955. In Game 6, the Dodgers weren't even competitive. Karl Spooner was knocked out in a five-run first inning, and Whitey Ford pitched a complete-game four-hitter for a series-tying 5–1 victory.

Game 7, however, attained the unattainable. Here was a generation of Brooklyn history in one contest. Tension, as the game remained scoreless after three innings. Hope, as the Dodgers took the lead on Hodges' RBI in the top of the fourth and his sacrifice fly in top of the sixth.

Then came the bottom of the sixth. The Yankees put two runners on. And then, after Yogi Berra went the other way with a long fly ball, leftfielder Sandy Amoros, who entered the game that inning, ran into the frame of history, his neck tilted back as if trying to spot an airplane, his arm fully outstretched at a perfect line to the ground, his weight back to keep from pushing too far toward the stands. He makes the catch close enough to the foul-line seats for an entire city to exult him, and in a continuous motion, he pivots on that back foot that is bearing the weight of the moment and fires the ball back to shortstop Pee Wee Reese, who relays it to Hodges to double up Gil McDougald.

It's entirely conceivable that history was setting up Brooklyn for the most crushing disappointment possible, but Podres fought back. With two on in the eighth, Podres survived Berra again, getting him to fly to right, before striking out Hank Bauer.

The final inning. Moose Skowron nearly drilled Podres into oblivion, his one-hopper ripping the webbing of Podres' glove before sticking between its fingers. Podres freed the ball and fed Hodges for the first out. Amoros then made an easy play on Bob Cerv's pop fly to left.

The final batter. With a 2–2 count, Elston Howard fouled off five Podres fastballs. "Podres had had enough," wrote Stewart Wolpin in *Bums No More!: The Championship Season of the 1955*

Brooklyn Dodgers. "Campy called for another heater, but Podres shook him off. The tired but stubborn lefty wanted to throw one last changeup."

Howard hit a grounder to short. Could this be it? Reese's throw to first base was wide—would there be another defeat ripped from victory? Hodges, stretching forward and low and to his left, flagged the ball with the tip of his shoe clinging to the bag.

The 1955 season proves it. The harder the journey, the sweeter the arrival. Euphoria.

5 The Sweetheart from '88

"A high fly ball to right field. She is ..."

She is heavenly in our memory, still vivid, still true.

She is sailing from the pitcher's hand toward a man on knotted stilts, all torso and determination and even a little secular prayer, but no legs, none to speak of. His bent front peg trembles, elevating slightly, the rear one already buckling.

She rises so slightly off an invisible cushion of air, then starts to settle, trailing away but not far enough away. The front peg descends under the weight of arms, strong, driving down into the strike zone.

She is inside the circumference of the catcher's mitt, but the bat intercedes. The arms look horribly awkward, the back elbow bent at almost 90 degrees, the front arm cutting down in front to form a triangle. The back leg elevates at the heel as the batter lunges, almost to the point of falling down.

But she meets flush with the bat, ceasing to be a sphere, transforming into a comet. She is launched by a popgun, a

"GONE!" Dodgers pinch-hitter Kirk Gibson rounds the bases in celebration after hitting a game-winning two-run home run in the bottom of the ninth inning to beat the Oakland A's 5–4 in the first game of the World Series at Dodger Stadium October 15, 1988.

croquet swing. The left wrist twists, then the hand loses the bat entirely. The follow-through whimpers like that of a novice tennis player, but it doesn't change anything.

He looks up. His back leg comes down again, spread across home plate from his right. His left arm is cocked like a puncher. His first motion out of the batter's box is of a runner. There's been a mirage. The living, breathing, conquering athlete was in there all along.

She travels at the speed of light. The right fielder breaks back, taking one, two, three…four…five…six steps, slowing down, his mind and hope retreating before his legs even know. A single set of identical red lights, that's all, prominently glowing but orphaned, can be seen under the peak of the pavilion roof, behind the brimming, jammed bleacher seats, not abandoned, not at all. Arms are soaring into the air in exultation.

She is crashing down from the sky; mass times acceleration, a shooting star at mission completion. She is in the crowd, she is in our heads, she is in our astonishment, she is in our incredulous joy, she has broken into our ever-loving, unappeasable souls and exploded.

She is …

"GONE!!!"

It had to be something astonishing, something brain-defying. To paraphrase Vin Scully, quoted above making his preeminent call of Kirk Gibson's pinch-hit, two-run 1988 World Series Game 1-winning home run, it had to be something impossible in a year so improbable.

And in a Series so unbelievable, there was also:

- Mickey Hatcher, a journeyman with 56 hits and one home run all year, bookending the Series with two-run homers in the first innings of Game 1 and Game 5, racing around the bases like the kid we wish all major league players still had inside them.
- Mike Davis, an unadulterated free-agent bust for six months, with 55 hits and two home runs after knocking 419 and 65 the previous three seasons, drawing his second walk since September 3 from none other than Dennis Eckersley, who had walked 13 men the entire year—with two out in the ninth inning of Game 1.

Scioscia's Swat

Did anyone mention Mike Scioscia? If it weren't for the onion-shaped Dodger catcher, Kirk Gibson's remarkable World Series homer never would have happened. Orel Hershiser's scoreless inning streak would have been the postscript to a disappointing year.

The Dodgers were three outs away from losing their third game of the first four in the 1988 NL Championship Series when, after John Shelby walked, Scioscia no-doubted a Dwight Gooden pitch over the right-field wall and tying the game at 4. Scioscia's blast, as much as anything, set up the remarkable string of events that included a home run by Gibson (a 1-for-16 postseason goat up to that point) in the top of the 12th to give the Dodgers a 5–4 lead and Hershiser's emergence from the bullpen after pitching 15⅓ innings in the previous five days—events that would propel the Dodgers back on track to their last World Series title of the 20th century.

Scioscia hit only three regular-season home runs in 1988 and 68 in 1,441 career games. When he came up to face Gooden in the ninth inning at Shea, Scioscia was 7-for-41 with one walk (.190 on-base percentage), one home run, and two doubles lifetime against Gooden. For his part, Gooden had allowed only one hit since the first inning. Scioscia was not hopeless with the bat: three years earlier, he had an on-base percentage of .407. But as stunned as the Oakland A's would be by Kirk Gibson's Game 1 homer six days later, the Mets were almost that floored when Scioscia knocked his out.

- Orel Hershiser, continuing his unprecedented heroics, getting as many hits of his own in Game 2 as he allowed in a 6–0 shutout, then finishing off the A's in Game 5. For his final 124⅔ innings in 1988, from August 19 through the end of the playoffs, Hershiser had an ERA of 0.65.
- An enfeebled Dodger lineup, including a Game 4 crew with 36 combined home runs in 1988, outshining an Oakland squad bursting with strength. For the series, Jose Canseco (.345 EQA in 1988) and Mark McGwire (.309) combine to go 2-for-36 at the plate with five walks.

> Canseco hits a second-inning grand slam in Game 1 that should have closed the door on the Dodgers; McGwire wins Game 3 with a ninth-inning homer that should have reopened it for the A's. Nothing else.

Gibson is done after his Mt. Olympus moment; Hatcher steps in. Mike Marshall goes down with an injury; Davis steps in. John Tudor's elbow gives way; Tim Leary steps in. Mike Scioscia wrenches his knee after a busted hit-and-run; Rick Dempsey steps in. No matter how hard the wind blew or the ground shook, the pennant never touched the ground.

Baseball is not a sport that embraces upsets. Baseball likes to see the best team win. In the age of the wild card, there's an undercurrent of dissatisfaction when a lesser team takes advantage of a short series to defeat a greater team. Postseason baseball doesn't light a candle for Cinderella; it nods to her politely, almost grudgingly, and moves on.

Except for a team like the '88 Dodgers. When a team wins with such drama and such style, when a team wins with eternal moments, that team can't be left unacknowledged; they are embraced.

The 1988 World Series title for the Dodgers is one of the greatest in baseball history.

6 '47, Heaven and Hell on Earth

You're a fan, and you're on the edge of your seat at the ballpark.

Someone's about to shout something filthy, absolutely vile. You're straight-backed rigid because you know it's coming. Or because it's already come, hitting you like burning pricks of spit. Or because you're the bullheaded angry man himself, incensed at the black man running inside the white lines of Major League Baseball.

It's April. It's the Dodgers, it's Brooklyn, and there's no mystique here. It's 1947, the century almost halfway over, and they've got all of four NL pennants to show for it. They had tied for the flag the year before, only to get swept by the Cards in baseball's first league playoff. Now, they're victims of cards again—a bad hand to be sure. Manager Leo Durocher has been shoved off for a year, suspended on account of being on the good side of some gamblers, the bad side of some baseball brass or some combination therein.

But they're up to something now. Insolent are these Dodgers with their Jackie Robinson. And some of you, maybe most of you, fell in love with them for that insolence. But it wasn't safe love, it was Romeo and Juliet love—love that causes blood to spill; love with arrows flying from the stands and on the field; love that induced joy or even serenity but also hate and hardly a moment's relaxation.

It's April. It's May. Robinson and the Dodgers are setting the world on fire in one sense, but not on the scoreboard, where they're flickering in and out. In first place one week, in fourth place the next. It's the end of June, and still it's a jumble; Brooklyn and the Boston Braves tied for first, but four other teams within six games of the leaders.

But time is on the Dodgers' side. Robinson isn't being defeated. Spikes still fly at his legs, barbs everywhere. He hasn't won everyone over. But he's winning. He can start to breathe at the ballpark. So can you. The fear is abating. If you're angry, your anger is becoming more patently pointless.

From the inferno, a baseball season is emerging. Thirteen wins in a row, and suddenly with a 10-game lead heading into August, the Dodgers take control. Except, wait—nope, they haven't. Eight losses in 11 games later, the lead's down to 3½. But never lower, and on September 22, the Dodgers clinch the pennant. Robinson plays 151 games, has a .383 on-base percentage, 48 extra-base hits, and 29 stolen bases to win the first Rookie of the Year award.

You're a fan, and the Dodgers are going to the World Series. And that's all that matters now.

In the Bronx, the Yankees get a five-run fifth in Game 1 and a four-run seventh in Game 2 to take the Series lead. Back in Brooklyn, the Dodgers score six in the second inning of Game 3 and hang on for a 9–8 win.

And then, Game 4. Game 4.

Harry Taylor walks the Yanks' Joe DiMaggio with the bases loaded in the first inning for a run. Hal Gregg relieves and pitches admirably for seven innings, allowing only a run in the fourth. The Dodgers scratch for a run in the bottom of the fifth without the aid of a hit, a Pee Wee Reese grounder scoring Spider Jorgensen, who had walked.

Walks. Bill Bevens of the Yankees had a whole different idea for infusing an entire ballpark with tension. One out, bottom of the ninth inning, Yankees lead the game 2–1, and Bevens has walked eight batters while retiring the other 25.

It doesn't stop. Carl Furillo walks. Jorgensen fouls out. After pinch-runner Al Gionfriddo steals second, pinch-hitter Pete Reiser, standing at the plate with an ankle swollen twice as thick as his bat, is walked intentionally. He's the winning run of the game—you don't do that. Then again, how's he gonna score? Bevens has walked 10—a World Series record—but he won't walk three more. And somehow, God knows why, the man who stepped into Durocher's spats, Burt Shotton, has decided to remove Eddie Stanky and replace him with Cookie Lavagetto, who had 18 hits in his final major league season. Lavagetto thought Shotton wanted him to pinch-run. "He had to tell me twice that he wanted me to go up and hit," Lavagetto said in all sincerity, according to Glenn Stout in *The Dodgers*.

But Eddie Miksis went out to be Reiser's legs. Lavagetto was really batting. Bevens, who had struck out five, got ahead in the count with Lavagetto whiffing at the first pitch. On the second, Lavagetto sliced one toward right field, diving, landing...fair! Gionfriddo scores! Miksis...SCORES!

You're a fan, and—Holy Mother of Mercy!—you're beside yourself. It's incredible!

"This was then, and still is to this day, the biggest explosion of noise in the history of Brooklyn," Red Barber would later recall in his appropriately titled book, *1947—When All Hell Broke Loose in Baseball*. "The Dodgers started pounding Lavagetto, then picked him up, and carried him off. I recall I said, 'The Dodgers are beating Lavagetto to death.' They almost did."

Momentum took a holiday in this Series. The Yanks eked out a 2–1 victory in a taut Game 5, then rallied from a 4–0 deficit to take the lead in a potential season-ending Game 6, only to drop an 8–6 decision. The 1947 season was down to the final nine innings.

The Dodgers struck with two runs in the top of the second inning, but their exhausted pitching staff couldn't hold back New York. An RBI single by Tommy Henrich in the bottom of the fourth put the Yankees up to stay. Joe Page entered in relief and faced the minimum 15 batters over the final five innings, preserving a 5–2 victory for the World Champion Yankees.

You're a fan, and you've never been so exhausted in your life. Maybe you've never been so crushed. Yet you've never had so much to look forward to. It's going to be some kind of roller coaster, but Jackie Robinson and the Dodgers are here to stay.

7 Fernandomania

The word "Fernandomania" first appeared in the *Los Angeles Times* as the headline of a Scott Ostler column on April 27, 1981. "The morning after Fernando Valenzuela's most recent shutout," Ostler began, "sports announcer Jaime Jarrin arrived at the studios of radio station KTNQ and saw the phone switchboard lit up like a Mexican Christmas tree. 'I've been doing Dodger games for [23] years and I've never seen this kind of reaction to a ballplayer,' said Jarrin."

Fernandomania was a multicultural phenomenon. *Time* and *Newsweek* began planning cover stories on Valenzuela by May. That month, 59 percent of TV viewers in Los Angeles watched a broadcast of a Valenzuela start in Montreal. KABC radio deejays Ken & Bob campaigned to rename the San Fernando Valley "The San Fernando Valenzuela," wrote Howard Rosenberg in the *Times.*

At the heart of all this—it can too easily be forgotten—was an athlete. Valenzuela was impossibly youthful, charismatic with a winking innocence, and tubbier than life. For a heady period in the 1980s, he mesmerized a sport, drew attention to his culture, and charmed an entire city. He was absolutely a phenomenon. But he was a phenomenon rooted in an all-around athletic ability that, despite the unlikely package it came in, doesn't get enough credit.

Those who saw him game after game remember. They remember, among other things, his batting prowess—upon arrival, the greatest hitting Dodger pitcher since Don Drysdale. They remember him being one of the most agile, astute fielders ever on the mound, with brilliant reflexes and the precise knowledge of what to do in a rundown. "If Valenzuela had been 100 years old and in the

When a 20-year old pitcher from a small, Mexican farm pitched a shutout to Houston on Opening Day in 1981, the city and the media fell in love with the youthful and jovial powerhouse. Fernandomania was born.

majors for 90 of them, he couldn't have looked more in control," wrote Mark Heisler of the *Times* in describing Valenzuela's reaction to a hard comebacker on Opening Day 1981.

Above all, of course, was his pitching, propelled by his remarkable ability to learn the screwball from Dodger teammate Bobby Castillo. "Pitchers have taken years to learn it," Heisler wrote, "and others couldn't learn it at all." Valenzuela picked it up in a week.

This preternatural talent set the stage for Fernandomania to take off. Because what Los Angeles and the baseball world fundamentally responded to was this amazing man's ability to put zeroes on the scoreboard. Fanning the flames were his mythic backstory (growing up beyond poor with 11 older siblings on a Navojoa, Mexico farm), the constant skepticism about his November 1, 1960, birthdate, and

Pure Joy Amid a Hopeless Cause

You can't find a moment fitting the above description that surpasses Pedro Astacio's July 3, 1992 major league debut. Called up to pitch the second game of a doubleheader—one of four twin bills (thanks to the riots that ripped through the city two months earlier), the Dodgers had to play in a six-day stretch during their desultory 99-loss season—Astacio had struck out 10 batters while shutting out the Phillies for 8⅔ innings when he faced Mariano Duncan. As Duncan's fly ball to right field headed for and settled into Mitch Webster's glove, Astacio jumped up and down like his team was winning the World Series.

Was it in bad taste for him to celebrate? Hardly. Astacio reminded us that we can never become too jaded. There's never a day in baseball when there can't be magic.

the fascination with his pudgy build and habit of looking up at the sky while in his pitching motion. But the kindling was his ability.

The prelude came in 1980, when the Dodgers called up Valenzuela before his 20th birthday for the September stretch run in the wake of his scoreless inning streak of 35 innings in AA ball. Valenzuela pitched 17⅔ more innings without allowing an earned run. "Teen-Age Beer-Drinker Is Now Dodger Stopper," headlined the *Times*. That positioned Valenzuela to join the Dodger starting rotation in 1981—he was to battle Rick Sutcliffe for the No. 5 spot. But, as if choreographed by fate, with Burt Hooton already dealing with an ingrown toenail, Bob Welch a right elbow bone spur, and Dave Goltz a groin pull, scheduled starter Jerry Reuss strained a calf muscle the afternoon before Opening Day. It would be up to the boy who spoke no English, the boy who had thrown batting practice hours before, to start the Dodger season.

When Valenzuela then shut out Houston 2–0 before 50,511 in attendance at Dodger Stadium, Fernandomania was launched.

The scoreless inning streaks of Don Drysdale and Orel Hershiser have received due attention, but one wonders if they actually compare to what Valenzuela accomplished given his level of experience: pitching nine innings in each of his first eight starts, he allowed four earned runs, chalking up five shutouts and an 8–0 record. In the first 89⅔ innings of his major league career, Valenzuela allowed 51 hits, walked 22, and struck out 84. His ERA was 0.40.

A 4–0 loss to the Phillies ended the increasingly legitimate dreams of an undefeated season for Valenzuela, at which point he settled into simply having a very good season, one that would win him the National League Rookie of the Year and Cy Young awards. Valenzuela then passed several postseason tests. He held Houston to two runs over 17 innings in the first round of the playoffs, recovered from an NLCS Game 2 loss to pitch 8⅔ innings of one-run ball in the clinching Game 5, and in his final start of the year, survived when he had nothing, hanging on to defeat the Yankees 4–3 in a 147-pitch complete game in which he allowed 16 base runners.

It was Valenzuela's propensity for complete games that might have sidetracked what could have been his path to the Hall of Fame. In his first seven full seasons, Valenzuela averaged 14 complete games and 255 innings. That's a tortuous workload for someone throwing a pitch like the screwball, which comes with a horror movie–like reverse twist of the arm. For a player of Valenzuela's age, it put him on the fast track for arm trouble.

Nevertheless, the highlights continued. He began the 1985 season by allowing one earned run in his first five starts and 42 innings and having a 2–3 record to show for it. Later that year, he had a memorable showdown with Dwight Gooden and pitched 11 shutout innings. In the 1986 All-Star game, Valenzuela struck out five consecutive American Leaguers. In 1990, reduced to a back-end member of the Dodger rotation, Valenzuela made history by joining former teammate Dave Stewart of Oakland to become the first combo of pitchers to throw no-hitters in two different games on the same day, prompting Vin Scully to utter another of his most memorable lines: "If you have a sombrero, throw it to the sky."

Fernandomania came to a bitter end in Los Angeles when Valenzuela was released before the end of spring training in 1991. But what figured to be an unpleasant end denouement to his career instead was transformed into a fitting epilogue. Valenzuela would periodically find the magic again—a 3.00 ERA (143 ERA+) in 32 games with Baltimore in 1993, and a 3.62 ERA (111 ERA+) in 33 games with San Diego in 1996. Valenzuela wrapped up his career with 2,074 strikeouts and a 3.54 ERA (104 ERA+) in 2,930 innings, along with a .200 career batting average and 10 home runs. Well into his 40s, well after one wouldn't have thought it possible, Valenzuela added to his mystique. After he made peace with the Dodgers and quietly assumed a role as a Spanish-language game commentator for them, Valenzuela returned to his roots, mesmerizing hitters in the Mexican League. And it made sense. Wherever Fernando Valenzuela has gone, the crowds have always been transfixed.

8 1951

Why is it Ralph Branca's fault?

Did Branca spit in the face of caution like Dodgers manager Charlie Dressen, who had famously told the world, "The Giants is dead," after the Dodgers had built a 13-game lead over second-place

New York on August 11 of the 1951 NL pennant race? Did Branca cause the Giants to go on an astonishing 38–8 run, winning 83 percent of their games from August 12 through the end of the season? Did Branca compel Giants reserves Sal Yvars and Hank Schenz to lead an elaborate system of stealing signs that has been determined to have helped the Polo Grounds' home team get any number of hits? Did Branca, who pitched 204 innings with a 3.26 ERA (120 ERA+) do more harm than good for the cause?

No.

It wasn't Branca's fault, after all, that the Dodgers pitching was bone-dry by the end of the season, with Dressen using Branca, Don Newcombe, Preacher Roe, and Carl Erskine for 65 percent of the team's 1,423 innings. One day after pitching 1⅓ innings in relief as the Dodgers rallied from a 6–1 deficit to a 9–8, 14-inning, season-extending victory—a game that required Jackie Robinson to spear a bases-loaded line drive in the 12th inning to preserve the tie and then homer in the 14th to win it—Branca was chosen to start the first game of the three-game playoff with the Giants. Branca pitched eight innings and allowed three runs, but the Dodger offense mustered only one off Jim Hearn and lost.

The next day, Clem Labine got 10 runs of support on a day he didn't need it, shutting out New York to bring the NL pennant to the final game. Despite pitching 23⅔ innings in the previous week including 14⅔ in the final two games before the playoff, Newcombe got the start and went 8⅓ more. And when he needed relief after allowing three hits and a run in the ninth, it wasn't a member of the Dodgers bullpen that got the call. It was, once more into the breach, Branca.

Branca would face Bobby Thomson. Thomson was the hero of Game 1, hitting a two-run homer off Branca in the fourth inning to give New York the lead. Thomson was also, potentially, a goat of

Game 3. He inadvertently ran into an out on the base paths in the second inning. With the Giants trailing 2–1 in the eighth inning, the third baseman couldn't handle shots by Andy Pafko and Billy Cox that doubled the Dodger run total.

In recent years, a predominant question has been whether Thomson got a stolen sign for Branca's pitch. Thomson has denied it. For that matter, research by baseball historian Dave Smith has questioned the value of the entire sign-stealing enterprise because the team's overall offensive performance at the Polo Grounds declined after the scheme reportedly began. Branca did come to believe that Thomson had a hint of what was coming.

In the end, did Branca throw a fastball that caught too much of the strike zone, a fastball that Thomson surrounded with his bat like a boy bear-hugging his old man? It was the pitch that gave the Giants a 5–4 victory and the NL pennant, and the Dodgers the most infamous defeat in baseball history. Yes. But in a season that probably saw the Dodgers throw about 20,000 pitches, should the fella whose principal crime was simply throwing the last one be forgiven? No doubt about it.

9 Ebbets Field: The Center Cannot Hold

"Ebbets Field was simultaneously the best ballpark in the world and the worst ballfield for the long-term future of baseball in Brooklyn." Glenn Stout's Dickensian declaration in *The Dodgers* sums up how the replacement of Washington Park with a brand new ballfield on April 9, 1913, helped foster the diehard Brooklyn fan base while setting the stage for its abandonment.

Hilda Chester

She started by bringing a frying pan to the Ebbets Field bleachers and banging it with a ladle, then graduated to shaking a cowbell. She was the loudest, most raucous fan in Dodgers history—even though two heart attacks forced her to abandon her ceaseless razzing of Brooklyn's rivals. Like no one else, Hilda Chester brought on the noise.

"During the games," wrote Peter Golenbock in *Bums: An Oral History of the Brooklyn Dodgers*, "Hilda lived in the bleacher seats with her bell. [Leo] Durocher had given her a lifetime pass to the grandstand, but she preferred sitting in the bleachers with her entourage of fellow rowdies. With her fish peddler voice, she'd say, 'You know me. Hilda wit da bell. Ain't it trillin'? Home wuz never like dis, mac.'"

Like Dodger Stadium, Ebbets Field was more than some seats and a baseball diamond; it had character born of its construction that its fabled residents would later enhance. Ceaselessly visionary, team owner Charles Ebbets wanted a work of art for his team to play in and, in several ways, he succeeded. A rotunda, resplendent with Italian marble, glazed brick, and a grand chandelier (constructed with 12 arms in the shape of baseball bats supporting 12 globes resembling baseballs) greeted visitors. Roman columns and arches provided the support for the grandstand. Ebbets Field felt special from the outset.

But it was such an accomplishment for Ebbets to buy the parcels that would form the ballpark's 4½ acre base (an area that until that point had been a veritable slum popularly known as Pigtown) that he was in denial about how quickly his park would fight against itself, like a baseball bursting from the inside out. The ballpark could not contain the energy it attracted and redoubled. "From the moment ground was first broken, Ebbets Field was an anachronism, one that in each ensuing season would prove to be less and less adequate," Stout wrote. "That is not to say it was not a wonderful place to watch a baseball game—it was that and more,

The entry into Ebbets Field, the vision of Charles Ebbets in 1912, was a large rotunda featuring a marble floor that reads "Ebbets Field" around a large baseball and signature chandelier, made of baseball bats and globes painted with stitching to resemble baseballs. Ebbets Field opened April 9, 1913.
Photo courtesy of www.walteromalley.com.

a glorious Globe Theater of a place where the mob felt like part of the game, for its cozy dimensions, and double-decked grandstand put fans almost on the field."

In fact, Ebbets Field became a character in its own plays. Extending the second deck around the entire stadium—which was almost all that could be done to increase capacity—had a catalytic effect on the action within. The dimensions of the playing field shrunk and the slants of the walls, always a physical manifestation of a geometrist's fiendish mind, multiplied. By one count on Ballparks.com, the right-field wall and post-1930 scoreboard offered nearly 300 different angles.

Spiritually, the evolution of Ebbets Field fell in step with the evolution of the Brooklyn baseball franchise, which featured characters like Casey Stengel and Babe Herman along with classic heroes like Zack Wheat and ultimately, the Boys of Summer. There could be no greater emblem for the ballpark than Hilda Chester, a Brooklyn fan with a booming voice and head-ringing cowbell, who wanted nothing more than victory. By the end, Ebbets Field was an acquired taste for some, an annoyance for others.

"There was no escaping the person in the next seat, or the drunk a few rows down," Brooklyn-born Michael Shapiro wrote in *The Last Good Season.* "The fans' close proximity to the field, which made it possible to talk with outfielders during a pitching change and to hear voices from everywhere in the park, felt as confining as life in a brownstone with neighbors who asked too many questions. Ebbets Field was a row house street, a railroad flat, a kitchen window looking out onto a red brick wall. It was not the way people wanted to live anymore."

Ebbets Field was built not to last, and you'd have to have blinders not to recognize that some sort of transition needed to be made. Compared to Brooklyn's fading edifice, Wrigley Field and Fenway Park were modern mansions. Ebbets Field was a ticking clock. On September 24, 1957, the Dodgers played their final game there before 6,702 in attendance. In fewer than three years, the ballpark was demolished. While Chavez Ravine in Los Angeles was being transformed from a former residential area into a ballpark, Brooklyn's ballpark was reborn as a 1,300-unit apartment complex, Ebbets Field Apartments.

10 The Move

The real history of the Dodgers' move from Brooklyn to Los Angeles is much more nuanced than most people realize, as the following timeline only begins to indicate.

The Dodgers made a huge splash upon their arrival to Los Angeles on October 23, 1957, just 15 days after the announcement that they'd leave Brooklyn and head west. Despite a two-hour delay, an enthusiastic crowd anxiously waited for their new professional baseball team. Photo courtesy of www.walteromalley.com. All rights reserved.

Back in 1946, with Ebbets Field clearly aging, Dodger vice president Walter O'Malley began soliciting ideas for enlarging or replacing the ballpark. Five years of research and investigation passed before, in 1951—a year after gaining majority ownership of the Dodgers—O'Malley asked to have the city help assemble land for him to purchase in Brooklyn for the building of a privately financed stadium with parking.

O'Malley directed his request to New York parks commissioner Robert Moses, the biggest hurdle to the Dodgers' continued residence in Brooklyn. In an August 1955 letter to O'Malley, Moses explained the rationale for his opposition, saying that it was not in the public interest to aid the Dodgers in this quest.

"I can only repeat what we have told you verbally and in writing, namely, that a new ball field for the Dodgers cannot be dressed up as a 'Title I' project," Moses wrote. "If the Board of Estimate on the advice of the Borough President of Brooklyn wants to put through a reasonable sensible plan for highway, railroad terminal, traffic, street, market, and relative conventional public improvements, and incidentally, wants to provide a new Dodgers Field at Flatbush and Atlantic, you can be sure that my boys will fully respect the wishes of the Board and do everything possible to help."

Flatbush and Atlantic was the location of the deteriorating Fort Greene meat market but also a subway and Long Island Railroad nexus with room for considerable parking as well. It stood as the preferred site among approximately a dozen locations in Brooklyn that were explored for accommodating a new stadium. "Our present attendance studies show the need for greater parking," O'Malley said in a press release that announced the Dodgers would begin scheduling select regular season games in New Jersey's Roosevelt Stadium in preparation for the inevitable transition out of Ebbets Field. "The public used to come to Ebbets Field by trolley cars, now they come by automobile. We can only park 700 cars. Our fans require a modern stadium—one with greater comforts, short walks, no posts, absolute protection from inclement weather, convenient rest rooms, and a self-selection first-come, first-served method of buying tickets."

O'Malley argued that these weren't luxuries, but necessities. "Baseball, with its heavy night schedule, is now competing with many attractions for the consumer's dollar and it had better spend some money if it expects to hold its fans," he said, "Racing has found a way to get State legislation and financing for a super-colossal proposed race track. I shudder to think of this future competition if we do not produce something modern for our fans. We will consider other locations only if we are finally unsuccessful in our ambition to build in Brooklyn."

In the coming months, the Dodgers won their first World Series, and O'Malley got his first look at a model of a domed stadium that, if given the space, would address the needs of baseball in Brooklyn. In April 1956, with the support of New York mayor Robert Wagner and 100 civic leaders, Governor Averell Harriman raised hopes for a Brooklyn solution by signing into law the creation of the Brooklyn Sports Center Authority "for the purpose of constructing and operating a sports center in the Borough of Brooklyn at a suitable location."

But the momentum soon fizzled.

Three years earlier, Roz Wyman, running in part on a campaign to bring baseball to Los Angeles, became the youngest person ever elected to the L.A. City Council. The following year, the council wrote to Major League Baseball's owners asking them to consider moving a team there. None of this had the slightest significance until dreams of a new Brooklyn ballpark began to fade before the year was out. A decade after O'Malley had begun trying to address the demise of Ebbets Field, a cross-country move emerged as an option. Almost as if to give the Dodgers a little push, Moses recommended that the city of Brooklyn excise the proposed stadium from the redevelopment of downtown Brooklyn.

Moses did have an idea for keeping the Dodgers in New York, however, and proposed to throw support to a 50,000-seat stadium in Flushing Meadows, the geographic center of Queens. O'Malley visited the site and said afterward it had "possibilities."

"To me it has a chance, [but] there are obviously some deterrents," he wrote in another internal document. "Rapid transit facilities are minimum.... Grand Central Parkway is already bumper to bumper but the future might mean widening. The site would be more acceptable to Westchester and Queens people than to Brooklynites. There is no well-defined network of buses serving the area. We might get by on the parking but it would be minimum with little likelihood of being expanded to maximum requirements."

Also discouraging was the fact that the site was on swampland that, according to Emil Praeger, past designer of Holman Stadium in Vero Beach and future designer of Dodger Stadium, would make securing the proposed ballpark's foundation a challenge.

Meanwhile, numerous other cities, from Oakland to Dallas, soon began making inquiries regarding the Dodgers. The ensuing issue, which remains open to debate, is this: Should O'Malley have

On October 28, 1957, the Dodgers attended a civic luncheon welcoming them to their new home, Los Angeles. Dodgers owner Walter O'Malley (center) is joined with Rosalind Wyman, the L.A. City Councilmember most responsible for encouraging the Dodgers to relocate, and Los Angeles mayor Norris Poulson. Standing behind them are Dodgers manager Walter Alston (left), former Dodgers player and manager Casey Stengel (middle) and an unidentified man (right). Photo courtesy of www.walteromalley.com.

shown favoritism to a site that was in New York but not in Brooklyn? He chose not to. "If the Dodgers would have to go out of Brooklyn any site would have to be weighed against such available locations such as Los Angeles," he wrote in an April 1957 internal memo. "In other words, the Brooklyn Dodgers would not be Brooklyn anywhere else."

Within a month, O'Malley was the terrified single passenger in an open-door helicopter above Los Angeles, examining potential sites for a ballpark. He saw from overhead the Chavez Ravine site that was among those he had been told about for years, a site offering ample room to build and access to the freeways converging to nearby downtown. As O'Malley's interest in Los Angeles grew, the New York Giants were also closing in on a West Coast move to San Francisco. By the time the Giants made their formal announcement in August, further research had convinced O'Malley that Los Angeles was superior to Queens.

To the end, O'Malley still favored staying in Brooklyn over any kind of move out of town, but Moses would not pull the strings to make the Flatbush and Atlantic site available. On October 7, 1957, the L.A. City Council officially approved the contract agreed to on its behalf by lead negotiator Chad McClellan, and the following day, citing the aging Ebbets Field, insufficient parking, dwindling attendance, and a 5 percent New York City admissions tax, O'Malley announced the Dodgers' intention to move.

If it's true that O'Malley sought a stadium outcome that would be best for his franchise and its financial well-being, it's also true that Moses stood firmly in the way of what the people of Brooklyn professed to desire. O'Malley never wavered from his willingness to pay for the land in Brooklyn and the stadium that he would erect upon it, if only the site would be made available for purchase. Though it was ultimately O'Malley's decision for the Dodgers to leave the City of Churches, Moses and other officials gave them little reason to stay.

11 Chavez Ravine

"Back in the 1880s," wrote baseball historian Bob Timmermann, a senior librarian at the Los Angeles Central Library, "a Los Angeles County Supervisor named Julian Chavez owned a hilly tract of land north of downtown, and it eventually took his name and became known as Chavez Ravine after the most prominent geographic feature. The area became home to a number of Mexican-American families over time, and was also called Palo Verde, Bishop, and La Loma. Chris-Pin Martin, who appeared as a character actor in numerous films—mostly Westerns including the Cisco Kid series—was its most notable resident. But for the most part, it was not a part of the city that most people even knew existed or how to get to."

A child of that area born in those 19th-century days would still have had all those memories in 1949, when a federal housing act offered money to cities for public housing. Los Angeles approved a 10,000-unit project, a huge chunk of which would encroach upon Chavez Ravine's 300 acres. Sounds like a plan, except for the not-so-minor issue of the existing 300 households (as counted by the *New York Times*). To facilitate the transformation of the area, Los Angeles accompanied its demand for the residents to sell their homes with a promise that they would have the first opportunity to live in the new project designed by architect Richard Neutra and featuring new playgrounds and schools.

As you can imagine, some agreed to the terms, others held out for better offers, and still others dug in their heels and prepared for a battle. These were their homes, after all, and in many cases more valuable to them than the compensation they were getting. What happened next forms the wound upon which Dodger Stadium rests.

Of those people in Los Angeles who had the city's political and economic ear, few fretted over the fate of the Chavez Ravine population. But things changed when the Los Angeles real estate business, hardly thrilled that valuable property was being transacted at rates well below market, exploited a timely political and public relations problem for the housing project and its assistant housing director, Frank Wilkinson.

"We had tremendous support for the program," Wilkinson said years later in the PBS documentary, *Chavez Ravine: A Los Angeles Story*. "We were pretty well finished. And the only people opposing were what is commonly called the real estate lobby, which was headed up by the department of house owners association and other people like that. They called [the public housing project] creeping socialism. They were trying to discredit us every way they could. They had petitions, they had initiatives to try to kill the program. We should have been more suspicious than we were.

"As I remember, [the piece of property discussed at the hearing] was a very large site. It was vacant land, but the owner of that property was a prominent person in downtown L.A., and he demanded, I think, a hundred thousand dollars, and we were fighting with them over value. He wanted as much as he could get, when out of nowhere this lawyer for the property owner turned to me and said, 'Now, Mr. Wilkinson, I want to ask you what organizations, political or otherwise, did you belong to since 1931?'"

When Wilkinson exercised his right not to answer the question, the Chavez Ravine housing project became wrapped up in the Red Scare.

"After a City Council hearing, in which Mayor Fletcher Bowron punched a man in the audience who had called him a 'servant of Stalin,' Mr. Wilkinson was questioned by the California Anti-Subversive Committee," wrote Rick Lyman of the *New York Times* in Wilkinson's 2006 obituary. Still resisting, Wilkinson was fired.

"I'm out," Wilkinson recalled. "Destroyed. Really destroyed. 'Neutralized,' they, the FBI, listed it. They successfully neutralized me. Crews of television people walked in, arrived to take pictures of the whole scene. Mayor Bowron [who wanted to preserve the project] was removed—he would have been a shoo-in in 1953. After this was reported in the press, the *Times* and other papers crusaded against the mayor."

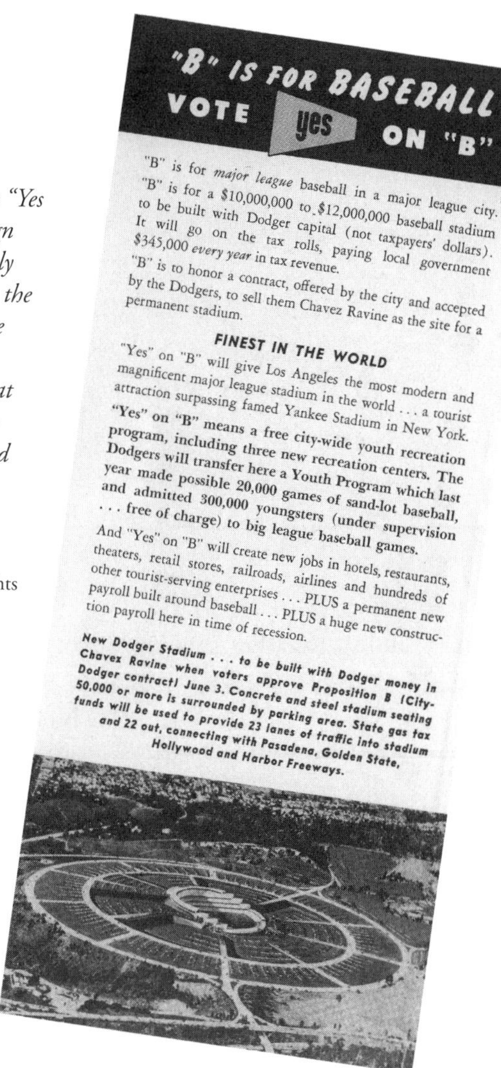

A 1958 brochure from the "Yes on Proposition B" campaign explains what the previously approved contract between the City of Los Angeles and the Dodgers means to the Southland. It also notes that Walter O'Malley pledges to build, privately finance and maintain a 50,000-seat stadium, and pay property taxes. Photo courtesy of www.walteromalley.com.

With Norris Poulson defeating Bowron at the polls in 1953, a public vote on the Chavez Ravine situation took place despite a California Supreme Court ruling declaring it unenforceable. Los Angeles canceled its public housing contracts (except for two that had already had construction started on them) and later sealed their end by negotiating to buy back the land from the United States at a discount, on the condition that it still be used for a public purpose, though not limited to housing. Los Angeles ultimately determined that purpose should be a baseball stadium, one that would host the team the city lured west from Brooklyn after the 1957 baseball season.

Though the Dodgers had nothing to do with its controversial history, Chavez Ravine was falling into their lap. But opponents to the new Dodger Stadium (including business interests who had hoped to profit from the property themselves) stalled construction by forcing a public referendum, contested to the final hour but boosted to narrow approval by a live five-hour "Dodgerthon" on KTTV in Los Angeles that took place two days before the June 3, 1958, vote. Even in the ensuing months, it took continued legal wrangling before the Dodgers were almost free to build their stadium.

By this time, Chavez Ravine had almost been emptied of its residents. "The land titles would never be returned to the original owners, and in the following years the houses would be sold, auctioned, and even set on fire to be used as practice sites by the local fire department," according to PBS. But approximately 20 parcels remained.

Two months after the California Supreme Court unanimously denied a Los Angeles Superior Court injunction that had continued to preclude Dodger Stadium's construction, eviction notices for those who remained at Chavez Ravine came in March 1959. In the following month, the legal battle ended when the U.S. Supreme Court did not find sufficient merit to further explore the case. But there was one final showdown. "On May 8, 1959," wrote Neil J.

Sullivan in *The Dodgers Move West*, "as deputies forcibly removed the Arechigas from their dwelling, Mrs. Avrana Arechiga, the 68-year old matriarch, threw rocks at them while her daughter, Mrs. Aurora Vargas, a war widow, was carried kicking and screaming from the premises. Mrs. Victoria Angustain also physically resisted the eviction, while children cried and pets, chickens, and goats added to the chaos. The grim scene was televised by local stations in the city."

The footage seemed to sum up 10 years of conflict in the area, though sympathy for the Arechigas—who remain a cause célèbre today—dissipated at the time when it was revealed that they were actually owners of numerous properties elsewhere in Los Angeles, had been occupying the land tax-free for years and had been awarded compensation for their lots from the courts but were holding out for more. In subsequent decades, they became a symbol both of the anguish enveloping the area and the misunderstandings—on both sides—of its history.

The specter of looted art hovers over Chavez Ravine, but the Dodgers weren't complicit. The expulsion of Chavez Ravine's homeowners lay at the feet of the city, which was going to dictate a new fate for the land, with or without the Dodgers. One could further argue that Dodger Stadium does serve a public purpose, albeit one that profits private ownership; you can decide whether that's fair or hypocritical, clear-eyed or naive. But the Dodgers shouldn't be counted among any villains in the story of Chavez Ravine.

12 'The Worst Club Ever To Win a World Series'

No, it wasn't the 1988 Dodgers—at least, not yet. Dodger general manager Buzzie Bavasi's quote referred to the 1959 team, which aside from Kirk Gibson's home run, could boast all the improbable success its successors 29 years later would.

Coming off a seventh-place finish in their Los Angeles debut the year before, the Dodgers were swept in a doubleheader June 14 by the Pirates to fall into fifth place with a record of 31–30 that placed manager Walter Alston's job in jeopardy, four years after winning the franchise's first World Series title.

But '59 was really a story of two Dodger teams, thanks to the midsummer arrival of two pitchers: Roger Craig and Larry Sherry. A regular starter on the '56 Dodgers who had since been banished to the minors, Craig was recalled June 19 and pitched 152⅔ innings down the stretch—including a stunning 11 innings of shutout

Following the Dodgers' 1959 World Championship in Chicago against the White Sox, broadcaster Vin Scully interviews Dodgers owner Walter O'Malley at the Chicago Hilton. Dodgers executives and their spouses celebrated the 9–3 triumph in Game 6 over the "Go-Go Sox" on October 8. Visible right behind Scully in the second row are Lela Alston, wife of Dodgers manager Walter Alston, and Kay O'Malley, wife of Walter O'Malley. Photo courtesy of www.walteromalley.com.

relief in a 4–3 July 9 victory—with an eye-catching ERA of 2.06 (205 ERA+). And yet Craig would be overshadowed by Sherry, a Fairfax High grad who, along with Don Drysdale, became the Dodgers' first local heroes in their new home. With 4⅓ career innings under his belt when he joined the Dodgers on Independence Day, Sherry was the glue of the pitching staff that featured two vets named Podres and Labine and two younger pitchers named Drysdale and Koufax. Sherry pitched 94⅓ innings as a swingman with an ERA of 2.19 (192 ERA+).

Thirteen wins in 22 games propelled the Dodgers into first place July 29, but only for a day, and they hovered below the league-leading Giants heading into September. Los Angeles swept a series in San Francisco to move into first, dropped a heartbreaking 11–10 decision to seventh-place St. Louis to fall back into second, then won three of their last four to forge a tie with—not the Giants—but the Milwaukee Braves at the end of the regular season.

In the first game of the best-of-three series (the Dodgers having lost playoffs in 1946 and of course '51), Sherry relieved Danny McDevitt in the second inning and pitched 7⅔ innings of shutout ball, long enough for Johnny Roseboro to hit a go-ahead sixth-inning homer for a 3–2 victory.

Even more drama followed the next day. Down 5–2 in the bottom of the ninth, Wally Moon, Duke Snider, Gil Hodges, and Norm Larker all singled to pull the Dodgers within one, and then 37-year-old Carl Furillo hit a sacrifice fly to tie the game. The teams continued into the 12th, when with two out, after Hodges walked and Joe Pignatano singled, Furillo again had the key blow, hitting a grounder near second base that Felix Mantilla fielded. Mantilla threw wildly in the dirt and off Dodger coach Greg Mulleavy into the stands, allowing Hodges to score the pennant-clinching run.

Opening the World Series in Chicago against the White Sox two days later, the Dodgers were practically absent. Chicago jumped out to a 9–0 lead in the third inning and won 11–0 on the

Buzzie

Branch Rickey cast a large shadow atop the Dodgers front office, but it was Buzzie Bavasi who was the general manager of the team when the Dodgers achieved their greatest success, from 1951 to 1968.

He had come to work for the Dodgers back in the late 1930s, and was the GM in Nashua, New Hampshire, in 1946, looking out for Roy Campanella and Don Newcombe while they were preparing to become Dodgers. When Rickey departed for Pittsburgh after the 1950 season, Bavasi inherited the Boys of Summer team that Rickey had built, but it wasn't long before Bavasi made his own imprint. By the time the Dodgers won their second title in 1959, all but just a few of the players had come into the organization under Bavasi's leadership—and the glory days continued for most of the next decade.

strength of two Ted Kluszewski homers. In fact, it wouldn't be until Charlie Neal's fifth-inning homer in Game 2 that the Dodgers would score—a homer made famous because a fan reaching for the ball spilled his beer on Chicago left fielder Al Smith's head.

But mirroring the regular season, once the Dodgers got their act together, they became almost unstoppable. Pinch-hitter Chuck Essegian homered in the seventh to tie the score at 2, and then after a walk to Jim Gilliam, Neal hit his second homer for a 4–2 lead. In the bottom of the eighth with two on, Smith doubled. Earl Torgeson scored, but a relay from Moon to Maury Wills to Roseboro nailed Sherm Lollar. Sherry completed a three-inning save to even the Series by shutting out the Sox in the ninth.

Game 3 was scoreless through six, thanks in part to Roseboro throwing out three White Sox base stealers. Furillo struck again with a pinch-hit single to drive in two in the seventh, and Sherry struck out the side in the ninth after relieving Drysdale to seal a 3–1 win.

Game 4 might have been the key to the Series. Early Wynn, who had breezed in Game 1, allowed four runs in the third inning. But in the seventh, Kluszewski singled in a run, and Lollar hit a game-tying three-run homer. It was another old Brooklyn hero, Hodges, who gave the Dodgers back the lead by homering in the bottom of the eighth. This time, Sherry would be credited with the win, and the Dodgers were one game away from a title.

A tense Game 5 saw the Dodgers set the all-time World Series attendance record of 92,706, but ended with the White Sox extending their season thanks to a 1–0 victory over Sandy Koufax, the run coming on a fourth-inning double play. The Dodgers had five base runners in the seventh and eighth innings and so emptied their bench trying to score that Alston had to turn to Sherry as a pinch-hitter leading off the ninth, and thus couldn't avoid a return trip to Chicago.

But Game 6 was over quickly. Moon homered to cap a six-run fourth inning, and Sherry did his thing, finishing off the White Sox with 5⅔ innings of shutout relief to give him a 0.71 ERA for the Series. When Luis Aparicio flied to left field, the city of Los Angeles had its first World Series title in its second major league season.

The worst team ever to win a series? Try telling that to Alston, who all but foreshadowed his successor Tommy Lasorda's 1988 exuberance.

"This is the greatest team I ever was connected with," Alston shouted to Al Wolf of the *Los Angeles Times,* "or any manager ever was connected with.... This team would make any manager look good, because whatever you did, they came through."

13 Family Affair

One was as tough a cuss as you'd find on the mound, a rough-and-tumble warden of the strike zone who'd knock you down if you so much as breathed on his part of the territory. "I hate all hitters," he said. "I start a game mad and stay that way until it's over.... If they knocked two of your guys down, I'd get four."

The other had the carriage of a professor. He was nicknamed "Bulldog" to coax the he-means-business side of his personality, but even when that succeeded, the moniker retained its irony when juxtaposed with the man.

Don Drysdale and Orel Hershiser were heroes of a different stripe, at least if you buy into the mythology. By their reputations, you wouldn't assume they'd necessarily get along. But when Hershiser broke Drysdale's major league record for consecutive scoreless innings, the Dodger world saw how sincere a bond had formed between them.

"Where is Drysdale? I've got to find Drysdale," Hershiser said, according to Bill Plaschke of the *Los Angeles Times*, upon reaching the dugout moments after completing his 59th goose egg in a row. "It couldn't happen to a better kid," Drysdale, who had become a Dodger announcer, told Hershiser after they embraced.

"At least it stays in the family," the older pitcher added.

It was Drysdale, the Van Nuys native, who in 1968 brought the record home. He was 31 years old, but already in his twilight as a ballplayer. His left-handed complement, Sandy Koufax, had retired at the end of the 1966 season at 30, and the Dodgers had since plunged from the World Series into losing more games than they were winning. Drysdale himself had barely a year left before his own retirement when he threw a two-hit shutout against the Cubs on May 14.

Two blankings of Houston sandwiched one of St. Louis, and by the end of the month, Carl Hubbell's 35-year-old NL record of 46⅓ consecutive scoreless innings was coming in sight. Famously, in the ninth inning against the San Francisco descendants of Hubbell's New York Giants on May 31, Drysdale lost the streak—then regained it. Perhaps it would have been an appropriate touch for

Drysdale's streak to end on a hit batter such as the Giants' Dick Dietz. But as the bases full of Giants began their advance, umpire Harry Wendelstedt ruled the pitch a ball on the grounds that Dietz hadn't tried enough to avoid it, thus making the count 3–2. Dietz then flied out to left, and two more edge-of-your-seat outs later, Drysdale's streak was at 45.

Drysdale broke Hubbell's record June 4 against Pittsburgh during his sixth straight shutout—a feat Robert F. Kennedy would mention hours later in the opening of his California Democratic Primary victory speech at the Ambassador Hotel, moments before his assassination. Drysdale was primed to pass Walter Johnson's major league record of 56 against Philadelphia in four days.

As Dan Hafner of the *Times* noted, Drysdale began with seven balls in his first eight pitches. But he settled down long enough to get a 1–2–3 second inning to tie Johnson, then retired shortstop Roberto Pena and, after a single by Larry Jackson, struck out Cookie Rojas and Johnny Briggs to make it 57.

At the end of that inning, upon the request of Phillies manager Gene Mauch who suspected a foreign substance in play, Drysdale was warned by umpire Augie Donatelli not to touch the back of his head for the rest of the game. Howie Bedell broke the streak—at $58\frac{2}{3}$ innings—in the fifth inning with a sacrifice fly, though Drysdale denied that the warning was the reason.

"I wanted the record so badly," he said, "but I'm relieved that it's over. I could feel myself go 'blah' when the run scored. I just let down completely. I'm sure it was the mental strain."

Drysdale retired with a 2.95 career ERA (121 ERA+) and 2,486 strikeouts in 3,432 innings, and most assumed that the scoreless inning streak—reduced officially to a fraction-free 58 innings—retired with him. But then came the tall, reedy Hershiser, whose first full season was 1984, the year the Hall of Fame inducted Drysdale.

Hershiser hinted at his record-setting potential by unfurling 33⅔ consecutive scoreless innings in the summer of '84 and established himself as a frontline pitcher with a 2.03 ERA (170 ERA+) the following year. But that didn't mean his run in 1988 was anything less than stunning.

It began with four shutout innings after allowing two runs in the fifth to Montreal on August 30. Five shutouts later, thanks in part to another favorable umpire ruling for the Dodgers against the Giants—an interference call on sliding Giant Brett Butler that nullified a Jose Uribe run in inning 43—the streak was at 49 innings, exactly one shutout away from Drysdale's official record of 58. And Hershiser had only one start remaining in the regular season.

There was talk about Hershiser sneaking in a relief appearance if he needed a chance to break the tie, but the Dodgers offense paid homage to the era Drysdale pitched in by simplifying matters to match Hershiser zero for zero on September 28 at San Diego. With two out in the ninth inning of the scoreless game, the Padres' Carmelo Martinez grounded out to give Hershiser a tie for the record.

"I really didn't want to break it," Hershiser told Plaschke. "I wanted to stop at 58. I wanted me and Don to be together at the top. But the higher sources [Lasorda and Perranoski] told me they weren't taking me out of the game, so I figured, what the heck, I might as well get the guy out."

Drysdale, always the competitive type, laughed when told of Hershiser's statement. "I'd have kicked him right in the rear if I'd have known that," Drysdale said. "I'd have told him to get his buns out there and get them."

It wasn't automatic. Hershiser struck out Marvell Wynne, but with a wild pitch that allowed him to reach first base. Two outs later, there were runners at second and third. But Keith Moreland flied to Jose Gonzalez in right field, and the record was Hershiser's.

Though he would later allow runs in the ninth inning of his next game in the NL Championship Series as well as his first regular season inning of 1989, Hershiser's record season was even more memorable than Drysdale's. Counting the 42⅔ innings he pitched in the '88 postseason, including NLCS- and World Series-clinching victories, Hershiser ended the year by allowing five earned runs in 101⅔ innings, a 0.44 ERA in the most pressure-packed situations.

Like Drysdale, Hershiser began to have arm trouble not long after the streak, though he stretched out his career all the way to 2000, retiring at age 42 with a 3.89 ERA (112 ERA+) and 2,014 strikeouts in 3,130⅓ innings. Hershiser won't make the Hall, but he'll remain a legend. And the record is safe—for now, though the humble Hershiser isn't holding his breath.

"I never thought I would break this record," Hershiser told Sam McManis of the *Times*. "I thought nobody would break this record. But now, I think somebody can break it from me, because I'm nobody special."

14 Hall of Fame Businessman

In early 1958, Walter O'Malley started talking about his passion for baseball, but he just as easily could have been talking about business.

"It's a virus, my boy," he told Robert Shaplen of *Sports Illustrated*. "Baseball is in my Irish bloodstream and I revel in it. Dr. Salk hasn't found a vaccine for it yet, and I'm glad."

O'Malley loved the game as a child (like Vin Scully, he was raised a New York Giants fan), but if he ever pictured himself in

Walter O'Malley, future Hall of Fame owner of the Dodgers, received the highest honor of his University of Pennsylvania graduating class in 1926, when he was named "Spoon Man" as the outstanding overall student. Photo from the Collections of the University of Pennsylvania Archives.

one of those Mayday situations—bases loaded, two out, 3–2 count, the whole world watching, the fans living and dying with every pitch—he was dead on, except that it would all be metaphor. He would be the owner, playing a game of exponentially higher stakes. He wouldn't win every game, but you don't win every game. It's a long season, measured not in days or weeks but years. You play to be on top at the end, and on top is where O'Malley finished.

By the time he attended the Culver Military Academy in Indiana and couldn't crack the varsity as a first baseman, O'Malley's feats of academia began surpassing his athletics—ultimately, he would become something of a five-tool coat-and-tie. As his official biography at Walteromalley.com notes, he was named senior class salutatorian and outstanding student at Penn, then earned his law degree at Fordham. In between, he wrote a widely circulated legal guide to New York Building Codes and established first a drilling company and then a surveying company.

When he began to practice law in the post-Depression era of the 1930s, his focus gravitated toward business reorganizations and financing. That's when baseball and business began to meld into a single playing field for O'Malley.

"I had season seats at Ebbets Field," O'Malley would later recall in a KFI radio interview, "and I found that that was a great way of entertaining clients, active or potential. I used my seats quite effectively for that purpose. It became pretty generally known that you could find Walter O'Malley at a Dodger ballgame in Ebbets Field almost each night. [That] led [to] my active association with the ballclub. I represented the Brooklyn Trust Company; the bank was

Danny Goodman

Dodgers fans of a certain age will remember Danny Goodman as the man they were told via radio and TV ads to send a couple bucks to if they wanted to purchase the Dodgers' latest souvenir special. But Goodman was much more than a guy receiving checks and money orders. Any time you leave the ballpark with a T-shirt, a bobblehead, or some other souvenir of various niftiness, you can thank Goodman.

In the 1930s, when pretty much the only thing you could buy at a ballpark was food, Goodman essentially invented the ballpark souvenir industry while working concessions for the minor league Newark Bears. He came to the West Coast in 1938 as concessions manager for the Hollywood Stars, but soon made Los Angeles the center of the baseball novelty universe, long before the majors had ventured that far. Goodman supervised concessions for major and minor league teams across the country, so it was natural that when the Dodgers moved to Los Angeles, Goodman would come to work for them.

In 1962, Goodman—who also parlayed his experience into pioneering the Dodgers' annual Hollywood Stars Game—and team public relations head Red Patterson suggested to Walter O'Malley that they give away Dodger caps to attendees at a game as a means to boost interest. The giveaway was a wild success, and led to the ubiquitous tradition of giveaways to lure fans to the ballpark. The success of this gimmick would seem to go without saying, but it didn't go without Goodman.

a trustee of 50 percent of the Dodgers' stock. The ballclub was badly involved in a mortgage they could not pay off, and the president of the bank assigned me as a troubleshooter to step into the picture and see what could be done."

Though his professional interests would further diversify for the next 10 years, O'Malley would become more than a fringe major leaguer, joining the Dodgers wholeheartedly in 1943 as vice president and general counsel before becoming a co-owner inside of two years. In 1950, when he became majority owner of the team, he had been a part of the team's life and guiding it through difficulties for more than a decade.

"The First Lady of the Dodgers" Kay O'Malley was honored by her husband Walter to toss the ceremonial first pitch at Opening Day of Dodger Stadium on April 10, 1962. Standing by her side was son Peter O'Malley, who later became Dodgers president in 1970. Photo courtesy of www.walteromalley.com.

As owner, O'Malley studied the game, worked doggedly, and played to win. His effort to keep the team in Brooklyn is well-chronicled and undeniable, but aging Ebbets Field was a pitch he ultimately couldn't drive. Like a savvy hitter, O'Malley went the other way for a hit, and smacked an opposite-country home run.

It wasn't that he had invented the notion of moving to the West Coast. It was inevitable that the major leagues would take up residence there. What wasn't inevitable was that it would be done well. In Los Angeles, he built the finest stadium and the finest franchise in the National League. From 1958 to 1978, the year before his passing at age 75, no team in baseball was more successful: seven NL pennants and three World Series titles. The organization averaged 89 victories per year and became a role model in baseball, epitomizing excellence while remaining family-friendly in price and atmosphere. As great as the team was in Brooklyn, it became greater in Los Angeles.

You can choose to care about one part more than another, but the game of Major League Baseball is inseparable from its business. Achievements in each arena matter. O'Malley wasn't perfect, but baseball isn't an endeavor that allows perfection. What Walter O'Malley was, though, was a baseball man par excellence and a champion of his game. That's why he's in the Baseball Hall of Fame.

15 Walter Alston

For most, Walter Alston presents a stoic if upbeat memory; a solemn but avuncular gent surrounded by an aura of 2,040 victories as Dodgers manager from 1954–1976. The Dodgers won four World Series under Alston, including their first. In his second

The path from obscure major league player to minor league manager to manager of the Dodgers eventually led Walter Alston directly to the National Baseball Hall of Fame in 1983. Alston, who played one game for the St. Louis Cardinals in the majors, was hired by Dodgers owner Walter O'Malley to skipper the team in the 1954 season, and he successfully remained at the post for 23 seasons, winning 2,040 games and World Championships in 1955, 1959, 1963, and 1965. Photo courtesy of www.walteromalley.com.

season in Brooklyn *and* his second season in Los Angeles, Alston piloted the team to World Series titles. Publicly, Alston projected the manner of the schoolteacher he used to be before his managerial career. A Hall of Famer with relatively little fame, his Cooperstown plaque calls him the "soft-spoken, low-profile organization man."

Further review reveals a more complicated existence because the stately Alston, the man who worked under 23 one-year contracts, was steadily under the gun. He was second-guessed from the moment he was hired when a headline shouted "Walter Who?" He would only be thankful he didn't work in today's media-saturated age. In *The Bill James Guide to Baseball Managers*, James studied Alston's career in detail. His style of managing, which at times involved extreme use of stolen bases, sacrifice bunts, pinch-hitters, pitching changes, defensive changes, intentional walks, and the hit-and-run would have come under even more intense scrutiny.

The attacks on Alston peaked in October 1962, when the Dodgers, who led the NL by four games with seven to play, surrendered the pennant in the final inning of a three-game playoff to the San Francisco Giants. Alston was blistered by fans, by the press, and by his coach (well, not really *his* coach, but a Dodger coach) Leo Durocher, who directly told reporters that he blamed Alston for the Dodgers' failure to make the World Series. Not only was Durocher the Dodgers manager from 1939–46 and also part of '48, and back as a coach in 1963, the team also hired the man Alston replaced, Charlie Dressen, in the front office.

"Throughout his career in the majors," Robert Creamer wrote in a 1963 *Sports Illustrated* story, "Alston has been jeered, booed, mocked, hooted, taunted, derided, maligned, criticized, satirized, ridiculed, hung in effigy, and generally made out to be an incompetent boob holding his job only because of the incredible patience or shortsightedness of the Dodger front office." Yet Alston not only survived, he won three pennants and two World Series in the next four seasons.

After the retirement of Sandy Koufax following the 1966 season, however, the best of times were over for Alston. In his 10 remaining seasons, the Dodgers made the postseason once.

In retrospect, Alston was anything but an emotionless presence with the Dodgers. Though he was renowned for not showing up his players in public, stories of fierce confrontations with his players, including Jackie Robinson and Don Newcombe, have become part of the backroom Alston legend. A chapter could be written on the Robinson-Alston dynamic, which began with Robinson's dim view of Alston's savvy and culminated with Alston's benching of the 36-year-old Robinson for Game 7 of the 1955 World Series. If there's a quintessential Alston story, it's the tale of him challenging any and all members of the '63 Dodgers to step off the team bus and fight him.

Alston's successor, Tommy Lasorda, quickly gained his reputation as the piss-and-vinegar manager of the Los Angeles Dodgers, but Alston, a man whose major league career was limited to one single strikeout, still burned. He may have burned on a low flame, but he burned.

16 The Two Tommys

The Dodgers' biggest cheerleader had the mouth of a sailor. He was a Dodgers Blue carnival barker who could give you the greatest show on earth, even as his insides churned like a freight train.

It is no disservice to Tommy Lasorda to point out that he, like Walter Alston before him, was more coiled than his popular image (in this case, his famous exuberance) would suggest. Lasorda was born with aggression. In front of a camera, where the kids or the True Blue fans might see him, he was just a big ol' bear. In more private arenas, he was, well, a *big old bear.* Either way, he channeled that agita into crazy, indelible memories for the Dodgers, and you can hardly talk about the team without talking about him.

Lasorda spoiled for fights long before he won 1,599 regular season games, eight division titles, four league pennants, and two

Pitching to Jack Clark

Tommy Lasorda has not been criticized more for a single managerial decision than his choice to let Tom Niedenfuer pitch to Jack Clark with runners on second and third for St. Louis, two out in the top of the ninth inning of Game 6 of the 1985 NL Championship Series, and the Dodgers one out away from a 5–4 victory. Clark had an outstanding season (.322 EQA) for the Cardinals; the next Cardinals batter Andy Van Slyke was a rising talent at age 24, but not yet in Clark's class overall.

However, in the 1986 *Baseball Abstract*, Bill James makes a powerful argument in favor of Lasorda, noting that the Dodgers had a greater chance of preserving their lead by pitching to Clark with two on than loading the bases for Van Slyke, who had higher on-base and slugging percentages then Clark against right-handed pitching. Wrote James:

"If you walk Clark: 1) You're bringing a better hitter to the plate facing a right-hander, 2) You're allowing the Cardinals to tie the game with a walk, 3) You're using up the margin of error for the pitcher, and, 4) You're making an extra-base hit as damaging as a home run.

"Against this you have one advantage—the fact that the veteran Clark has a well-deserved reputation as a clutch terror, while the young Van Slyke does not... Lasorda made the only reasonable move in the circumstances. It just didn't work."

Nope, not at all, as Pedro Guerrero slamming his glove to the left-field ground can attest. Clark's homer over Guerrero's head—the second game-winning blast off Niedenfuer in as many games for St. Louis, following Ozzie Smith's first career homer as a left-handed batter in Game 5—ended the Series, the Cardinals winning four straight games after the Dodgers had taken a 2–0 lead.

One more option for the Dodgers would have been to walk Clark and bring in a left-hander like Jerry Reuss, who was warming up in the bullpen, to face a pinch-hitter for Van Slyke, but Reuss himself had been struggling, which made that matchup less desirable as well. It won't end the debate, but you can make a very strong case that Niedenfuer was the right guy, in the right situation—with the wrong result.

World Series as a Dodgers manager from the end of 1976 through the middle of 1996. After Wally Moon slashed Lasorda's leg in a home-plate collision during his first major league start with Brooklyn (as Lasorda wrote with David Fisher in *The Artful Dodger*), Lasorda had to be dragged away from staying in the game to pitch. Later with the Kansas City A's, Lasorda decided he was going to throw at every batter he saw in retaliation for the way New York Yankee pitcher Tom Sturdivant was knocking his teammates down—and he did, until Billy Martin charged out for a fight.

The methods at times might have bordered on madness, but never was there a doubt—push; push himself, push the team, push the sport. Fatigue and fear were irrelevant. Twenty years passed between Lasorda's last major league game as a pitcher and his first major league game as a manager. Fight and spirit together got him there; one without the other would have stranded him.

That's how a man who was all business when it came to winning could also find time to dress Don Rickles up in a Dodgers uniform and send him out to the mound to pull Elias Sosa from a game after the Dodgers had clinched the NL West title in Lasorda's first season. If Lasorda heard a kid say he was a fan of another team, he could proselytize on behalf the Dodgers until heaven's blue gates opened. If Lasorda heard a reporter ask what he thought of Dave Kingman's three-homer performance, he could profanitize until the Apocalypse.

And so, as appealingly or menacingly cocksure Lasorda could be at times, when he asked his players for that something extra, they couldn't argue that he wasn't giving it himself. When it came to winning, you could never say a Lasorda opponent wanted it more.

This included strategy. When it came to the mind games of baseball, Lasorda was anything but passive. Not only was he always looking for opportunities to squeeze, steal, or hit-and-run, he was also looking for opportunities not to. Lasorda was all too happy to have home run hitters who could put runs on the board in a hurry.

He just didn't always have them. He truly does deserve credit for his guidance in the improbable 1988 World Series upset over the A's. Between Kirk Gibson's homer and Orel Hershiser's pitching mastery were numerous decisions in which Lasorda out-maneuvered his Oakland rival, Tony LaRussa—and that could only be pulled off if his team were prepared to execute his maneuvers.

Not surprisingly, Lasorda did not go gently into that good night. It took a heart attack to wrestle the managerial reins away from him and, even after that, he remained a figure determined to be heard, whether as general manager or special advisor. In significant ways, Lasorda represents the evolution of the Dodgers from the relatively genteel organization of Koufax and Alston to the multifaceted behemoth they are today. Lasorda has a little bit of Brooklyn bum in him, which became a chip on his shoulder that sometimes could be self-defeating but every so often became the means to some very good ends.

"Nobody thought we could win the division!" Lasorda shouted in 1988's postgame celebration. "Nobody thought we could beat the mighty Mets! Nobody thought we could beat the team that won 104 games!

"But WE BELIEVED IT!"

Or at least two people did. The two-and-only Tommys.

17 Newk

I want to write a book about Don Newcombe. I want to because apparently no one has yet, and that seems incredible.

The Dodgers signed him out of the Negro Leagues before his 20th birthday, making him a teammate of Roy Campanella in

Dodgers pitcher Don Newcombe is the only man to win the three major awards in baseball—the Cy Young Award, Most Valuable Player, and Rookie of the Year. Newcombe was also the first African-American to start a World Series game, in 1949. Photo courtesy of www.walteromalley.com.

Nashua, New Hampshire, in 1946. Three years later, Newcombe followed Campy and Jackie Robinson into the majors as the youngest black player of his time.

And like Robinson, Newk's impression was immediate. Shutting out Cincinnati in his first major league start, he pitched 244⅓ innings with an ERA of 3.17 (130 ERA+) for the pennant-winning Dodgers, led the league in strikeouts per nine innings, won the NL Rookie of the Year award, and finished eighth in the voting for NL MVP (Robinson won). The Newcombe book-to-be would talk about him being a sensation.

The World Series began a run of dramatic late-season appearances for Newcombe. For example, in his first World Series start—the black rookie taking the mound in Game 1, only 2½ years after Robinson broke the color line—he took a scoreless duel into the ninth inning before allowing a homer to Tommy Henrich and losing 1–0. And then, following a solid second year (3.70 ERA, 111 ERA+), he gave up a three-run homer in the 10th inning of a game the Dodgers needed to win to force a playoff with Philadelphia. His next year he was worked to the bone, pitching often on rest of two days or less, including 16 innings in a doubleheader against those same Phillies. To cap his third year (3.28 ERA, 120 ERA+, NL-high 164 strikeouts), he found redemption with a critical shutout over...what, the Phillies again?... followed by four shutout innings the next day to help get the Dodgers into a playoff with the Giants. And after just two more days of rest, another 8⅓ innings in the final game of the playoffs, leaving with a two-run ninth-inning lead for Ralph Branca. The book would talk about the relentless heat of these moments.

Newcombe didn't get another chance to pitch in the majors until 1954. In the interim, he was on military duty. The book would talk about his experiences as a black man in the service, and how that affected the rest of his life in and out of baseball.

After initially struggling during a partial season in '54, Newcombe fully flowered in the next two years, the ace pitcher of the '55 World Series champions (233⅔ innings, 3.20 ERA, 128 ERA+)—not to mention batting .359 in 117 at-bats with seven homers and a steal of home before winning the 1956 MVP and Cy Young Awards with a 3.06 ERA (132 ERA+). The book would talk about his reign as baseball's most dominant player.

And then the book would talk about his stumbles. About his battle with alcoholism…

"In 1956 I was the best pitcher in baseball. Four years later, I was out of the major leagues," he once said. "It must have been the drinking. When you're young, you can handle it, but the older you get, the more it bothers you."

…And about how, for the second half of his life—his life after baseball—he maintained his sobriety and helped others do the same.

"I'm glad to be anywhere when I think about my life back then," Newcombe told Ben Platt of MLB.com. "What I have done after my baseball career and being able to help people with their lives and getting their lives back on track and they become human beings again—means more to me than all the things I did in baseball."

In my book-to-be, this would be put into context within the world Newcombe lived in, into the 21st century, and how that world evolved from his childhood and earliest playing days.

"We'd finally get a cab that would take us to a substandard hotel with no air-conditioning," Newcombe is quoted as saying in Cal Fussman's *After Jackie: Pride, Prejudice and Baseball's Forgotten Heroes*, "while the white players went on their air-conditioned bus from Union Station to the Chase Hotel and didn't have to even so much as touch their shaving kits until they got to their rooms. Not one of them—not one of the white guys on the Brooklyn Dodgers—ever got off that bus and said, 'I'm going to go with

Jackie, Don, and Roy just to see how they have to live, just to find out.'

"The first St. Louis hotel Jackie had to stay in back in 1947, then Roy in 1948, and me in 1949, was called the Princess. It was a slum. We moved to the Adams Hotel after a friend of ours bought it, but he couldn't afford air-conditioning. Many nights, we had to soak our sheets in ice water and put them on the bed just to get a little relief from the heat and humidity. Try that sometime. We kept our windows open even with the trolleys running up and down the street below, because in that heat, you needed to get some air.

"There we were, members of the great Brooklyn Dodgers."

And there he is, the great Don Newcombe. If I don't write a book about him, someone should.

18 Dodger Stadium

In the center is a pitcher's mound, enclosed by four bases forming the corners of a diamond, 90 feet apart. That's standard. Everything else that surrounds it is a matter of choice.

At Dodger Stadium, the diamond is surrounded on two sides by a symmetrical outfield, laden with the most pristine grass in Southern California. Since 1962, this has never been anything less than perfect. It hasn't been limited to baseball players; it has been the earth under Beatles, Globetrotters, Olympians, Tenors, and a Pope.

At the rim of the outfield is a fence, eight feet high from the left field bullpen to the right, waist-high as you near the foul poles. The wall has changed with the times, alternating different shades of blue; in later years adorned with homages to Dodgers history; still

April 10, 1962, was Opening Day at Dodger Stadium, and no one was prouder of the $23 million stadium than visionary Dodgers owner Walter O'Malley (center). Next to him was the popular Dodgers manager Walter Alston (No. 24) and farther right is Dodgers coach Leo Durocher. All three are now members of the National Baseball Hall of Fame. Photo courtesy of www.walteromalley.com.

later with welcome-to-the-real-world advertising. In the 21st century, scoreboards were embedded in its face. The walls have not always been forgiving; for decades they went without sufficient padding, contributing to a key shoulder injury to Darryl Strawberry in the 1990s. James Loney lasted one experimental inning in the outfield in 2007 before his knee fought a losing battle with the joint between the scoreboard and the fence.

Beyond the walls—closer to home plate today than they were when the stadium opened—are the pavilions, which can be the Sahara on a day game but a grand ol' time otherwise. Famously, in the initial decade, Willie Stargell became the first player to hit a ball over the pavilion roofs—and the second as well. For nearly two decades, no one else duplicated the feat until Mike Piazza and Mark McGwire in the '90s, homering over the roof-level ring of retired Dodger numbers.

Above the pavilion are two scoreboards at left and right. Despite a remodel, the latter at its heart hasn't changed, offering the lineups and score-by-innings. Its partner used to be made of similar stuff, offering messages and spelling out graphics in text boxes, like a giant number 19 to mourn Junior Gilliam, who was stolen from the team and this world too soon. Then, in time for the 1980 All-Star Game, the left-field scoreboard led ballparks into the video age with DiamondVision and forever changed the experience of attending a game.

Center field offers no seating, just a black batter's eye and a spot for the TV camera, like the one that got thudded by Jose Canseco's World Series Game 1 grand slam that should have spelled the end of the '88 Dodgers, the camera through which most baseball fans in their bars and living rooms see every pitch. The center-field walls open for new-model cars to drive through on Fan Appreciation Day and for ambulances to come to the aid of the stricken, like Alex Cora, Kazuhisa Ishii, or umpire Kerwin Danley.

Out beyond center field lies the mammoth parking where Dodgers fans safely in their seats can gloat at those struggling to arrive. As stolid a fixture as any in Dodger Stadium's first 46 years, even this became positioned for change with the 2008 announcement that the Dodgers would breed shops and restaurants—along

Our Little Secret

They're not foolproof, but here are three good bets for cutting through the traffic to Dodger Stadium.

1) From the southbound Harbor/Pasadena (110) Freeway:
   - Take the Academy Road exit.
   - Follow Academy Road to Solano Canyon Drive and turn left.
   - Proceed ahead to Dodger Stadium entrance.
2) From the northbound Harbor/Pasadena (110) Freeway:
   - Take the Academy Road exit.
   - Turn right on Solano Avenue.
   - Turn right on Amador Street.
   - Turn right on Jarvis Street.
   - Turn left back onto Solano Avenue.
   - Turn left onto Solano Canyon Drive.
   - Proceed ahead to Dodger Stadium entrance.
3) From the intersection of Sunset Boulevard and Beaudry Avenue:
   - Head northeast on Beaudry to Alpine Street and turn right.
   - Turn left on Figueroa Terrace.
   - Continue on Figueroa Terrace, bearing left.
   - Turn right on College Street.
   - Turn left on Chavez Ravine Place.
   - Bear right onto Stadium Way.
   - Continue toward Dodger Stadium entrance, which will be on your left.

with the nirvana of a Dodger historical museum—over the pavement. One only hopes that the view beyond the parking never changes: the hills of Elysian Park with "THINK BLUE" in bold letters resting atop, and further back, the San Gabriel Mountains offering as resplendent a backdrop as any in baseball.

Circle around the perimeter, and you come to the rear of the stadium, offering a reminder to those who might otherwise have no idea that, yes, Los Angeles does have a downtown, and you can spy on it from here and even fantasize about a tram or *Simpsons*-esque escalator that would link the stadium to the city's public transportation nexus. But back to reality. Turn around with your ticket, and find your seat: in the Top Deck with its vertigo-inducing but rewarding view; or in the Reserved Level that is the most populated part of the stadium; or among the affluent on the Club Level (which evolved from exclusivity to downright largesse when suites were added between the Stadium Club in right field and the Dodger executive offices in left); or down to the Loge Level where the seats are upper class if not Hearstian; or down to the Field Level that just seems to expand, expand, expand, encroaching into and populating what used to be roomy foul territory. The home and visitor dugouts have expanded as well. It's all about real estate in Southern California, after all, and you've got to keep up with the Joneses.

It's a short walk from the on-deck circle to home plate, back to that central, fixed diamond of Dodger Stadium. Who knows how often a batter steps out of the batter's box and takes a look around and realizes what the people in the stands realize: that much of the wonder of Dodger Stadium remains, even on your 100th or 1,000th visit. For all the changes, for however loud or lewd it has gotten in some ways, it is still a *ballpark*. It is a tremendous place to watch a baseball game.

19 Don't Turn Your Back on a Hero Who's Down on His Luck

After Fernandomania, there was Nomonia (or, as the less eloquent called it, Nomomania). Allowing one hit in five shutout innings in his first major league game, allowing two hits in seven shutout innings while striking out 14 in his fourth, Hideo Nomo whipped the Dodger faithful into a frenzy. It wasn't the rags-to-riches, babe-in-the-woods mind-spinner that Valenzuela caused, but it was a phenomenon nonetheless.

Other than one game started by Giants reliever Masanori Murakami in 1965, no Japan native had ever been a starting pitcher in the NL or AL. And here was the 26-year-old Nomo, the first Japan League player to come to America in his prime, posting 16 strikeouts June 14, then back-to-back games of 13 later that month—11 double-digit strikeout games in 28 starts overall during his rookie season. His average of 11.1 strikeouts per nine innings was the fifth-highest single-season total in major league history at the time. He emerged as the ace of the '95 Dodgers (2.54 ERA/150 ERA+), not to mention the NL Rookie of the Year. With two days remaining in the regular season and the Dodgers leading the Colorado Rockies by one game in the NL West, Nomo struck out 11 while allowing one earned run in eight innings, enabling the Dodgers to clinch a tie. One game is the margin by which the Dodgers won the division, and they almost certainly wouldn't have done so without him.

In 1996, Nomo remained strong, even climbing the Mt. Everest of pitching feats by throwing a no-hitter at the hitting capital of baseball, Colorado's Coors Field. Chris Jaffe, writing for *The Hardball Times*, called it the second-most impressive no-hitter in baseball history. But like so many other pitchers, Nomo would battle arm issues—violently high pitch counts were a featured element of his Japan-era backstory—and his performance declined in subsequent years for the Dodgers. After starting the 1998 season with a 5.05 ERA (80 ERA+) in 67⅔ innings, Los Angeles shipped him with Brad Clontz to New York in a trade for journeymen Dave Mlicki and Greg McMichael. Thus began the peripatetic phase of his career. The Mets, Cubs, Brewers, and Tigers would all release him over the next 30 months, and the Red Sox let him leave as a free agent even though he pitched his second career no-hitter in his first start of the 2001 season.

Nomo found his way back to Los Angeles, and just like that, Nomonia started spreading all over town again. He had a 3.39 ERA (112 ERA+) and 193 strikeouts in 220⅓ innings in 2002, and then in 2003, he helped anchor one of the great Dodgers pitching staffs of all time with a 3.09 ERA (130 ERA+) and 177 strikeouts in 218⅓ innings.

And then, in 2004, it all vanished. Stunned by a six-run fifth inning in his first start of the season, Nomo never got his ERA below 6.00. He struck out more than three batters in only four of 18 starts. As far as being a competent pitcher, Nomo was done. Yet Dodgers manager Jim Tracy kept sending him out to the mound every fifth game. Dodger Stadium fans—not all of them, but enough to make an impact—started booing him.

Booing, in its many forms, is part of baseball. Some fans are raised in it, some can't help it. Some feel it's harmless venting; some intend it as anything but. Few would call it a particularly mature act, but who ever said you had to be mature at a baseball game?

At some point, however, there has to be a line. There has to be a barrier you don't cross, even if you're unhappy that you've shelled out big bucks to see what's turning into a big loss. And if nowhere else, that barrier has to come with the kind of player that has won huge games for you, thrilled you, that has given his all for you, that has been nothing but professional for you. And if he's gotten well-paid for the work, well, ask yourself if you'd turn down the money.

If you're a Dodgers fan, or any kind of sports fan, remember Hideo Nomo. Remember context. When someone's been a hero for you, cut him some slack during the rough times. Then, more than ever, is the time to cheer him.

20 Dodger Dogs

Dodger Dogs are controversial, and not for Upton Sinclair *The Jungle* reasons.

The fact is, Dodger Dogs are not a single, static entity. Dodger Dogs, like the Dodgers, are different from moment to moment.

First, the Dodgers sell more than one type of hot dog. The nominal Dodger Dog is a footlong tube that out-stretches the bun, but some prefer the shorter, squatter, and arguably tastier all-beef dog.

Depending on where in the ballpark you purchase them, Dodger Dogs are sometimes grilled, sometimes boiled. And if you end up at a boiled stand, you might as well not even bother. Not that it's bad, but it doesn't have the snap that you'd like from a hot dog. Essentially, a Dodger Dog isn't a Dodger Dog without the taste of char. It's part of the food's character, and it's frankly a little silly that the Dodgers sometimes ignore this. And then, even on the grill, Dodger Dogs can be undercooked or overcooked—there's no doubt that the dog is a precision instrument.

Condiments are also an issue. The Dodgers have been better in recent years at providing spicy mustard in addition to yellow, but the relish can sometimes err on the runny side. Ketchup seems to go well on a Dodger Dog, though of course there are some regions in this country that would consider a ketchup-laden dog a sin against nature.

All of this might seem to make the Dodger Dog an impossible dream, something mythological rather than achievable, and to be sure, some longtime fans have given up on the pursuit and warned other visitors and first-timers off the chase.

Face the Music

Maybe Dodgers fans don't think much about the organ player the first time they go to the ballpark. Maybe they took Gladys Goodding for granted at Ebbets Field, or paid no mind to Bob Mitchell, Don Beamsley, teenager Donna Parker, Helen Dell, or Nancy Bea Hefley while absorbing the Dodger Stadium experience.

But when it comes to memories, that's when the organ player is important. You can hear rock music anywhere. The organist gives Dodger Stadium its own personality. It's swimming against the 21st-century tide, but the organist needs to be celebrated, not diminished.

But you can get an ideal Dodger Dog. And when you do get one and take it to your seat at the ballpark, it can seem as perfect as the Dodger Stadium grass and the white uniform with blue lettering, as perfect anything you've ever tasted.

It's worth it to endure the subpar Dodger dogs for the champion dogs. I mean, this is baseball, right? If they were all great, that'd be nice, but just a little too easy, wouldn't it?

21 Campy

"The old gentleman's roundness, like the outward geniality, was deceptive. When Campanella took off his uniform, there was no fat. His arms were short and huge up toward the shoulder. Fat housewives have arms like that, but Campy's arms were sinew. His thighs bulged with muscle and his belly was swollen, but firm. He was a little sumo wrestler of a man, a giant scaled down rather than a midget fleshed out. He had grown up in a Philadelphia ghetto called Nicetown and he made you laugh with his stories of barnstorming through Venezuela with colored teams where [he said] you always had to play doubleheaders and meal money was fifty cents a day. But he would second-guess a manager and then deny what he had said. He accepted no criticism and his amiability was punctuated by brief combative outbursts. Still, it was difficult to resist him. . . ."

— Roger Kahn,
The Boys of Summer

The accident happened on the road. It was January 1958. The Brooklyn Dodgers were heading for Los Angeles. Jackie Robinson had just retired, but Roy Campanella, 36 years old, would be part of the caravan and had grown optimistic about the trip. Though he had suffered through consecutive subpar seasons for the first time since becoming a major leaguer in 1948, everyone had heard by now about the peculiar dimensions of the Dodgers' West Coast lodgings, the Los Angeles Memorial Coliseum. Barely 250 feet to left field. Even at his age, even after hitting only 13 home runs in his final Brooklyn season—two after July 1—Los Angeles would be easy pickings for Campy.

Campanella's road was taking him to the Hall of Fame. His 10 Dodgers seasons produced three NL Most Valuable Player awards, eight All-Star seasons, 242 home runs, and a .291 EQA—numbers that were limited by how tardy his big-league promotion was, seeing as he had been playing pro ball since he was 15 years old with the Baltimore Elite Giants of the Negro Leagues. In 1953, his most astonishing season, he had an on-base percentage of .395 and slugging percentage of .611 (.320 EQA), hitting 41 homers and driving in 142 runs. In his painstaking research, historian Bill James determined that Campanella was the sport's greatest catcher at his peak, adding that he also probably had "the best throwing arm of his generation."

"The managers would say to the young pitchers, 'If you shake Campy off, you better have a darn good reason,'" Dodger pitcher Carl Erskine said in an interview. "Everyone who played with him agrees, he would have been the first black manager in the big leagues if he hadn't had his accident, because he was that style of player and thinker."

The stature of his accomplishments was underscored by the way his baseball mortality occasionally emerged, such as when 1954's injuries and slumps held him to 111 games, a .207 batting average, and 19 homers (.230 EQA). Although Campanella looked forward to Los Angeles, he had been building his life outside of baseball by the time the move was happening. Roy Campanella's Choice Wines and Liquors stood on the corner of Seventh and 134th in Harlem, and it was from there that Campanella was driving home at 1:30 in the morning, January 28, 1958.

The Chevy hit a patch of ice, and Roy Campanella skidded off the road. Paralyzed below the shoulders, his upper arms capable of only the slightest movement, Campanella struggled mightily. His playing days were over, but not his life.

He lived for almost as long after the accident as he had lived before it: 35 more years. He lived to see more than 93,000 fans pay stirring, heartbreaking tribute to him at that Coliseum field on the other side of the country. He published a book, *It's Good To Be Alive*. He completed his journey to the Hall of Fame in 1969. Peter O'Malley hired Campanella to be a catching instructor, and he tutored three generations of Dodger backstops in Steve Yeager and Joe Ferguson, Mike Scioscia, and Mike Piazza.

This was his painful yet rewarding path.

"I've accepted the chair," he told Kahn. "My family has accepted it. My wife has made a wonderful home. I'm not wanting many things. Sure, I'd love to walk. Sure I would. But I'm not gonna worry myself to death because I can't. I've accepted the chair, and I've accepted my life."

And Kahn reflected:

"He pushed the lever and the wheelchair started bearing the broken body and leaving me, and perhaps Roxie Campanella as well, to marvel at the vaulting human spirit, imprisoned yet free, in the noble wreckage of the athlete, in the dazzling palace of the man."

22 Sweep!

What if the Dodgers overwhelmed the Yankees in a World Series the same way Sandy Koufax typically overwhelmed NL batters? It's a question that Dodgers fans of either coast could hardly have dared ask.

But in 1963, it happened. The Dodgers not only beat the Yankees in the '63 Series, they swept them. They not only swept them, they never trailed in any game. And of course, it had to start with Koufax.

The left-hander was 27 years old at the time and about to win his first Cy Young Award. He began the World Series by striking out the first five Yankees he faced: Tony Kubek, Bobby Richardson, Tom Tresh, Mickey Mantle, and Roger Maris. After five innings, he had 11 Ks, and when pinch-hitter Harry Bright went down in the bottom of the ninth, Koufax set a World Series record with his 15th.

A good sign for the Dodgers was that although Koufax was supreme in his success, he wasn't alone. Johnny Roseboro hit a three-run homer off future Hall of Famer Whitey Ford to cap a four-run second inning, and second baseman Dick Tracewski knocked down a low liner by Clete Boyer to keep the Yankees from scoring in the fifth after two earlier singles broke up Koufax's no-hit bid. Though the Yankees got a two-run homer from Tresh in the

The celebration begins at Dodger Stadium after the Dodgers swept the New York Yankees in the 1963 World Series. Pitcher Sandy Koufax won two games in the four-game sweep, including the last game 2–1. Photo courtesy of Los Angeles Dodgers, Inc.

eighth and a single in the ninth, Koufax was resilient enough to put them away.

Oh, and by the way—Koufax didn't feel good.

"I felt a little weak," he told the press afterward. "I just felt a little tired in general early in the game. Then I felt a little weak in the middle of the game. Then I got some of my strength back, but I was a little weak again at the end."

Cautious in their optimism in the clubhouse after the initial victory, the Dodgers kept an all-business approach in Game 2. Willie Davis followed singles by Maury Wills and Jim Gilliam with

Dick Nen

Dick Nen's first major league at-bat came against St. Louis Cardinals ace Bob Gibson, which means that Dick Nen's first major league at-bat resulted in an out. The product of Banning High and Long Beach State had joined the major league roster of his now-local team earlier in the day—September 18, 1963—although Nen made his debut far from home and comfort. The host Cardinals led the Los Angeles Dodgers 5–1 in the top of the eighth behind four-hit, no-walk pitching by Gibson, and were six outs away from cutting the Dodgers' NL lead to two games with 11 days remaining in the regular season.

Nen did make solid contact against Gibson, lining out to center field, and if anything that might have been a sign that Gibson was tiring—letting a scrub get wood on him. Maury Wills and Jim Gilliam followed with singles, Wally Moon walked to load the bases, and then Tommy Davis singled to left field to cut the Cardinal lead in half. Bobby Shantz relieved Gibson and walked Frank Howard to load the bases, then gave up a sacrifice fly to Willie Davis. But a second reliever, Ron Taylor, retired Bill Skowron on a groundout, leaving the Dodgers down by a run. Nen stayed in the game at first as part of a triple switch, which meant that he would be due up again as the second batter of the ninth.

Dick Nen's second major league at-bat is still going on. When you mention unsung heroes in Dodgers history, Nen is one of the first names to enter the conversation because against Taylor, the left-handed Nen slugged a long drive over the right-field wall to tie the game. Dick Nen. Dick Nen! The Dodgers then rode Ron Perranoski's six innings of shutout relief to a 6–5, 13-inning victory, and ended up burying the Cardinals six games back.

Dick Nen's second major league hit would come nearly 21 months later with another team in another league and before a crowd of 4,294—at Dodger Stadium of all places, but as a member of the Washington Senators in a road game against the California Angels. Nen, the father of major league reliever Robb Nen, never had another moment like he had in St. Louis in his first major league game. Then again, most of us have never had a moment like that, period.

a two-run double past a slipping Roger Maris in right field. Tommy Davis later added two triples, and Johnny Podres pitched $8\frac{1}{3}$ innings of shutout ball to send the Dodgers back to Los Angeles with a 4–1 victory and 2–0 series lead.

Despite getting only six hits in their next two games, the Dodgers closed out the series. Don Drysdale made a first-inning RBI single by Tommy Davis stand up for a 1–0 victory in Game 3. Then in Game 4, Frank Howard broke up a scoreless rematch between Koufax and Ford with the first-ever home run to the Loge level of Dodger Stadium. Mickey Mantle homered off Koufax in the seventh to give the Yankees their first tie of the postseason, but then came the final, fateful play of the Series. Gilliam grounded to Boyer at third base, but first baseman Joe Pepitone couldn't pick up the throw and let it get past him.

"I didn't see it," Pepitone told John Hall of the *Los Angeles Times.* "It got lost in the shirts behind third base. It hit me on the side of the glove and the wrist and went on by.... Nothing like that happened to me all year."

Gilliam zipped all the way to third base, and Willie Davis brought him home with a sacrifice fly for a 2–1 lead.

For those who didn't think the Yankees could ever be disposed of so easily, one play in the ninth gave pause. After Richardson singled off Koufax to open the inning, Tresh and Mantle struck out looking. But Elston Howard reached base on what was ruled an error by Tracewski catching a throw from Maury Wills, and suddenly the tying run was in scoring position. However, Koufax again was up to the task, inducing a 6–3 groundout from Hector Lopez.

Just like that, the Yankees, 104-game winners in the regular season, were swept away like yesteryear's dust, held to four runs in four games while striking out 37 times.

"For one of the few times since the electric light, the Bombers were forced to depart with a borrowed line that once belonged to the Dodgers," Hall wrote. "Wait 'til next year."

23 Piazza

The 1970s brought the Popeye arms of Steve Garvey and the 1980s had the majestic swing of Pedro Guerrero. But in the history of the Los Angeles Dodgers, there might not have been a hitter as startling, as eye-popping, as fall-back-in-your-seat-in-amazing as Mike Piazza.

His story as a Dodger was forever poisoned by his ungracious, day-the-music-died trade by the Dodgers to the Florida Marlins shortly after the O'Malley family sold the team to News Corp.-owned Fox and without the consent of general manager Fred Claire. Piazza's name evokes as much lament as wonder. Sandy Koufax retired young, but he retired as a Dodger. Garvey and Fernando Valenzuela gave Los Angeles their best years, Kirk Gibson his best moment. All had the time they needed to celebrate a World Series title.

Piazza was unique in Los Angeles history: a player firmly established as a future Hall of Famer that the Dodgers *aloha*'ed with several Cooperstown-caliber years remaining. That the hitter who replaced him, Gary Sheffield, was his measure with the bat (with a higher career Los Angeles Dodger OPS+ than Piazza) footnotes the shock, but doesn't reduce it.

Piazza emerged from an obscurity quite differently from Valenzuela's, but from obscurity nonetheless. He began his professional career as an anecdote. He was the scion of a Tommy Lasorda boyhood chum named Vince Piazza, and the Dodgers selected him in the 62nd round of the June 1988 draft, after 1,389 other players and before only 43 others, as a favor. The ties between Lasorda and the elder Piazza were such that when Piazza briefly joined a group

Mike Piazza may go down in history as the greatest hitting catcher of all time, but it's important to know that he first wore Dodger Blue. Piazza became the first Dodger ever to hit a ball out of Dodger Stadium.

interested in purchasing the San Francisco Giants, reports stated Lasorda would leave Los Angeles and become manager of the Dodgers' archrivals.

What few realized at the time was that the team had unwittingly acquired the ultimate late bloomer. When he was a teen, the Piazza family installed a batting cage in the backyard, and Mike developed a hitting stroke that even impressed Ted Williams, according to Maryann Hudson of the *Los Angeles Times.* That nascent skill was hidden by how unrefined the rest of his game was. Piazza went undrafted out of high school, and ended up walking on at the University of Miami before transferring to Miami-Dade Community College.

After the Dodgers drafted him, following Lasorda's encouragement to move from first base to catcher, he became the first U.S. ballplayer to attend the Dodgers' Dominican Republic academy. "After more than two months, he had lost 25 pounds and suffered prolonged bouts of homesickness," wrote Bill Plaschke in the *Times.* "But he learned to catch."

He got a September trial at the end of the Dodgers' lost 1992 season, going 3-for-3 with a walk in his major league debut. He presented such impressive potential that the Dodgers allowed 13-year vet Mike Scioscia to sign with San Diego. "He hits the ball so hard," wrote Hudson during spring training 1993, "that even his teammates crowd around the cage to watch him during batting practice."

So true. It's no surprise that Piazza became the first Dodger ever to hit a ball out of Dodger Stadium. He lashed the ball; he sledgehammered it. In his first full season, he set what was then a Los Angeles Dodgers record with 35 home runs, including two in the final game of the year to help knock the Giants out of a playoff berth. In a 1995 season limited by injury, he hit 32 in 112 games. In 1996, he broke his team record by hitting 36. A year later, he topped himself again with 40.

Never an all-or-nothing hitter, that '97 season represented the full flowering of Piazza as a batsman. He developed the plate discipline (or the awe of opposing pitchers) that gave him the greatest offensive season in Los Angeles Dodgers history. He batted .362 with a .431 on-base percentage and .638 slugging percentage, a 185 OPS+ never approached for the previous 40 years or the following 10 (except for Manny Ramirez's two months in 2008).

Thirty-seven games later, Piazza was wearing a Florida Marlins uniform. In 726 games as a Dodger, he batted .331, on-based .394 and slugged .572, hitting 177 homers, and averaging one every four games. That wasn't even the halfway point of the back of his baseball card. In his post-Dodgers career, he added 1,186 games and 250 homers, at a .293/.365/.528 pace. Overall, he will go down in history as the greatest hitting catcher of all time.

It wasn't that the Dodgers were robbed of talent. Sheffield was a tremendous hitter. It was that the Dodgers were robbed of half of a great novel. They got the *War* without the *Peace*.

That first half was a heck of a read, though.

24 4+1

The idea that the 2006 Dodgers could come back from a four-run deficit against San Diego Padres ace Jake Peavy—even with nine innings to go and even with Peavy having what was for him an off year—tested all credibility.

The idea that the 2006 Dodgers, 15th in a 16-team NL in home runs, could hit four home runs in a week, let alone a game, let alone an inning, let alone a ninth inning with career saves leader Trevor Hoffman in the opposing bullpen, was utterly implausible.

Hitless Wonders

The ball cued off Matt Kemp's bat like a trick shot from a pool shark, rolling about 50 feet up the first base line before suddenly darting under the glove of Angels pitcher Jered Weaver. Weaver still had the time and opportunity to make the play but was unable to before Kemp reached first base on what was ruled an error.

With the game scoreless in the fifth inning, Kemp took off for second base. The throw from catcher Jeff Mathis sailed into center field for another Angel error, allowing Kemp to head over to third. Blake DeWitt hit a fly ball to fairly deep right field, but even an on-the-money one-hopper from Vladimir Guerrero couldn't keep Kemp from scoring on the sacrifice fly.

And with that, the Dodgers had all of the runs (one) and all of the hits (zero!) they would need on June 28, 2008, becoming the fifth team since 1900 to win while being no-hit. It was a quintessential game to add to Dodgers lore—and as if to further magnify the accomplishment, on August 25 of the same year, the Dodgers got 13 hits but were shut out by Philadelphia.

The idea that both events could happen in the same night? We can only answer that question by asking another: How many people sold their souls to swing this one?

Monday, September 18, 2006. The Dodgers had just dropped two games in a row at home to San Diego to fall a half-game behind the Padres in the NL West with two weeks of regular-season play remaining. They had scored three runs in those previous two contests, which made their task all the more daunting once they found themselves down 4–0 in the first inning to Peavy, who in 10 previous starts against the Dodgers had a 1.66 ERA with 65 strikeouts in 65 innings.

But the Dodgers managed to make Peavy look human for once; perhaps he was rattled by an on-field shouting match with Dodger first-base coach Mariano Duncan in the bottom of the first. By the bottom of the third, they had tied the game, thanks to Jeff Kent

On September 18, 2006, the Dodgers hit four homeruns back to back (to back to back) against Trevor Hoffman and the San Diego Padres to a 9–9 tie in the bottom of the ninth. Another homer in the tenth by Nomar Garciaparra pushed the Dodgers to an 11–10 victory.

(who drove in one run and scored another with a pair of doubles) and a small-print August 31 acquisition, Marlon Anderson, who homered in the second inning.

If this all seemed too good to be true to Dodgers fans, it was. Even after getting Peavy out of the game and loading the bases with one out in the sixth inning, the Dodgers couldn't take the lead. Then, the whole idea of completing the comeback became a farce, an apparition. Against the Dodgers' top two relievers, Jonathan Broxton and Takashi Saito, San Diego scored a total of five runs in the eighth and ninth innings. Anderson tripled (his fourth hit) and scored in the bottom of the eighth, but still the Dodgers trailed 9–5 heading into the bottom of the ninth.

And then, *magic*. On the second pitch from Padres reliever Jon Adkins, Kent homers over the center-field wall. A strike and two balls later, J.D. Drew crushes one deep into the right-field bleachers. Hoffman enters. Rookie Russell Martin homers on his first offering. And on the very next pitch, unbelievably, Anderson does the same. A 9–9 tie. A 5-for-5 night for Anderson. Back-to-back-to-back-to-back back back back back backs. Four straight home runs—the first time that had happened in the majors in 42 years, and the only time it ever happened in the bottom of the ninth.

And still it wasn't over. Padres catcher Josh Bard singled in Brian Giles in the top of the 10th inning, threatening to make this comeback of all comebacks go for naught. But as easy as it was to give up on the Dodgers in the first and in the ninth, it was impossible for fans to surrender now.

In the bottom of the 10th, Dodger center fielder Kenny Lofton worked out a leadoff walk from Rudy Seanez. Nomar Garciaparra, who had struck out in the bottom of the eighth with two runners on, worked the count to 3–1.

One swing. Nirvana. "A high fly ball to left field," calls Vin Scully, "It is a-way out and...gone! The Dodgers win it 11–10! Ha ha ha—unbelievable!" And later: "I forgot to tell you—the Dodgers are in first place."

It became, from start to finish, the most incredible game in Los Angeles history.

25 The SQUEEZE

In a darkening Southern California afternoon, Pedro Guerrero breaks down the third-base line. A rookie pinch-hitter, R.J. Reynolds, making his 27th career plate appearance, watches Atlanta pitcher Gene Garber begin his follow-through, and drops the bat from his shoulder into bunting position like water flowing downstream.

It's the final play of a game that stood for more than 20 years as the greatest in Dodger Stadium history. The play comes during the softening glow of a heated September pennant race, the Dodgers clinging to a two-game lead in the NL West after losing in extra innings to the Braves the previous night.

It comes hours after Jack Fimple, one of those temporary heroes the Dodgers find from time to time, adds to his fleeting legend by doubling in two second-inning runs. It comes hours after Atlanta center fielder Dale Murphy almost single-handedly throttles the Dodgers, hitting a three-run homer in the top of the third and then going above and nearly through the outfield fence in the bottom of the inning to steal Guerrero's two-run bid. It comes hours after the Dodgers use four pitchers in the fourth inning to try to keep the game from becoming a complete runaway; the home team is fortunate to escape the inning with only a 6–2 deficit.

The play comes through a small opening in the fabric of baseball reality, a pathway carved by the truly bizarre. Future Dodgers manager Joe Torre, then helming the Braves, signals for relief pitcher Tony Brizzolara to come into a bases-loaded sixth without having him warm-up that inning. Four balls to Steve Sax later, Brizzolara leaves the game with the Dodgers one run closer.

In a game that could be subtitled *A Series of Improbable Events*, the play comes after a ninth inning full of them.

Leading off, 38-year-old pinch-hitter Jose Morales offers a textbook-rejected swing, a Leaning Tower of Pisa flick of the wrists sending Donnie Moore's pitch into left field, far enough from Atlanta outfielder Brett Butler that Morales can come in standing with a double.

After Moore walks Sax, Garber enters the game and strikes out Bill Russell, and for a penetrating moment, there's a sense that the surreal has finally expired.

But then Dusty Baker hits a seeing-eye blooper to right field for a single to load the bases. And to a Dodgers fan base watching from home, Vin Scully rises:

This crowd is on its feet and pleading. They're all getting up. It is that time of day. Never mind the seventh-inning stretch. This is the wire.

And then Pedro Guerrero, in a nine-pitch at-bat that lasts a full six minutes, ekes out a walk to cut the deficit to 6–4.

It is almost too much to take. You'd have to be a block of wood not to feel it.

And then Mike Marshall hits a fly to right field that dovetails into one of the sun's gallant rays, stymieing Claudell Washington, who spins around but can't find the ball before it lands at the base of the outfield fence and allowing the tying runs to score.

The play comes with the infield in, with the outfield in. The play comes with Dodgers fans begging, imploring Reynolds to find a hole within or beyond that shortened field.

Guerrero breaks down the third-base line.

The SQUEEZE! And here comes the run!!

Dodgers 7, Braves 6. Bedlam.

26 And a Manny Shall Lead Them

As their 2008 season wound down to its final innings, the Dodgers' hopes appeared to rest on Manny Ramirez's ability to hit a five-run homer.

Based on what he had done to that point, you half-believed he could.

The Dodgers were not a one-man band in 2008, their 20th season since the heroics of Kirk Gibson. But they did need something of a hero: someone who could push them past the two decades of postseason struggles that had limited them to a single victory. Someone who could provide the power for a team that hadn't seen anyone hit more than 20 homers in a season since 2005.

In 2008, the Dodgers needed someone who could push them past the two decades of postseason struggles and bring in the runs. Manny Ramirez was nothing less than a dream hitter, hitting 17 home runs and slugging .743, and was one hit shy of batting .400.

Joe Torre, the celebrated Yankee manager who had come out to helm the Dodgers following the 2007 season, couldn't exactly be expected to drive in the runs.

It was for that reason that the Dodgers went out in December 2007 and got a big-name, slugging outfielder. The team signed free agent Andruw Jones, who had averaged 31 home runs per season with the Atlanta Braves and was still only 30, to a two-year, $36.1 million contract—the highest average annual salary ever for a Dodger. Jones was coming off the poorest season of his career to that point, but most people found easy enough to explain away to injury.

Instead, Jones faltered to an almost unprecedented extent. Arriving at Spring Training overweight, Jones never, at any point, found his swing. He had a .275 on-base percentage and .273 slugging percentage through May 18, when he was sidelined by torn cartilage in his right knee. Unable to salvage his season, Jones finished with three home runs and a 32 OPS+, the lowest by a Dodger with at least 200 plate appearances in 97 years. Instead of being carried by Jones, the Dodgers had to carry his dead weight.

For a while, Rafael Furcal helped them do exactly that. The shortstop—a former teammate of Jones in Atlanta—was his solar opposite, a ball of flame in contrast to Jones' ice-cold bat. In his first 32 games, Furcal on-based .448 and slugged .597, positioning himself arguably as the NL's most valuable player to that point. But the injury bug didn't play favorites, striking Furcal in his back and taking him out of the Dodger lineup from May 5 to the final week of September. Within a week, the Dodgers had lost their projected and actual best hitters.

Add to this the struggles of 2007 staff ace Brad Penny, whose ERA more than doubled (3.03 in 2007, 6.27 in 2008) as he foolishly tried to pitch in pain before going on the disabled list for half the season, and the two-in-one-day Spring Training injuries to third basemen Andy LaRoche and Nomar Garciaparra, and you could get the sense that the 2008 Dodgers were a star-crossed team.

Still, they weren't entirely bereft. The team's emerging home-grown core continued to take more responsibility. At age 24, Chad Billingsley finished ninth in the NL with a 135 ERA+ (3.14 ERA) and fifth with 201 strikeouts. Jonathan Broxton, Hong-Chih Kuo and rookie surprise Cory Wade sharply backed him in the bullpen, and heralded 20-year-old phenom Clayton Kershaw took a spot in the back end of the rotation. James Loney and Matt Kemp joined Russell Martin in the everyday lineup, while at age 22, Blake DeWitt, who had been three levels below the majors a year earlier, stepped up in the absence of LaRoche and Garciaparra with a .837 OPS through the end of May, earning himself the nickname "The Solution."

But the Dodgers' path to success was at best meandering. Los Angeles was seven games out of first place in the NL West before the end of April, and even though the division-leading Arizona Diamondbacks faded from their hot start, the Dodgers found themselves in the confounding position of being one game out of first place yet two under .500 (49-51) on July 22, when Colorado slaughtered them 10–1.

Four days later, the Dodgers acquired third baseman Casey Blake from Cleveland (at the cost of minor league pitcher Jonathan Meloan and catcher Carlos Santana, the 2008 California League MVP) to supplant DeWitt and LaRoche. As the morning of the July 31 non-waiver trade deadline came, it seemed Blake would be the team's big move for success.

Then came Manny.

Despite leading the Boston Red Sox to its first two World Series titles in nearly a century, hammering 274 homers in 7½ seasons and posting a .430 on-base percentage and .601 slugging percentage for them in 2008, Ramirez had earned the enmity of much of Boston through some malcontent behavior—an incident of pushing a front-office employee here, allegations of dogging it there. His actions seemed a transparent ploy—in theory with the encouragement of his new agent, Scott Boras—to force his employer to void the two remaining option years on his contract and render him a free agent, although the Red Sox never chose to suspend him. They did, however, decide they had had enough of him. So, in a three-way deal completed minutes before the deadline, the Dodgers sent LaRoche and minor-league pitcher Bryan Morris to Pittsburgh, which sent All-Star outfielder Jason Bay to Boston, which sent two minor leaguers to the Pirates and one Manny Ramirez to Los Angeles.

That's when things really got crazy. Ramirez was every bit as fantastic as Jones was not. In 53 regular-season games, Ramirez hit 17 home runs and slugged .743. He reached base in nearly half his at-bats. He was one hit shy of batting .400. He whipped Dodger Stadium crowds and cash registers into delirium. He was nothing less than a dream hitter, providing, by all indications, the single greatest hitting performance by a trade-deadline acquisition ever.

Even so, three weeks after he arrived, the Dodgers went on an eight-game losing streak. Everything else had stopped working. This was worse than meandering—this was a death spiral. The team dropped 4½ games behind the Diamondbacks, and faced two weekend games in Arizona against two of the best pitchers in the league: Dan Haren and Brandon Webb.

Improbably, in their darkest hour, the Dodgers responded. They won both games, kicking off a stretch in which the team went 18-5. Both young and old contributed, with Andre Ethier and starting pitcher Derek Lowe particularly catching fire. The Diamondbacks, who hadn't been able to bury the Dodgers when they had the chance, paid for it dearly. When they lost an afternoon game in St. Louis on September 25, they officially handed the NL West to the Dodgers.

That was all well and good, but there was still that matter of a postseason drought to contend with. The 84-78 Dodgers had to face the NL's top team, the 97–64 Chicago Cubs, in the best-of-five NL Division Series. Los Angeles was a decided underdog, a fate the team seemed destined to fulfill after Lowe, who had an ERA of 0.94 in his final nine regular-season starts, gave up a two-run second-inning home run to Mark DeRosa in the NLDS opener.

But Loney, facing Cubs starter Ryan Dempster (who was left in the game with two out in the fifth inning even though he had just walked his seventh batter), blasted a grand slam to center field to give the Dodgers a lead they wouldn't relinquish for the rest of the series. They won 7–2 in Game 1, 10–3 in Game 2, and thanks to a taut performance by 33-year-old Japanese rookie Hiroki Kuroda, 3–1 in Game 3, sending the Dodgers into the best-of-seven NLCS for the first time since '88.

The Dodgers had been so dominant that they suddenly went from underdogs to favorites in their next matchup, even though they faced a team with a better record, the 92–70 NL East champion Philadelphia Phillies. Vexingly for Los Angeles, the Dodgers led in each of the first four games, but squandered the lead in three of them. Furcal, who had just come back from his long injury absence to excel against the Cubs, threw away a ball in the fifth inning of Game 1, setting the stage for Lowe to give up a two-run home run in what became a 3–2 loss at Philadelphia. Billingsley, so exquisite during the regular season, quickly surrendered a 1-0 lead in Game 2 by allowing eight runs in 2⅔ innings. The Dodgers tried to rally, but Blake's bid for a three-run game-tying home run was caught at the deepest part of the ballpark, and the Phillies held on 8–5.

Returning to Los Angeles, the Dodgers chased Phillies starter Jamie Moyer with six early runs in a 7–2 win behind Kuroda. And leading 5–3 with five outs to go in Game 4, the Dodgers were on the verge of tying the series. But there, the good times ended.

Wade and Broxton, who between them had allowed three home runs at Dodger Stadium all year, each gave up two-run shots in the top of the eighth, and Philadelphia rallied for a 7–5 victory. Game 5 presented chances for the Dodgers to start one more back-to-the-wall comeback, but they couldn't take advantage, losing the final game of the series and the season 5–1.

The only Dodgers run of that game came on a home run by Ramirez, who was 13-for-25 with four homers and 11 walks in the playoffs, and the lingering question for people heading out of Chavez Ravine was whether Manny would return to the Dodgers—and if not, how would they replace him? While their youth movement remained poised to proceed in 2009, the team was in the same offensive boat, wondering where the power would come from. Jones had one more year left on his contract, but pessimism about him could hardly be higher.

As the Dodgers and their fans watched the Phillies defeat a young, spunky Tampa Bay Rays team in the World Series, they could comfort themselves with this. No longer were wins in the postseason an albatross. The Dodgers had made it back to baseball's Final Four.

How soon before they would go farther?

27 Arrive Late, Leave Early

So, whenever a book about the Dodgers is published, does a fan of another team joke that the readers start reading in the third chapter and finish in the seventh? Maybe. And maybe it's even funny the first time someone says it. But not the second, or the third, or the three-hundredth.

What Goes Around, Comes Around—And Smacks You

If you don't like seeing dramatic comebacks at the Dodgers expense, then August 21, 1990, was the night to leave Dodger Stadium early. Los Angeles built an 11–1 lead over Philadelphia, thanks largely to an eight-run fifth inning, and still led 11–3 heading into the ninth.

But the Phillies started stringing some singles and walks (with two errors by Dodger shortstop Jose Offerman tying it all together) that cut into the Dodger lead. Dale Murphy doubled off Tim Crews with the bases loaded to pull the Phillies within reach at 11–8, and John Kruk immediately followed with a pinch-hit three-run homer to tie the game. Two batters later, Jay Howell then gave up a double to Carmelo Martinez that drove in Philadelphia's ninth run in the ninth, the deathblow in a 12–11 loss for the Dodgers.

Postgame traffic was light, but heavy-hearted.

If you're taking in a national or out-of-town broadcast from Dodger Stadium, it's inevitable that the so-called wit of some announcer will find its target in the ritual late arrival and early departure of Dodgers fans. If it's true fans are like this in Los Angeles, it's also true they're like this at major league parks across the country, with nary a person commenting. And this doesn't even address the ballparks where most of the seats are empty from start to finish.

It may be fair to say, however, that no city is quite like Los Angeles for a *laissez-faire* attitude toward seeing nine innings of baseball. Part of this is inspired by the geographical spread of Los Angeles, its epic traffic, and the notoriously crowded Dodger Stadium parking lots that are barely mitigated by the area's patchy public transportation system. Given those elements, it's no wonder fans are late or fear a homeward struggle.

There are Dodgers fans who will leave at a certain inning by rote, regardless of the hour, how close the game is, or how quickly the game is moving. When Montreal righty Dennis Martinez was pitching the 13th perfect game in major league history at Dodger Stadium in 1991, more than a few folks headed for the exits before the ninth.

But you know what? Not every person in the ballpark that day was a baseball fan. Not everyone who goes to a baseball game lives and dies with the sport. Not everyone has the kind of life that allows one to get to a game on time or stay until the end. So? Isn't it better that people get a taste of the ballpark, however shortened, than no taste at all?

To interject a personal moment…one time my shift at work ended in the neighborhood of midnight. In my car, I listened to a Dodgers game that had entered extra innings. Instead of heading home, I decided to drive to the ballpark and see if the game was still going by the time I got there. Sure enough, I entered Dodger Stadium in the top of the 12th inning—and left triumphantly after the Dodgers won it in the bottom of the 12th. I saw one inning, and it was one of the most memorable games I have ever attended.

On some level, it's been decided that giving tardy slips or detention to baseball fans is a way of measuring their dedication, their innate "fanness". That's not going to change, but the methodology isn't fail-safe. The Dodgers have sold more tickets than any franchise in history. Even after accounting for those who don't see a full game, it's doubtful there are many other fan bases that have seen more innings of baseball than the one in Los Angeles. And the passion of Dodgers fans, whether they're at the game or listening to Vinny (the No. 1 reason for not rushing to one's seat), has always been underrated.

Baseball is supposed to be fun. Baseball is not football or basketball with rigid time constraints. Baseball is a carefree day at the park, a night to unwind. No doubt, there are some of you who want to see nine innings of ball but just can't. But if you're pleased with less, then be pleased. Arrive late and leave early, and do it to your hearts' content. This is not a test.

28 Hail the Duke of Flatbush

"With two runners on base and the Dodgers leading 5–4 in the 12th inning, Willie Jones drove a 405-footer up against the left-center-field wall. Duke isn't a look-and-run outfielder like Mays. He prefers to keep the ball in view all the time if possible, and he was judging this one every step of his long run to the wall. There it

Longtime Dodgers center fielder Duke Snider greets invited guests to the "sneak peek" of the new Dodger Stadium on April 9, 1962. "The Duke of Flatbush" played his final season at Dodger Stadium, was the franchise leader in home runs at 389, and played on two Dodgers World Championship teams in 1955 and 1959. Photo courtesy of Los Angeles Times Collection, UCLA Library Special Collections.

seemed he was climbing the concrete 'on his knees,' as awed Dodger coach Ted Lyons put it. Up and up he went like a human fly to spear the ball, give a confirming wave of his glove and fall backward to the turf. The wooden bracing on the wall showed spike marks almost as high as his head. It was such a catch that, although it saved the game for Brooklyn, admiring Philly fans swarmed the field by the dozens. Duke lost his cap and part of his shirt and almost lost his belt."

– Al Stump, *Sport*

Edwin Donald Snider gets third billing in the Terry Cashman song, "Willie, Mickey, and the Duke"—a placement that seems to celebrate as well as diminish his legacy. Snider was one of the greatest center fielders of all time, up there with Willie Mays and Mickey Mantle, but he was forever proving himself to the Dodgers and to baseball history.

"Duke was so talented, and he had a grace about him," said his Dodgers roommate for 10 years, Carl Erskine. "They talk about [Joe] DiMaggio and how he carried himself on the field.... His outfield play and his running the bases and his trot for the home run, he just looked class, man.

"The thing that bothered Duke was, no matter how well he did, the coaches [and] managers always said, 'He can do better than that.' They always kind of made Duke feel no matter how hard he tried, he couldn't satisfy everybody. It was bothersome for him."

Snider, a Compton High School graduate from Los Angeles, even had a love-hate relationship with Ebbets Field fans, as Maury Allen writes in *Brooklyn Remembered.* "Snider always wore his emotions on his sleeve," Allen said. "A home run in a key spot would produce that Hollywood handsome grin. A strikeout with the bases loaded and the Brooklyn fans booing his very name announcement the next day would result in a week of sulkiness."

15-Love

May 21, 1952: Just another lovely night at Ebbets Field, the Dodgers facing the Cincinnati Reds. Billy Cox leads off the bottom of the first by grounding out, but Pee Wee Reese walks and Duke Snider homers over the right-field scoreboard. Would that be enough?

Maybe this would help: Jackie Robinson speeds to a double on a Texas leaguer, then after an Andy Pafko walk, scores on a George Shuba single. Pafko was thrown out at third on an attempted double steal, but perhaps a 3–0 lead would suffice.

Just in case it wouldn't, the Dodgers eke across...12 more runs. The next 14 Dodger batters all reach base on seven singles, five walks, and two batters hit by pitches. Reese alone notches a single and two walks in the inning. Finally, with the bases loaded, Snider takes a curveball from Frank Smith, the fourth Reds pitcher, for a called strike three, and the Dodgers settle for a 15–0 lead, the biggest first-inning onslaught in big league history.

And yes, pitcher Chris Van Cuyk, who went 4-for-5 at the plate, is able to make the lead stand up for a 19–1 Dodger victory.

Ultimately, like the way he climbed that Ebbets Field wall to save the game against the Phillies, Snider reached magnificent heights. He had eight full seasons and two partial seasons with EQAs of .300 or better, more than any other Dodger ever. He had at least 40 homers in the Dodgers' five final seasons in Brooklyn, and a career .295 batting average, .380 on-base percentage, and .540 slugging percentage. He hit an all-time Dodgers record 389 homers.

In a 1955 article, *Sports Illustrated* chose Snider over Willie Mays: "In every sense, the contemporary hero of Flatbush, prematurely gray at the temples in his 29th year, is a picture player with a classic stance that seldom develops a hitch. Next to [Ted] Williams, Snider probably has the best hitting form in the game. And, like Williams, he has amazing eyes—large, clear, calm, and probing. With each oncoming pitch, Snider tenses and then throws his full 195 pounds into it, if he swings, with a smooth, lashing motion."

The Duke was much, much more than a name in a song.

1965

A catharsis of a different kind. Two years after their fulfilling, resounding sweep of the Yankees, the once-snakebitten Dodgers won another World Series—the team's third in Los Angeles and fourth since 1955. But 1965's triumph came at the end of an exhausting season of scratching and clawing and self-medicating that elicited as much relief as elation.

It was a year most remembered for two grit-your-teeth moments: Giants pitcher Juan Marichal using Dodgers catcher Johnny Roseboro's head for batting practice, and Sandy Koufax's perfect game that the Dodgers offense backed with a single hit. It was a year that the only Dodger to bat .300 or slug .400 was pitcher Don Drysdale, who was 39-for-130 with seven homers.

Down 4½ games to the Giants on September 15, the Dodgers found the way to win 13 straight and 15 of their final 16, allowing only 17 runs over that stretch. On October 1, Koufax struck out 13 in clinching the title for the Dodgers with a 3–1 victory over the Milwaukee Braves. How did the Dodger offense break a 1–1 tie in the fifth? Almost inexplicable bases-loaded walks to Roseboro and Koufax.

There was every indication that the Dodgers were spent by the time the World Series began in Minnesota on October 6: Yom Kippur that year. Famously, Drysdale got the Game 1 start instead of Koufax, and when Walter Alston met Roseboro and Drysdale at the pitcher's mound to pull him during a six-run third inning, the pitcher supposedly quipped, "I bet you wish I was Jewish, too." (Rob Neyer, in his *Big Book of Baseball Legends,* investigated the story and found that "all three of these men later composed their memoirs [Alston twice], and yet none of them happened to mention this seemingly memorable joke that Drysdale made.... A check of various newspaper archives doesn't find it attributed to Drysdale until the 1980s, usually in reference to Sandy Koufax and the status of the Jewish ballplayer.") No matter—the tale spoke volumes, with the added irony that on Game 2 the following afternoon, Alston

Sandy Koufax and Lou Johnson were Game 7 heroes of the 1965 World Series. The Dodgers defeated the Minnesota Twins 2–0. Koufax pitched a complete-game shutout and Johnson drove in the initial run with a home run.
Photo courtesy of Los Angeles Dodgers, Inc.

Zero for '66

Dodgers futility never got a more public airing than the 1966 World Series against the Baltimore Orioles. In Game 1, Jim Lefebvre homered in the bottom of the second inning, and Jim Gilliam walked with the bases loaded in the third. That was it—the team was done. For the remaining 33 innings, the Dodgers did not score. Only two Dodger base runners reached third base. The nadir was Game 2, when the Dodgers made six errors, three in the space of two batters by center fielder Willie Davis, though back-to-back 1–0 losses in Games 3 and 4 offered their own special brand of excruciation. The Dodger doldrums began in earnest in 1967, after Sandy Koufax retired, but the entry point was here.

probably wished Yom Kippur had returned in time to prevent Koufax from allowing two runs in the sixth inning of a scoreless contest. The Dodgers lost the game 5–1 and headed back to Los Angeles in a 2–0 Series hole.

In Game 3, the Dodgers' one major preseason acquisition paid its greatest dividend. Claude Osteen, acquired in a deal that marked the departure of slugger Frank Howard, threw a 4–0 shutout backed by RBI hits from Roseboro, Lou Johnson, and Maury Wills that put the Dodgers back in Series contention. A three-run sixth gave Drysdale breathing room in a 7–2 Game 4 victory, and then Wills' four hits helped Koufax cruise to a 7–0 Game 5 shutout, in which he took a perfect game into the fifth inning and a two-hitter into the ninth.

But nothing was going to be entirely easy for the Dodgers, not this year. Back in Mnnesota, Mudcat Grant hit a three-run homer while pitching a complete-game 5–1 victory on two days' rest, setting up the Dodgers' first Game 7 since '55.

Koufax and Jim Kaat, also pitching on two days' rest, started out scoreless through three innings. Then, leading off the top of the fourth, "Sweet" Lou hooked one off the left-field foul pole to put the Dodgers on the scoreboard and give Koufax the only run anyone ever hoped he would need. Wes Parker's high chopper over first base to drive in Ron Fairly that same inning seemed almost luxurious in context.

Koufax, who later said he relied on fastballs because his curveball had abandoned him, would get even more help. In the bottom of the fifth, with runners on first and second and one out, Jim Gilliam—who began the season as a Dodgers coach—made a sprawling, backhanded stop of Zoilo Versailles' grounder for a force play that helped preserve Koufax's shutout.

In the ninth, a one-out single by Harmon Killebrew gave the Twins two final chances to tie the score. But Koufax fanned Earl Battey and Bob Allison to end it. A very much non-leaping Koufax, who had struck out 29 in 24 innings over nine days while allowing one earned run, joined the Dodgers in thankful celebration. In the clubhouse after the game, Vin Scully reminded Koufax that after that Game 5, Koufax said he felt 100 years old. "So today," Scully asked him, "how do you feel?"

"A hundred and one," Koufax replied. "I feel great, Vinny, and I know that I don't have to go out there any more for about four months."

30 Steve Garvey

There has never been another Steve Garvey. There has never been anyone to match his Popeye-sized forearms, his senatorial presence, and his 200-hit regimen straight out of Jack LaLanne. Never someone who was every bit the athlete—he was a star college football player at Michigan State, after all—but who wouldn't have seemed out of place heading to first base in briefcase, coat, and tie.

For Dodgers fans in the 1970s, underneath that metaphorical coat and tie was a big red *S*. Once Garvey moved over from third base to first and shed the need for his scattershot throwing arm, he became a legend straight out of baseball pulp fiction: a Dodger batboy and son of a team bus driver who rose up to become its conquering hero. He never missed a game. He could scoop an errant throw out of quicksand. Most of all, it always seemed, if you needed a hit, he got it for you. Starting in 1974, the year he became a write-in starter in fan balloting for the All-Star Game and later NL MVP, Garvey had at least 200 hits for six out of seven seasons, averaging 23 homers and 104 RBI. He was an All-Star every one of those seasons.

"He moves precisely, with a textbook stride, almost in slow motion," wrote Pat Jordan in his renowned *Inside Sports* article on Garvey. "He is conscious of the way he runs and of the fact that he is being watched. His pumping arms are properly bent into L's at his sides, and held away from his body a bit, like wings, as if to keep his shirt from wrinkling. He resembles a man trotting to catch a bus in a new silk shirt on a hot day... His are the movements of a man with a single-focus concentration, a man for whom nothing—running, picking up a ball, smiling—is natural and everything is learned."

Separating his performance from his persona was nearly impossible. While still a player, Garvey got a junior high school named after him. It wasn't speculated, it was assumed that Garvey would run for public office after his playing career was over. Immortalization in bronze was invented for guys like Garvey.

"Steve Garvey is the only ballplayer I ever saw who, when he began to talk, you could almost feel the organ music and candlelight and incense," Jim Murray wrote for the *Los Angeles Times* on December 23, 1982. "Who, when the choir struck up 'Ave Maria,' could turn to his date and murmur, 'Listen, darling, they're playing our song.'"

Murray wrote that column in the aftermath of Garvey's departure for San Diego and away from the Dodgers, who negotiated with Garvey but chose to go with touted minor league prospect Greg Brock rather than meet the demands of the soon-to-be 34-year-old. Garvey's consecutive game streak ended the following season at an NL record 1,207 games when he injured his thumb sliding into home, but he had one more World Series appearance and two more All-Star games with the Padres before retiring in 1987. So powerful was Garvey's presence in Southern California that even though he played only 645 games with San Diego, the team retired his number. That's something the Dodgers haven't done, because the Dodgers almost without exception require you to make it to Cooperstown first.

There has never been another Steve Garvey, in part because Steve Garvey wasn't really Steve Garvey. Time has not treated his legacy kindly. His ostensible political ambitions became the stuff of parody as revelations emerged of a troubled marriage, children fathered out of wedlock, and financial troubles. More relevantly for pure baseball fans, his on-field record has suffered as well. A closer look reveals that his on-base percentage was never all that high because of how rarely he walked (career high of 50). Not once was he the top hitter on a Dodger team, according to OPS+ or EQA. That's not at all to say he wasn't good; from 1974 through 1980, his EQA never fell below .283. But there was a time when the public considered Garvey to have the inside track to the Hall of Fame. The revelation that his numbers don't compare so well to other players, even on his own team—Ron Cey, Reggie Smith, and Davey Lopes all have arguably better stats—combined with a certain *schadenfreude* among some about the decline of his public image, have left him on the outside looking in.

Garvey is best remembered if you place yourself back in the era in which he played. He was a winner, a rock, and he made you feel secure.

31 Peanuts!

Playing catch with the greatest lefties in Dodgers history would have been something to remember. But while he might not be Sandy Koufax or Fernando Valenzuela, a catch with Roger Owens is a pretty great alternative.

Owens is the most famous peanut vendor in history, and for good reason. He came out to sling snacks at Dodgers games in their 1958 debut season at the Coliseum, working his way up the ballpark food chain starting when he was 15 years old—first soft drinks, then ice cream—before cresting atop the exalted salted pinnacle. And then, like Raymond Chandler or Ray Charles, he reinvented the genre. Out of necessity when his path to a customer was blocked by some confused fans standing in front of him, Owens threw prudence and peanuts to the wind, flinging a bag behind his back and curving it around the clueless contingent right into the hands of his waiting patron.

Over time, Owens developed various circus throws such as under-the-legs and two-for-ones (two bags sent simultaneously to

The Cool-a-Coo

Of all the items that have ever been on the menu at Dodger Stadium, there might be no departure more lamented than that of the Cool-a-Coo: a thick, generous dose of vanilla ice cream sandwiched between two oatmeal cookies, the entire amalgamation sealed in a chocolate covering. A similar dessert is the It's It, but is an It's It it? It isn't.

Cool-a-Coos vanished without warning from Dodger Stadium around the turn of the 21st century. Periodically a movement begins to bring them back, to no avail. The manufacturer ceased to exist, thus taking the unforgettable treat with it.

two different customers). He became first a legend locally and then nationally after he began appearing on *The Tonight Show* with Johnny Carson. With his infectious enthusiasm, Owens is the Magic Johnson (or, if you prefer, the Mickey Hatcher) of the eager-to-be-pleased Dodgers crowd.

And he's still there—though he won't be there forever. So while you still have the opportunity, get yourself some tickets in Owens' usual section on the left-field side of the Loge level, bring cash and an appetite, and call out "Peanuts!" And then prepare to have one of the quintessential Dodger Stadium experiences.

32 Peter O'Malley

It was no accident that under the leadership of Peter O'Malley, the Dodgers had only six losing seasons in his nearly three decades as president, became the first team in the majors to break the 3 million barrier in season attendance, expanded their groundbreaking globalization of the game (a preoccupation that continued for O'Malley long after selling the Dodgers), and three times were the only sports franchise *Fortune* named as one of 1997's "100 Best Companies to work for in America."

O'Malley could have chosen any field to work in. He could have forgone a work ethic. Instead, he showed constant diligence and vision. The Dodgers were lucky to have him.

He was a child when his father became a Dodgers vice president, and not quite a teenager when the family gained majority ownership of the team in 1950. In those days, after returning home from spring training in Florida, O'Malley would take one of Brooklyn's famous trolleys to Ebbets Field, mingle with the players,

Not quite a teenager when his family gained majority ownership of the Dodgers in 1950, Peter O'Malley (left) followed the successful steps of his father Walter (right). It was no accident that under the leadership of Peter O'Malley, the Dodgers had only six losing seasons in his nearly three decades as president.
Photo courtesy of www.walteromalley.com.

then cheer for the Dodgers from a seat behind the dugout before grabbing a ride home from Dad after the game.

"Pete Reiser was a family favorite," O'Malley recalled. "[Roy] Campanella was always talking to me about what's going on, fishing or something like that. Kirby Higbe, I identified with him for some reason. Rex Barney, who lived in Vero Beach later on after he played, was another family favorite. All the players, they were terrific. My memory is they were just nice to me, and I was never in their way.

"I remember washing Joe Black's car in Vero Beach—that was the neatest thing. He gave me a dollar or whatever it was. I would say it was just a natural, comfortable feeling."

Unsurprisingly, the Dodgers figured heavily in O'Malley's future. But what drew him most to a life in baseball wasn't a fascination with who was on the field, but what was happening off the field.

"I thought about law school when I was an undergraduate at Penn," O'Malley said. "But then the move [of the Dodgers to Los Angeles] and the building of the stadium and all those issues convinced me, 'Did I really want to go to school another couple of years?' So then I put aside the law school idea and just came and started working for the Dodgers."

In 1962, O'Malley was named director of Dodgertown, then a January-April job, with the rest of the season spent rotating among the Dodgers' minor-league teams. From 1965–66, O'Malley was president and general manager of the team's AAA franchise in Spokane, and then he came to Los Angeles in 1967 as vice president of stadium operations.

What laid the foundation for his ultimate success was not that he had the family name, but that he had a thirst for understanding the Dodgers business inside and out, alongside his interaction with people at every level.

"Looking back now, it was helpful because the people in the organization—the scouts, the managers, whoever—they all saw me summers along the way," O'Malley said. "I didn't just arrive, whether they saw me in Vero Beach or a minor league city, or certainly those who came through Spokane. I met a lot of great people, not just in the organization, but umpires and managers of other teams in the [Pacific] Coast League in those days, owners of other teams, general managers, press people."

Observers are often surprised if not skeptical when a young person takes over a ballclub, but O'Malley was an exception despite being only 32 when he started running the Dodgers in 1970. He had been around the franchise for so long that it was easy to accept him, and by the time he succeeded his father as president, he was in a comfort zone that enabled productive working relationships on all the off-field issues that so intrigued him when he was a Penn student.

Yet O'Malley never lost sight of on-field performance. When asked what his biggest challenge was as team president, he quickly mentioned when the Dodgers fell into last place in July 1979, and close behind recalled the devastating injury suffered by Pedro Guerrero, coming off his overpowering 1985 season at the end of spring training in 1986.

By those years, however, the Dodgers philosophy—one that could be summarized as patient decisiveness—had become ingrained in him.

"Like a battleship," O'Malley said, "rarely did we make a sharp right turn. It was usually an adjustment—fine-tuning. We tried to make a decision with the long-term view of decisions you make every day. If we believed in the people who were there, and we did, and the strategy and the goal and everything else, you're going to have times you fall into last place or you get an injury.... 'Fire the manager, fire the pitching coach, fire the general manager, replace somebody else'—that really didn't enter. We may have thought about it, but not seriously and for any length of time, because we believed in the people."

33 Down Goes Jackson

Perhaps even more than the pitch, people remember the reaction: Reggie Jackson untwisting himself from a swing that almost corkscrewed him into the ground. He grabbed his bat high on the barrel and violently thundered a furious curse.

Powerhouse hitter Reggie Jackson is struck out by 21-year old Bob Welch on a 3–2 pitch in the ninth inning. Welch saved Game 2 of the 1978 World Series and brought one of the most exhilarating victories over the Yankees ever imaginable.

David slew Goliath. Jack brought down the Giant. Bob Welch—all 21 babyfaced years of him—struck out the Bronx Bomber on a 3–2 pitch in the ninth inning to save Game 2 of the 1978 World Series and bring on a deafening roar at Dodger Stadium.

The day the Series opened, rumors were spreading that fire-balling Dodgers rookie Welch had an arm problem. Nonsense, insisted Tommy Lasorda. "Bob had a soreness in his side, down along his rib cage," he told Scott Ostler of the *Los Angeles Times*. "Our trainer said he's fine."

Apparently. Clinging to a 4–3 lead in the top of the ninth, the Dodgers sent out Terry Forster for his third inning of work. Yankees hero Bucky Dent opened the inning with a single to left field and

Hip To Be Tied

The Yankees were on the ropes. They had lost two of the first three games of the 1978 World Series and trailed 3–1 in the sixth inning of Game 4. New York had Reggie Jackson and Thurman Munson on first and second with one out, but Lou Piniella hit a sinking line drive to Dodger shortstop Bill Russell, who dropped it. Alertly, he stepped on second base to force Jackson out. Russell needed only to get the ball to Steve Garvey at first base to end the inning, but the action was thwarted. Jackson turned his hip into the ball, deflecting it toward the right-field stands, allowing Munson to score.

A furious debate ensued—with both sides accusing each other of intentionally mucking up the works (Did Russell intentionally drop the ball? Did Jackson intentionally interfere?)—but the umpires let the play stand. The Yankees went on to beat the infuriated Dodgers in 10 innings 4–3 to even up the Series, then routed the Dodgers over Games 5 and 6.

moved to second on a groundout. A walk to Paul Blair put the go-ahead run on base, signaling that Forster had passed his expiration date.

Lasorda's do-or-die replacement had 24 career appearances, 11 in relief. The two batters he needed to get out, Thurman Munson and Jackson, had 465 career home runs between them, three of which were hit by Jackson in the last game of the previous year's World Series. Dodgers fans at the stadium and across the country waited for the roof to cave in.

Welch fed a strike in against Munson, who hit a sinking drive to right field that Reggie Smith caught at his knees.

It was Jackson time. This wasn't just any slugger. This was the enemy personified, a man, though well-liked in his later years, considered perhaps the most egotistical, vilified ballplayer in the game.

Welch began by inducing Jackson to overswing and miss. With Drysdale-like flair, he then sent in a high, tight fastball that sent Jackson spinning into the dirt.

Jackson later told Earl Gustkey of the *Times* that he was expecting Welch to mix in some of his good offspeed pitches, but instead came three fastballs, each of which were fouled off. Then there was a fastball high and outside to even the count at 2–2.

After another foul ball, another high and outside fastball brought a full count. The runners would be moving. Short of another foul, this would be it.

As everyone sucked in their breath, in came the heat. Amped up, Jackson swung for the fences—not the Dodger Stadium fences, but the fences all the way back in New York.

Only after Jackson missed the ball and nearly wrapped the bat around himself like a golf club, only through Jackson's rage, could Dodgers fans begin to comprehend what happened.

Jackson carried his fury into the dugout and clubhouse with him, pushing first a fan on his way to the dugout and then Yankees manager Bob Lemon once inside.

The only thing that could have made the event better for Dodgers fans would have been for them to have had longer to enjoy it. The Dodgers didn't win the World Series that year; they didn't win another game. Welch himself was the losing pitcher in Game 4, allowing a two-out, 10th-inning run in his third inning of work, and gave up a homer to Jackson in Game 6. But for a moment, the Dodgers and their fans enjoyed one of the most triumphant and exhilarating victories over the Yankees ever imaginable.

34 One Postseason, Three Comebacks

Two-strike hitters don't come much better than the 1981 Dodgers. After losing the first two games of a NL West division playoff, two of the first three of the NLCS and the first two of the World Series, the Dodgers went a combined 10–0 to bring Los Angeles its first Fall Classic title in 16 years.

The players' strike split the '81 season in half, and in the opening round of a first-of-its-kind postseason intra-division series, the Dodgers found the Astrodome in Houston every bit as inhospitable as it had been to them for years. Los Angeles scored one run in 20 innings, losing Game 1 by a 3–1 score and Game 2 in 11 innings 1–0. The Astros won both games in their last at-bats. But the Dodgers turned it around, holding the Astros to two runs over the final three games, Jerry Reuss capping the series with a 4–0 shutout in Game 5.

In the NLCS against Montreal, the Dodgers won Game 1 for the only time in the postseason, but lost the next two games to face elimination again. Burt Hooton came through with a 7–1 Game 4 victory to force another winner-take-all finale. With the score tied 1–1 in the ninth inning (Fernando Valenzuela had the RBI for the Dodgers on a groundout), Expos ace Steve Rogers came out of the bullpen to pitch. With two out, Rick Monday pounced on Rogers' hanging sinker for a raucous home run to give the Dodgers a 2–1 lead—arguably the biggest single hit for the Dodgers since the 1960s. Valenzuela was one out away from the pennant when he faltered, walking two batters, but Bob Welch entered to get Jerry White to ground out and send the Dodgers into the World Series.

For the third time in five years, the Dodgers would face the Yankees in the Fall Classic. In their last meeting three years earlier, the Dodgers had won the first two games before losing the final four. This time around, the Dodgers quickly had to cling to the hope they could reverse that circumstance and complete another comeback. Bob Watson's three-run first-inning homer put the Dodgers in an immediate hole with Game 1 going to New York at 5–3. Los Angeles lost quietly in Game 2 with 3–0.

In Game 3, Ron Cey hit a three-run first-inning homer of his own, but Valenzuela surrendered the lead by allowing two runs in the second and again in the third. However, Pedro Guerrero tied the game with an RBI double in the bottom of the fifth, and the Dodgers regained the lead on a double-play grounder.

Not to be forgotten from this game is the sparkling defensive play Ron Cey made on Bobby Murcer's pop bunt with two runners on. Cey dove to catch the ball in foul ground, then fired to first base to double up Larry Milbourne. With the Dodgers still winning by a 5–4 sliver, in the game that would define his ability to pitch in adversity, Valenzuela, after escaping a threat in the eighth, set the Yankees down in order in the ninth. Lou Piniella, the 40th batter Valenzuela faced went down swinging.

The fourth game was madness. Again, the Dodgers found themselves trailing 4–0 in the third, with Dave Goltz relieving 1978 hero Welch after he allowed three hits and a walk to the first four batters. Goltz allowed the second run to score on a sacrifice fly, then gave up single runs in the second and third.

It was 6–3 Yankees in the bottom of the sixth when team prankster/pinch-hitter Jay Johnstone hit a two-run homer to cut the lead to one. (According to Mark Heisler of the *Los Angeles Times*, the following exchange took place: "Johnstone was asked later if he'd hit a fastball. 'Does he throw anything else?' Johnstone asked. 'Can you hit anything else?' asked a man who has followed Johnstone's career closely.")

The next batter, Davey Lopes, lofted a fly ball to right field that hit Reggie Jackson inside the shoulder after he lost the ball in the sun. Lopes stole third, and Bill Russell singled to tie the contest. *Times* headline the next day: "Jackson Gets Something Off His Chest...It's the Ballgame."

In the bottom of the seventh, a dying fly ball by Monday landed just out of Bobby Brown's glove leading to a two-run rally, capped by an infield chopper by Lopes. Jackson homered in the eighth to cut the lead to 8–7, but Steve Howe pitched the final three innings and saved the game.

Game 5 provided the Yankees one more early lead, but the 1–0 margin could not withstand dramatic back-to-back homers in the seventh by Guerrero and Steve Yeager. That was enough for Jerry Reuss to survive a complete-game, 2–1 victory and give the Dodgers their first Series lead in '81.

Game 6 turned on a decision by Yankees manager Bob Lemon to pinch-hit for ex-Dodger pitcher Tommy John with two on in the bottom of the fourth and the game tied at 1–1. Murcer flied to the warning track, and George Frazier got hammered in the fifth. Cey, who was beaned by Goose Gossage in the eighth inning of Game 5, broke the tie with an RBI single, and Guerrero ended up driving in five runs. When Watson flied to Ken Landreaux in center field, the third and final comeback was complete. The Dodgers were champions again.

35 Pee Wee Reese

The regal career of Harold Reese has fallen more than a little under the shadow of Jackie Robinson. On May 13, 1947, the Dodgers shortstop from Louisville, Kentucky, legendarily wrapped his arm around his besieged teammate, casting a visual testament of their closeness. The irony is that while this memory is indicative of the close, meaningful bond the two developed, it offers myth mixed with fact. "No one else wrote about it...not in New York, not in Cincinnati, not in white papers, not in black—not in 1947," said Jonathan Eig after investigating the story for *Opening Day: The Story of Jackie Robinson's First Season.*

"It's possible that the Robinson-Reese moment took place just as...others remembered it, in 1947. But it seems unlikely." Eig and Arnold Rampersad (in 1997's *Jackie Robinson: A Biography*, noting that Robinson himself made no mention of the gesture in his 1948 autobiography) suggest that the substance for the tale of Reese's support for Robinson was real, even if the particulars of when and how it was expressed remain in doubt. While historians and fans, insiders and outsiders can natter over the details of this most famous moment, they risk overlooking the greatest shortstop the Dodgers ever had.

Dodgers captain Pee Wee Reese—shown here at Dodgertown in Vero Beach, Florida, with his wife Dottie and daughter Barbara—played shortstop for the Dodgers from 1940–42 and 1946–58 and was a 10-time National League All-Star. He played on seven Dodgers pennant-winning teams, and was a member of the 1955 World Champion Dodgers. Photo by Barney Stein.

The Handshake Deal

Before Pee Wee Reese, there was George Shuba. On April 18, 1946, playing for his first game the Dodgers' farm team in Montreal on Opening Day of the International League, Jackie Robinson homered in his second at-bat. Awaiting him at the plate was George Shuba, who extended his hand in the customary greeting—except that it was anything but customary for a white man to shake a black man's hand on a baseball field. On the first day of the Robinson's path to integrating baseball, a meaningful impression had been made.

Wasn't he, though? He provided 12 above-average seasons from the position, despite World War II waylaying his career in 1943, 1944, and 1945. He hit nothing like an Alex Rodriguez, but when it comes to the best offensive performances by Dodgers shortstops in OPS+, Reese has two of the top three, three of the top five and 11 of the top 30. Even though he didn't play a major league game from the time he was barely 24 years old until he was almost 28, Reese finished his Dodgers life as the team's all-time leader in runs and walks, second in hits and fifth in total bases. And for good measure, as baseball writer Rob Neyer notes in his *Big Book of Baseball Lineups,* Reese was the only man to play in every World Series game—44 in all—between the Brooklyn Dodgers and the Yankees.

At the turn of the present century, historian Bill James ranked Reese the 10th-best shortstop of all time and added that "among the shortstops who were leadoff men and who had long careers...Reese was the most effective leadoff man. [Maury] Wills was more celebrated in the role, but as a practical matter, Pee Wee's walks led to a lot more runs than Wills' stolen bases."

There's nothing wrong with being remembered for your personality, your good graces and, certainly your uncommon humanity in the face of opposing forces, but it shouldn't necessarily come at the expense of your accomplishments—even if you have trouble believing them yourself.

"Three themes sound through the years of Harold Henry Reese, son of a Southern railroad detective and catalyst of baseball integration," Roger Kahn wrote in *The Boys of Summer*. "The first was his drive to win, no less fierce because it was cloaked in civility. A second theme was that civility itself. Reese sought endlessly to understand other points of view, as with Robinson or with Leo Durocher or with a news photographer bawling after a doubleheader, 'Would ya hold it, Pee Wee, for a couple more?' The final theme echoed wonder. He played shortstop for three generations of Brooklyn teams. Yet near the end, sitting on a friend's front porch and watching a brown telephone truck scuttle by, he said with total seriousness, 'I still can't figure out why the guy driving that thing isn't me.'"

Instead, Reese drove an entirely different kind of vehicle, right to Cooperstown. He was his own kind of special. James passes along one more Reese anecdote to remember, an origin story specific to the man himself.

"In 1939, Tom Yawkey and two 'partners,' Donie Bush and a man named Frank McKinney, purchased the Louisville Colonels for $100,000," James wrote. "The Colonels had Pee Wee Reese on their roster, a year away from the majors, and Yawkey figured that Reese alone would be worth what he paid for the team. But Bush and McKinney, who were not Red Sox employees, decided they had no reason to let their partner have Reese for free, and voted 2–1 to sell Reese to the highest bidder. Yawkey refused to bid for his own player, and Bush and McKinney sold Reese to the Dodgers for $100,000—the same amount they had paid for the team."

36 Roseboro & Marichal

The idea of a bat hitting a skull is about as frightening an image as one can conjure at a baseball game. Baseball can be a surprisingly violent sport, from home-plate collisions to intentional beanballs, but in the modern game, few moments stand out as shockingly as what happened between the Dodgers and the Giants on August 22, 1965.

Tensions were usually heated between those two teams, of course, and a pennant race only turned up the flames. Entering the Sunday finale of a four-game series at Candlestick Park, the Dodgers led a tight NL by half a game over the Milwaukee Braves, with San Francisco just another game behind. Three days earlier, Lou Johnson had hit a game-winning, 15th-inning two-run home run off Gaylord Perry (in his seventh inning of relief work). In their previous game, Dodgers first baseman Wes Parker had hit a two-run homer in the 11th inning to beat San Francisco.

The pitching matchup on this Sunday was a beauty: Sandy Koufax against Juan Marichal. Koufax had already struck out 288 batters in his 248 innings at that point of the season; Marichal had an ERA of 1.73 and five consecutive complete games.

It wasn't long before the skirmishing began. Wills, who bunted for a base hit to lead off the game, dodged a knockdown pitch from Marichal before lining out to end the top of the second inning. In the bottom of the second, Koufax, who wasn't known for such actions, threw a fastball over San Francisco star Willie Mays' head. Then in the third, Marichal sent right fielder Ron Fairly to the ground with a near beanball.

In the bottom of the third, Marichal came up to bat, and Roseboro crafted a plan to send his own message. Returning one of Koufax's pitches, Roseboro zinged it so near Marichal's head that numerous reports stated it ticked his ear. (Roseboro would later say it was "too close.") What indisputably happened is it ticked Marichal off.

He raised his bat and struck several blows at Roseboro's head.

"Manager Walt Alston thought at first Roseboro might have lost his left eye," Sid Ziff wrote in the *Los Angeles Times*. " 'It was covered with blood,' he said. 'I thought Gabby was badly hurt. It's just lucky he had his arm up to ward off some of the blows.'"

The ensuing bench-clearing melee lasted nearly a quarter of an hour—and it would have been longer if not for the peacemaking efforts of Mays, who helped Alston wrap a towel around Roseboro's head and get him to the dugout amid the frenzy. That didn't stop Roseboro from trying to find Marichal again, nor did it stop other Dodgers such as Johnson from trying to get at anyone in a Giants uniform.

The battle for justice after the game was more protracted than the incident itself. Several Dodgers called for Marichal to be banned from baseball, and were incensed when the punishment by NL president Warren Giles was a nine-day suspension and a $1,750 fine. (Giles said he didn't want to penalize the entire Giants team in a close pennant race.) Roseboro, though he accepted an apology from Marichal, considered pressing criminal charges and ended up suing him in court, with the case ultimately being settled.

Meanwhile, the *San Francisco Chronicle* connected Marichal's rising animosity toward the Dodgers with a Don Drysdale pitch that knocked down Mays in May. According to a Ziff column on August 26, Giants fans and the team's manager, Herman Franks asserted that Roseboro got what was coming to him and wondered aloud why he wasn't being suspended. "Something brought this on," Franks told New York sportswriter Dick Young. "You don't believe this man would just start swinging a bat at people, do you?"

They lost not only the day of the incident (with a shaken Koufax walking two batters before serving up a three-run homer to Mays one out after the fight), but also two September games at home against the Giants after that (with Giles keeping Marichal from pitching in Los Angeles during the series), the Dodgers went on to win the NL pennant over San Francisco by two games, and ultimately the World Series.

In 1975, trying to stay in baseball at age 37, Marichal signed a one-year contract...with the Dodgers.

"Listen, nobody hated Juan Marichal more than I did," Dodgers vice president Al Campanis told Jeff Prugh of the *Times*. "But there are times when things change, when your affections replace any ill feeling... I'm excited."

Said Marichal: "I want to make the Dodgers fans forget the past and show them I'm not a bad guy." But he lasted only two games with the Dodgers, getting knocked out by the fourth inning in both starts, and made the decision to retire April 18. Roseboro had hung up his spikes five years before.

Eventually, Roseboro and Marichal hung up their dispute as well, becoming friends in their post-playing days. Fans at the 1982 Oldtimers Game at Dodger Stadium saw the two of them embrace, and that October, according to Rob Ruck in *The Tropic of Baseball: Baseball in the Dominican Republic*, Roseboro urged voters to forget about the brawl and elect Marichal to the Hall of Fame. That happened in 1983, and Roseboro was one of the first to call Marichal to congratulate him.

In August 1965, Roseboro was said to be hoping to see Marichal indicted, but two decades later, he journeyed to Cooperstown to see Marichal inducted.

"It was just another baseball fight," Roseboro said amid the 25th anniversary celebration of Dodger Stadium in 1987. "I never held that much animosity against Marichal, because if I was in a situation—one-on-one, going-to-fist-city situation—I'd be nervous, and if I didn't think I could kick the guy's butt, I'd probably take a bat and try to keep him off of me, too."

37 1962

Los Angeles, meet Brooklyn. Meet shock, meet despair, meet unremitting bitterness. Meet Murphy's Law. Meet the return of the Devil himself: "Wait 'til next year."

In 1962, the year Dodger Stadium opened, the Dodgers found themselves in a heated pennant race from the start. After losing their first game, they won 16 of their next 26, including an 18-strikeout performance by Sandy Koufax, tying his own NL record. Yet they still found themselves five games back of their 21–6 archrival San Francisco Giants. A 13-game winning streak only put Los Angeles in a tie for first place on June 1. It took a 41–18 record (.695) for the Dodgers to move into first place by themselves on June 8.

Los Angeles and San Francisco jockeyed for position over the next month. Koufax, who pitched his first career no-hitter June 30, combined with Don Drysdale on a 2–0 shutout of the Giants on July 8 to put the Dodgers once more in first, where they would stay into October. But nine days later, with a 2.06 ERA and 208 strikeouts in 174⅔ innings, Koufax was knocked out of action by injury. He would pitch only 8⅔ dreary innings for the remainder of the year, leaving behind a void that would redouble in the season's final days.

Even without Koufax, it looked like the Dodgers would edge the Giants without looking back. They led by 5½ games on August 9 and, after winning their 100th game on September 22, held a four-game advantage with seven left to play. But on the 23rd—the day Maury Wills broke Ty Cobb's single-season stolen base record—St. Louis hammered the Dodgers 12–2. Two more losses in their next three games followed, trimming the team's lead over San Francisco to two games with three left.

It still should have been enough, except Dodgers hitters showed their new, warm-weather hometown what a drought really looked like. "They didn't tail off," Dodgers vice president Fresco Thompson would later tell *Los Angeles Times* columnist Sid Ziff. "They just went to the edge of the precipice and jumped off."

Trailing the Cardinals 2–1 in the bottom of the seventh inning on September 28, the Dodgers tied the game on a Wills RBI single. Los Angeles wouldn't score again for 35 innings. St. Louis won in the 10th inning, and then on September 29, backed by two unearned runs off Drysdale, the Cardinals' Ernie Broglio two-hit Los Angeles, helping reduce the Giants' deficit to a single game heading into the final day of the regular season.

That afternoon, as Johnny Podres and Curt Simmons battled in a scoreless duel at Dodger Stadium, word came from the Bay Area that Willie Mays had homered in the eighth inning to break a 1–1 tie. Minutes later, the Giants sealed that victory. Then, when the same eighth inning rolled into Los Angeles, the Cardinals' Gene Oliver homered off Podres, dropping the Dodgers into the same three-game playoff series they had in New York with the Giants in 1951—the least awaited rerun in Dodgers history.

Upon the first game in San Francisco, the collapse of the Dodger offense—which despite it all was second in the NL in runs and on-base percentage—was joined by the full impact of Koufax's ailing digit. Having made three mostly ineffective appearances since returning to action September 21, Koufax tried again but lasted only seven batters, allowing three runs on four hits. Mays (3 for 3, two homers) and the Giants pounded six Dodger pitchers while San Francisco's Billy Pierce threw an 8–0 shutout. After 163 games, the Dodgers finally faced elimination.

By the time the Dodgers entered the sixth inning of the playoff, which moved to Los Angeles for the second game, they had amassed only 21 base runners in those 35 scoreless innings. Drysdale, who according to Baseball-Reference.com had thrown his 4,500th pitch of the season earlier in the game, ran out of gas and allowed a walk, a double, and two singles, adding to the damage by slipping while fielding a grounder for an error. Four runs came across, giving San Francisco what seemed obviously to be an insurmountable 5–0 lead.

Remarkably, the Dodgers actually scored. Even more remarkably, the Dodgers didn't stop scoring. Seven runs came across in the inning, with reserve Lee Walls doubling home three and then scoring for a 7–5 lead.

Although the offense had come to life, the Dodgers pitching and defense were still on life support. San Francisco tied the game

Fall of '42

Trailing the St. Louis Cardinals by 2½ games with a week to go in the 1942 NL pennant race, Brooklyn roared to the finish line by winning its final eight games.

The problem was that in the final third of the season, St. Louis was hotter than a Missouri summer's day, winning their final six games, capping a run that saw them lose only eight of their final 51 contests. The Dodgers had a 10-game lead over the Cardinals on August 5 and won 60 percent of their remaining games, and still it wasn't enough.

The pivotal swing came in a two-game series between the teams September 11–12 in Brooklyn. St. Louis held the Dodgers to one run in 18 innings, winning 3–0 and 2–1. That would be the difference between making and missing the World Series in 1942.

with two in the eighth, aided by another Dodgers error by Frank Howard. But in the bottom of the ninth, despite manager Alvin Dark's use of four pitchers, the Dodgers loaded the bases on three walks and then won the longest nine-inning game in major league history to that point on Ron Fairly's sacrifice fly. As in '51, one more game would decide it all.

Podres, whose 1–0 loss in the regular season finale had come three days earlier, started the finale. He allowed two runs in the third inning including yet another unearned run, but Los Angeles came back with one in the fourth, two in the sixth on a Tommy Davis homer, and one in the seventh when Wills singled, stole second and third and scored on a throwing error for a 4–2 lead.

In the bottom of the eighth, after Davis reached third base with two out, Alvin Dark dared the Dodgers to go for broke. He had reliever Don Larsen (of 1956 World Series perfect game fame) walk Johnny Roseboro and Willie Davis intentionally to get to the pitcher's spot. Rather than pinch-hit, Dodgers manager Walter Alston let bat Ed Roebuck, who had given him a much-needed three shutout innings.

"We had a two-run lead, and I'd rather have Roebuck pitching for us with a two-run lead than anybody I've got," Alston told John Hall of the *Times*.

Later, Jim Murray would write that "another baseball official couldn't believe his eyes, all four of them, when he wandered into the locker room in the late innings of the game where the wirephotos had rigged up machines and found Drysdale idly standing there watching the transmissions of pictures. 'Why the hell aren't you out there heating up?' he exploded. Drysdale shrugged. No one had asked him to." But considering how overworked his staff was, no option that Alston faced offered refuge once he committed to leaving Roebuck in.

Not only did Roebuck ground out to end the eighth, but needing only three outs for the pennant in the ninth, he ran into immediate trouble. Matty Alou singled, and after he was forced at second on a hard smash by Harvey Kuenn, Willie McCovey walked on four pitches. Then Alou's brother Felipe walked on a 3–2 pitch. Then Mays came up, and hit a ball that went off Roebuck's glove for an infield single and an RBI. Bases loaded, Dodger lead cut to one run, and Alston's gamble on Roebuck had busted. He called in Williams, the winning pitcher from the previous day.

"It had to be Williams," said Alston. "The only right-handers left in the bullpen were Stan and Larry Sherry. And Sherry couldn't get loose. His shoulder's been stiff. Williams was well warmed up."

Orlando Cepeda hit a sacrifice fly to tie the game, but at least it gave Williams and the Dodgers a second out. However, with catcher Ed Bailey up, Williams threw a wild pitch to move runners to second and third. That meant Williams would walk Bailey intentionally to load the bases again. And lacking any margin for error, Williams followed up by walking Jim Davenport on five pitches to force in the go-ahead run.

Appropriately, after Ron Perranoski relieved Williams, the Giants added another run on a bobble by Dodgers rookie reserve second baseman Larry Burright—the team's fourth error of the game. Though Perranoski got a strikeout to end the inning, the Dodgers were back in a hole. Game 1 winner Pierce came in to close the pennant out, and did so on 12 pitches, Walls flying to center to end it.

Reporters were held out of the Dodgers locker room for nearly an hour after the game. Eavesdroppers heard only silence punctuated by fierce cursing. When the doors finally opened, Hall observed, "There were several empty whisky bottles. Ripped uniforms were scattered on the floor." Said Duke Snider, the lone Dodgers remaining from the '51 defeat: "They're all still in a daze."

Though Los Angeles would find relief the following year, the collapse gave the team's new supporters their initiation. Truly, they were Dodgers fans now.

38 Go. Go. Go. Go. Go.

He was a vision of the word *go*; a living, racing vision, everything you think and feel when you close your eyes and say the word to yourself, as you hear 50,000 fans at brand new Dodger Stadium chanting it. Go. Go. Go. Go. Go.

After more than half a century of baseball that had been won and lost by the power of players' arms, Maury Wills brought legs back to the sport. He tore across the diamond like scissors through paper, carving his indelible place in Dodgers history.

In that 1962 season, Wills stole 104 bases, the most by a baseball player since 1891 and 41 more than anyone had swiped since 1920. His 31 steals in 35 attempts that year after August 31 were by themselves more than Jackie Robinson had in all of 1947 when he led the league.

"If the Los Angeles Dodgers hold together and win the National League pennant," Tom C. Brody wrote in *Sports Illustrated* just before the end of the regular season, "it may be said that they stole it. More accurately, a slight, almost frail Dodger stole it. Maurice Morning Wills is his name and the first time this larcenous son of a Baptist minister gets on base against the Yankees' left-handed Whitey Ford, possessor of one of the most unfathomable pick-off motions in baseball, a dramatic high point of the World Series already will have been reached. Will Ford pick him off? Will little Maury steal? For the answer, tune in next week."

The answer was that in the ninth inning of the third and final tiebreaker playoff game of '62, the Dodgers lost the pennant, forestalling Wills' World Series showcase. But Wills didn't lose his 1962 NL MVP award or his place in history.

It's true that the impact of Wills' revolution isn't quite what it's been touted to be. Baseball fans and insiders alike heralded him for bringing the stolen base back to the game, but NL stolen base totals declined in '63 and '64, and failed to return to '62 levels for another five years after that. Wills himself would only top 60 steals one more time in his career, perhaps not surprisingly since he turned 30 at the end of the '62 season.

But Wills' stolen bases meant something, no doubt about it. "Stolen bases in general were worth more in the lower-run scoring environment of the 1960s, and Wills' thefts were even more valuable in pitching-friendly Dodger Stadium," Rich Lederer of BaseballAnalysts.com said. "I don't necessarily think Wills is a Hall of Famer. I just believe he has gone somewhat unappreciated over time, partly due to his subsequent drug problems, disastrous managerial career, and a changed game that focuses more on power, including from the shortstop position. His No. 1 contemporary was Luis Aparicio, who was voted into the Hall of Fame.... Aparicio was a better fielder than Wills. But Wills was better offensively, both at the plate and on the bases."

Wills floated through the ballpark like a lifeline to Dodgers fans, who would all but give up on the team scoring if Wills didn't reach first base. When he was kept off the bases, the offense seemed to grind to a stop. But when he was on, it was all systems go...go...go. . .go...go!

39 *Nightline*

In the end, what you have to ask is not whether Al Campanis was a victim, but whether he was the only victim.

If he didn't deserve to see 19 years as Dodgers general manager and more than four decades in the organization come to an end over his grotesquely expressed remarks regarding African Americans on the April 6, 1987, ABC broadcast of *Nightline*, was his fate any worse than that of the nameless people deprived of career advancement in baseball because of the attitudes seeping through Campanis' inconsistent but telling comments? Even the most sympathetic interpretation of Campanis' use of the word "necessities," an interpretation that focuses on his contention that "you have to pay your dues," was disingenuous, as littered as baseball is with white managers who did no such thing. Black men were not getting past the gate, and Campanis could express no fault with the gatekeepers.

Excerpt from Ted Koppel's interview with Al Campanis

Koppel: Why is it that there are no black managers, no black general managers, no black owners?

Campanis: Well Mr. Koppel, there have been some black managers, but I really can't answer that question directly. The only thing I can say is that you have to pay your dues when you become a manager. Generally you have to go to the minor leagues; there's not very much pay involved. And some of the better-known black players have been able to get into other fields and make a pretty good living in that way.

Koppel: Yeah, but you know in your heart of hearts—and we're gonna take a break for a commercial—you know that that's a lot of baloney. [Campanis laughs.] I mean there are a lot of black players, there are a lot of great black baseball men who would dearly love to be in managerial positions, and I guess what I'm really asking you is to, you know, peel it away a little bit—just tell me why you think it is. Is there still that much prejudice in baseball today?

Campanis: No, I don't believe it's prejudice. I truly believe that they may not have some of the necessities to be, let's say, a field manager or perhaps a general manager.

And so if all Campanis was doing was channeling the prevailing attitudes of his time and his upbringing, does that make his forced departure unjust? There are undoubtedly those who got 19 fewer years as general manager than he did and who are less remembered, less celebrated, and less fulfilled than they might otherwise have been.

"I was shocked," baseball legend Henry Aaron said in response to Campanis' remarks, "and I think Mr. Campanis needs to apologize to every single black person in America for making comments like that."

Campanis did. "My statements have been construed as indicating a belief that blacks lack the ability to hold such positions," he said the next day. "I hold no such beliefs. However, I, and only I, am responsible for my statements. Therefore, I apologize to the American people, and particularly to all black Americans, for my

Koppel: Do you really believe that?

Campanis: Well, I don't say that all of them, but they certainly are short. How many quarterbacks do you have? How many pitchers do you have that are black?...

Koppel: Yeah, but I mean, yeah, I've got to tell you, that that sounds like the same kind of garbage we were hearing 40 years ago about players, when they were saying, "Ah not really..."

Campanis: Well—

Koppel: "Not really cut out"—remember the days when you hit a black football player in the knees. And you know—that really sounds like garbage if you forgive me for saying so.

Campanis: No, it's not garbage, Mr. Koppel, because I played on a college team and the centerfielder was black, in the backfield at NYU with a fullback who was black. Never knew the difference whether he was black or white—we were teammates. So it just might be that they, they...why are black men or black people not good swimmers? Because they don't have the buoyancy.

Koppel: Oh, I don't, I don't—It may just be they don't have access to all the country clubs and the pools....

statements and for my inability under the circumstances to express accurately my beliefs.... In my work and in my personal life, I have never distinguished a person by reason of his color, but only by reason of his abilities. For this reason, I feel that this is the saddest moment of my entire career."

Whether Campanis' failings were of discrimination or articulation, they should be considered alongside his humanity. They do not negate the way he openly befriended and supported Jackie Robinson when the two were the double-play combination of the 1946 Montreal Royals, at a time when that kind of support was anything but automatic. They do not eliminate the positive things he did, as a teammate, scout, and GM.

"There are a lot of racists in the world, on both sides, and he wasn't one of them," said Roy Campanella's widow Roxie to Matt McHale of the *Los Angeles Daily News*. "He helped Roy so much when he was coming through the minor leagues. He molded a lot of young men into men."

Campanis' legacy is necessarily two-pronged; it switch-hits on both sides of morality. No aspect of Campanis should be considered in a vacuum. It's a reminder that those of us who sit in judgment of others on any level still need to reexamine ourselves. We might or might not have Campanis' particular flaw, but we are all flawed, and we can all do better.

40 'The Best Hitter God Has Made in a Long Time'

After each home run he hit, Pedro Guerrero would look up in the stands and wag his index finger like a little puppet to his wife. In June 1985, the puppet show practically became a daily event.

In June 1985, Pedro Guerrero (on left, shown here with catcher Steve Yeager and third baseman Ron Cey) slammed 15 homeruns in one month, breaking the home-run record for June and second for all-time in a month. Guerrero slugged .860 and in the following month, reached base in14 straight plate appearances.

Though in his retirement Guerrero would generate a small bit of infamy for being acquitted on a drug conspiracy charge with a defense that his IQ was not high enough for him to have masterminded the deal, Pedro Guerrero was the thinking Dodgers fan's hitting hero in the 20th century. The genuine article.

Immediately before Guerrero, there was Steve Garvey and Ron Cey and Davey Lopes. There was Dusty Baker and the forever underrated Reggie Smith.

None of them quite swung the laser that Guerrero did.

"Pedro is the best hitter God has made in a long time," wrote Bill James in the 1985 edition of his *Baseball Abstract*. "His stats, for Dodger Stadium, are as good as [George] Brett's or [Jim] Rice's or anybody else's in their own context."

Born in 1956 in the Dominican Republic, Guerrero first reached the big leagues in 1978, EQAed .310 in 1980 while playing six positions, and shared the World Series MVP award with Cey and Steve Yeager in 1981. Always productive, Guerrero somehow topped himself in June 1985.

On the first day of the month, he hit a home run. Again on the fourth day, the seventh day, the eighth day. In a four-game stretch from June 10–16 (interrupted by rainouts), he hit five homers. He hit his 10th homer of the month on June 19, then homered again in four of his next six games.

He spent three days in pursuit of a 15th blast of the month, which at the time would give him the major league record for most homers in June and second-most for most homers in any month, behind Rudy York. In his final at-bat of a June 30 Sunday afternoon game at Dodger Stadium, Guerrero did it—winning the game to boot with his two-run dinger.

For the month, Guerrero averaged nearly a base per plate appearance (including walks) and slugged .860. And he wasn't done—at one point the following month, he reached base in 14 straight plate appearances. He finished the year with a .422 on-base percentage, .577 slugging percentage, and .360 EQA.

The Dodgers won the NL West in 1985 and had every expectation of repeating in 1986. But just before the end of spring training, Guerrero ruptured a tendon in his left knee. He came back strong in 1987 with a 154 OPS+, but he was traded in the middle of the Dodgers' championship season in 1988 for John Tudor. Still, for his Los Angeles Dodger career, Guerrero ranks fourth all-time in OPS+. In the 1980s, Guerrero was as good as there was.

41 Steady as She Goes

The loneliest job in the world this side of the Maytag repairman used to be that of Dodger human resources director. With only three general managers, two managers, and one Vin Scully employed during a four-decade stretch under O'Malley team ownership, Rip Van Winkle could have applied for a position and had a full nap waiting to hear the news.

Even after the dawn of free agency, even after years of the Garvey-Lopes-Russell-Cey infield gave way to more frequent change, stability remained the Dodgers' calling card well into the 1990s. And even when names did change, there was continuity.

"There was a process, a system in place that didn't have to be reinvented every year or two years and yet was enhanced with improvement year by year," former Dodger GM Fred Claire said in an interview.

"For example, if you take the critical role of pitching coach, at the time that I was fired, Glenn Gregson had been our pitching coach—not a name well known," Claire recalled. "He had started with us in Bakersfield in 1990. He replaced Dave Wallace, who came out of our system. Dave Wallace replaced Ron Perranoski, who came out of our system. Ron Perranoski replaced Red Adams, who came out of our system.... And if you look at all of this depth, that's not a rarity. That was the system. You can look at hitting coaches, you can look at field coordinator.

"And this applies not only to the major league level, but to the minor league level and to the scouting. This system had gone back literally to [Branch] Rickey days."

The flip side of stability and continuity, of course, is becoming so stuck in a rut, so addicted to formula, that you miss bolder

Foundation

As the 2008 regular season drew to a close, the Dodgers held their annual ceremony at Dodger Stadium honoring longtime employees. More than 50 had worked for at least a quarter-century at the ballpark. Some are well-known, such as Vin Scully, Tommy Lasorda, Jamie Jarrín or even traveling secretary Billy DeLury, but many more toil behind the scenes in anonymity: ushers, grounds crew, accountants, vendors, ticket takers, batting practice pitchers and administrative assistants. It's worth taking a moment to appreciate those who work, often from morning until well after the game ends, year after year.

chances for improvement and innovation. Surely, that happened to the Dodgers at times. But it wasn't as if changes never took place. In the meantime, the team's solid foundation worked as a security blanket, allowing the Dodgers to take a long-term view and, for the most part, avoid desperate, self-destructive decisions.

When Dodgers fans look back at life under the O'Malleys, they rarely lament the moves that weren't made, but rather those that were: namely, letting beloved team figures go. Stability wasn't a panacea for the Dodgers, but as a fail-safe, it was effective. Continuity with the humility to consider change seems like a pretty good model.

42 1980—The Final Weekend

In the 1980 season, from April 26 on, the Dodgers never lagged nor led by more than three games in a taut NL West. Tied for first place with Houston on September 24 with 10 games remaining, they suffered back-to-back 3–2 defeats to San Francisco and San Diego to fall two back. A week later, yet another 3–2 loss to the Giants put the Dodgers three back with three to play. The saving grace was that the Dodgers would be hosting Houston for the final three games of the regular season. But facing starting pitchers Ken Forsch (3.20 ERA), Nolan Ryan (3.35), and Vern Ruhle (2.37), the Dodgers faced a tall task.

What followed was one of the most memorable series in franchise history.

On Friday, October 3, Alan Ashby's sacrifice fly off Dodger starter Don Sutton gave Houston a 2–1 lead and put the Astros within two innings of clinching the division. Forsch got four consecutive groundouts to move Houston within two outs of the title. But with one out in the ninth, Rick Monday singled, and Dusty Baker reached on an error by second baseman and ex-Dodger Rafael Landestoy. Steve Garvey flied out, but down to their final at-bat before elimination, Ron Cey singled to center field, scoring pinch-runner Rudy Law. Forsch retired Pedro Guerrero to send the game into extra innings.

Fernando Valenzuela, in his eighth career game, retired the side in order in the 10th inning, his second inning of work. And then, in the bottom of the 10th, Joe Ferguson homered off Forsch, frenzying the crowd. Flinging his helmet like a frisbee as he crossed home, Ferguson kept the Dodgers alive for one more day. Finally, an important 3–2 game went the Dodgers' way.

On Saturday, Garvey's fourth-inning homer off Ryan broke a 1–1 tie, and Dodger starter Jerry Reuss made the advantage stand up, though not without some nail-biters. With two out in the top of the ninth, Reuss gave up singles to Cesar Cedeno and Art Howe, putting the tying run at third base. But Gary Woods, with a .396 on-base percentage, grounded out, and just like that, the Dodgers were playing for a tie on Sunday.

For the second time in three days, Houston moved within six outs of clinching the division. The Astros scored two early runs off

Burt Hooton, who was removed by desperate Dodgers manager Tommy Lasorda after recording only three outs in eight batters. Bobby Castillo gave up a third run in the fourth inning to put Los Angeles behind by three. Pitching two shutout innings for the second time in three days, Valenzuela kept the Astros at bay while the Dodgers got on the scoreboard with a fifth-inning RBI single by Davey Lopes.

In the bottom of the seventh, with runners at second and third, 42-year-old Manny Mota pinch-hit for the 19-year-old Valenzuela. Mota's pinch single—the final hit of the beloved Dodger's career—drove in Guerrero to cut the lead to 3–2. But Baker later fouled out with the bases loaded, and the Dodgers entered the eighth inning still down by a run.

NL Rookie of the Year Steve Howe retired the Astros in the eighth. Then, once more, the Astros made a pivotal error—Enos Cabell allowed Garvey to reach base—and the next batter, Cey, sent Dodgers fans into delirium with a homer.

When Howe allowed two singles in the top of the ninth, Lasorda continued to manage within an inch of his life. He brought in Sutton, who had gone eight innings fewer than 48 hours earlier, to get the final out. Denny Walling grounded to Lopes, and the NL West season had gone overtime.

Lasorda chose Dave Goltz, a tremendous disappointment in 1980 after signing a free-agent contract, to start the winner-take-all 163rd game. Subsequent legend has insisted Lasorda made a mistake here—that he should have instead started Valenzuela, who had yet to allow an earned run in his career and would go on to pitch that Opening Day shutout in 1981 to kick off Fernandomania. But, as indicated earlier, Valenzuela had pitched four innings in the past three days already, eliminating him from starting contention. Hooton had just been knocked out, Sutton and Reuss weren't available. Rick Sutcliffe, the 1979 NL Rookie of the Year, had been banished to the pen after posting a 7.51 ERA as a starting pitcher in 1980.

Though a disappointment, Goltz had a 2.56 ERA in 38⅔ innings since September 2. It might have been his luckiest stretch of the season, but it made Goltz the best available option.

In the end, Lasorda might have been better off coming out of retirement to make the start himself. Two Dodger errors helped put Goltz in a 2–0 hole in the first inning, and a two-run homer by Howe made it 4–0 in the third. Pitching in relief in the fourth, Sutcliffe surrendered three runs, and the Dodgers were done.

It was a deflating end to an incredible weekend. If the Dodgers had completed that four-game sweep to the title, it would have been a top–10 all-time moment. As it is, even in defeat, it was a weekend that the Dodgers could not forget.

43 Black and Blue and Purple Heart

This is the what-might-have-been story of the greatest player in Dodgers history. This is the bone-breaking, heartbreaking, hide-your-eyes story of the man for whom baseball was a playground and a brick wall.

The should've been greatest player in Dodgers history was named Pete Reiser, and he began once upon a 1939 by reaching base the first 12 times he came to bat in spring training, the month of his 20th birthday. Having made an unwritten agreement with Branch Rickey, then running the Cardinals, to sell Reiser back to his original team in St. Louis (Reiser was one of numerous minor leaguers Kenesaw Mountain Landis set free after

Roberto Clemente: What Happened?

Al Campanis saw a teenage Roberto Clemente while scouting for the Dodgers at a Puerto Rico tryout camp in 1952, and in February 1954, Brooklyn outbid the New York Giants and signed the 19-year-old to a $5,000 contract with a $10,000 bonus. However, the bonus required the Dodgers keep him on the major league roster or risk losing him at season's end. The Dodgers took the chance, assigning Clemente to their minor league affiliate in Montreal.

Clemente, writes Stew Thornley in his thoroughly researched piece for the Society of American Baseball Research's Baseball Biography Project, played only intermittently and not particularly well for Montreal much of the year, finishing with a .257 batting average and two home runs in 87 games, though he began to have success against lefties come July. And people recognized the talent. "You knew he was going to play in the big leagues," teammate Jack Cassini said. "He had a great arm and he could run."

The 1954 Rule 5 Draft, held in November, marked the occasion for major league teams to draft eligible minor leaguers from other organizations. Each franchise could lose at most one player, and the Pittsburgh Pirates—who had the worst record in baseball—would draft first. The Pirates were now Branch Rickey's club, and though he was still friendly with his replacement in Brooklyn, Buzzie Bavasi, he chose Clemente.

The rules of the time were simply not set up to allow the Dodgers to nurture a highly prized, highly priced minor leaguer without the peril of losing him. The rightfielder's legendary, 3,000-hit, 266-assist Hall of Fame career would begin in Pittsburgh in 1955, and end only with his tragic death in a plane crash on an aid mission to Nicaraguan earthquake victims on December 31, 1972.

calling into question the Cardinals' minor league operations), Dodger general manager Larry MacPhail hid the young outfielder in the minors with the team in Elmira.

Reiser spent three months of that season with his right arm in a cast, teaching himself to throw left-handed so that he could get back on the field sooner. And after he did, after his potential became obvious to everyone in Dodgerland, MacPhail found it impossible to fulfill his end of the secret bargain with the Cards.

The tornado came in 1941. Twenty-two years old, reaching base at a .406 clip, Reiser led the league in total bases (299 in 137 games), batting average (.343), slugging percentage (.558), doubles (39, tied with Johnny Mize), triples (17) and for good measure OPS+ (165). And, forebodingly, hit-by-pitches (11). From the outset of his career, his injuries warranted a revolving door at the hospital—as quickly after a beanball sent Reiser to the hospital, he'd plot his escape. W.C. Heinz, in his incomparable if loose-with-the-details story on Reiser, chronicled how Dodgers manager Leo Durocher would have him put on his uniform even though he wasn't supposed to play—just to buck up the spirit of his teammates—then find it impossible not to use him off the bench.

Twenty-two years old in 1941, a hero and a casualty, an emblem just in time for war.

Reiser had one more season before joining the service, and that was the season that did him in. July 19, 1942, bottom of the 11th inning, score tied at 6–6 in St. Louis. Enos Slaughter hits one over his head. "Out in center field, Pete Reiser tore back at top speed," wrote Tommy Holmes for *The Sporting News.* "He caught the ball a split second before he crashed into the concrete wall. The round, white thing spurted out of his glove. Reiser picked himself off the turf and staggered after it. He threw it and a double relay made the play at the plate reasonably close.

"That was the ball game and there wasn't anything to do except go out and pick up the pieces."

He had again been leading the NL, batting .379. He was back at the hospital—and then, just as soon out of it—on a train to Pittsburgh and back in action. Holmes wrote "just six days after he had rammed his skull against the center field wall at Sportsman's Park."

Over the next three seasons, Reiser played ball for different squads in the Army, challenging the common-sense notion that the ballfield was safer than the battlefield. He made it back to Brooklyn for the 1946 season, stealing a league-high 34 bases—including seven swipes of home, an NL record. He finished in the top 10 in the MVP voting, despite missing 34 games. "Twice," recalled Harold C. Burr of *The Sporting News,* "he went headlong into the concrete at Ebbets Field and near the end of the season broke his ankle, sliding back to first base against the Phillies, and watched the playoffs with the Cardinals with the limb in a plaster cast."

In 1947, on the fourth of June occurred another brutal collision with a wall. "Mercifully, he came out of this one, groggy and mumbling, but without a cracked skull," reported Burr. "Pete was taken to the Swedish Hospital with a wicked V-shaped cut along his hairline.... 'I don't even remember making the catch,' Pete said in the dressing room, smoking a cigarette while awaiting the arrival of the hospital ambulance." Within a week, Rickey, by this time reunited with his prize prospect in Brooklyn, put into work plans to rubberize the Ebbets Field outfield wall.

"The boy the fates delight in using as their plaything" was out for six weeks and still enduring dizzy spells when the Dodgers went into the 1947 Series against the Yankees. In Game 2, he misplayed three balls into triples, though he blamed it on the shadows at the Bronx ballpark. In the third game, he walked in the first inning, got the steal sign and, when he went into second, felt his right ankle snap, though no fracture was reported.

And yet, when Bill Bevens was in the ninth inning of his no-hit bid the next day, and Reiser pinch-hit, Yankees manager Bucky Harris walked him intentionally. He was still Pete Reiser, broken shell and all.

One more season in a Brooklyn uniform. Thirty more hits. The sensation at age 20 was traded away just before turning 30, struggling through four more campaigns before walking away from the playing field while he barely still could. He finished his major league career with a 128 career OPS+, but only 786 hits. Pete Reiser, the broken legend, the greatest Dodger that never was.

44 Know Red Barber

Once upon a time, Vin Scully was the young upstart, and the eminence of Dodgers broadcasting was a Columbus, Mississippi, native named Walter Lanier Barber. It was Barber who initially established the tradition of master storytellers in the Dodgers broadcasting booth.

"Red was so different that he made a tremendous impact on the community," Scully said. "If you can imagine a Southern gentleman broadcasting the Brooklyn Dodgers in the borough of Brooklyn, the contrast right there was really something. It wasn't an oxymoron exactly, but I think you understand, you're a Brooklyn fan listening to a fellow with this very soft, southern voice. And he was just marvelous; he did such a tremendous job."

Born in 1908, Barber began his baseball broadcasting career in 1934 with the Cincinnati Reds (he was on the air for the first major league game he ever attended), and then moved to do Brooklyn games in 1939. Along with Mel Allen, Barber was one of two original Ford C. Frick award winners from the Baseball Hall of Fame. He is responsible for a popularizing a chunk of baseball vernacular like "rhubarb" and "sitting in the catbird seat" and other phrases that remained uniquely his own, such as "wild as a hungry chicken hawk on a frosty morning" and "slicker than oiled okra." But reducing Barber to figures of speech does him an injustice.

Three legendary broadcasters in Dodgers history—Red Barber (left), Connie Desmond (center), and Vin Scully (right)—stand together during spring training at Dodgertown in Vero Beach, Florida, circa 1950. Barber, who worked for the Dodgers from 1939–53, became Scully's mentor when the young Fordham graduate joined the Dodgers in 1950. Desmond was a popular announcer with the Dodgers from 1943–56. Photo by Barney Stein.

Barber is best appreciated experientially, atmospherically. The rapid, high-pitched cadence, the lithe banter with his unseen, unheard but appreciative listeners are best when realized first-hand. Alternating with Connie Desmond and Scully, who joined the team in 1950, Barber set the tone not only for broadcasts of that era, but for decades to come.

"Red Barber moved people," wrote Bob Edwards, who hosted Barber's weekly commentaries for 12 years on National Public Radio called *Fridays with Red*. "A microphone was his magic wand. Either he knew what people cared about or he made them care simply because he raised the subject. It seemed to me that no one was indifferent to him or what he had to say. He knew how to reach listeners in a way that no one else on radio could."

"In Brooklyn," Scully added, "when we had Red, Connie, and the kid, what [fans of today] missed there was almost a familial thing. Red was the father, Connie was the older brother and I was the kid. And I don't think you'll ever quite see that again."

If it weren't for Barber, the Scully that Dodgers fans came to know over six decades might have become diminished. Barber taught Scully preparation, amongst a myriad of other things.

"When I started, just imagine, in New York you had Red Barber and Connie Desmond with the Dodgers," Scully recalled. "The Yankees had Mel Allen and Curt Gowdy. The Giants had Russ Hodges and Ernie Harwell. And what Red wanted was for me not to lose myself. It would be a tendency for a young broadcaster to tune in and maybe consciously or subconsciously pick up inflections, tonal qualities, expressions from the other announcers. And I guess you could say he was saying to me, 'Look, don't water your wine.' Because he said to me once—and I was shocked when he said it—he said, 'You know, you bring something into the booth that no one else does.' Well I looked at him; I had no idea what could that be. And he said, 'Yourself.' And that was the difference."

According to Edwards, Barber's departure from the Dodgers in 1953 was hastened by general manager Branch Rickey parting ways with the franchise a few years earlier. Barber and Walter O'Malley clashed, and Barber left after O'Malley didn't back him on a dispute with advertising manager Craig Smith of Gillette, which controlled broadcasting rights to the World Series. The next year, Barber was broadcasting from Yankee Stadium.

But when you think of Red Barber, you think of him as a Dodgers man. So charge yourself with a Red Barber treasure hunt. Check out his archived commentaries at NPR.org or the audio documentary on Barber available via WGUC.org. Find tapes of his old game broadcasts. For the truly adventurous, venture to the University of Florida's Smathers Libraries, which houses his personal collection of writings, photographs, memorabilia, film and video. Get his memoir, *Rhubarb in the Catbird Seat,* written with Robert W. Creamer. Immerse yourself in the founder of the Dodger broadcasting tradition. You'll be roundly rewarded.

45 Not This Time...

In October 2004, the Dodgers had been in first place since before the All-Star Break. But with the end of the regular season 24 hours away, with their pitching staff running on fumes, they were three outs away from seeing their lead in the NL West dwindle down to a single game. And of course, to paraphrase Vin Scully, it had to be the Giants.

The Dodgers had won two of three at San Francisco the previous weekend, but lost at Dodger Stadium on the final Friday of the season. If the Dodgers hadn't rallied in their final at-bat in three midweek games against Colorado, the Giants would have already caught them.

To make matters worse, the Dodgers' starting pitchers for the weekend were anything but reassuring. These were no longer the days of Newcombe or Koufax putting everything on the line on two days' rest. For the final Saturday of the season, it would be journeyman Elmer Dessens, making his first start since coming over from

Lima Time

The Dodgers' greatest playoff moment from 1987–2007 wasn't hard to pick—and no, it wasn't the 2006 game in which Jeff Kent and J.D. Drew were thrown out at home on the same play. Jose Lima, who had a 4.91 ERA the year before and a 6.99 ERA the year after (both times with Kansas City), stopped long enough in Los Angeles to give the Dodgers their most magical postseason night in ages. Facing a St. Louis Cardinals lineup led by all-world slugger Albert Pujols, Lima pitched a five-hit, one-walk shutout gem in Game 3 of the 2004 NL Division Series.

With a 4–0 lead in the eighth inning (thanks in part to two Shawn Green home runs), Lima allowed a two-out single and then threw a couple pitches in the dirt, signaling that it was getting near Eric Gagné time. But Lima got Larry Walker to ground out before retiring Pujols, Scott Rolen, and Jim Edmonds on 10 pitches in the ninth to seal the victory. The Dodger Stadium crowd rejoiced and rejoiced again. It had been 16 years without a postseason win up to that point. Thanks, Jose—we needed that.

Arizona as a reliever in August. Essentially, the Dodger bullpen would be counted on to go nine innings. If Dessens lost, it would be Kazuhisa Ishii (5.35 ERA since June 1) on Sunday.

Dessens actually pitched gamely, lasting four innings and allowing two runs, but the Dodgers bats truly could not hit a line drive to save their lives. Entering the bottom of the ninth inning, the Dodgers lacked an extra-base hit and trailed 3–0.

And then…a single by Shawn Green...a walk to Robin Ventura...after an Alex Cora strikeout, a walk to Jose Hernandez. Hee Seop Choi, part of the controversial Brad Penny-Paul Lo Duca trade two months earlier, worked out a walk after being down 1–2 in the count to drive in the Dodgers' first run.

And then, Cody Ransom booted Cesar Izturis's ground ball, allowing another run to score. And then, Jayson Werth knocked a 2–2 single to right field, scoring Hernandez to tie the game.

And then, and then, and then….

"The roar of the crowd, like waves crashing on the shore," Scully tells his audience. "They'll crash, and they'll be loud, and they'll back off and kind of build up more energy and then start to build again on the next pitch...0 and 1 the count to Finley. The outfield is shallow, the infield is up. Finley today is 1 for 4. Franklin set; Wayne ready and deals. Swung on—high fly ball to deep right field! Wherever it goes, the Dodgers have won—and it's a grand slam home run!"

Not this time, Giants. Steve Finley, another July 31 acquisition, had put the Dodgers over the top.

"I have always felt there are no words to describe a situation like this except the roar of the crowd," Scully continued after Finley circled the bases amid pandemonium, "and for those of us privileged to be there, watching the Dodgers just about jump out of their uniforms: What a finish, as Steve Finley hits it into the seats in right field, and the Dodgers come up and roll a seven in the bottom of the ninth inning, and beat the Giants 7–3. And in all the storied history and glory, frustrations and heartbreak, that both of these teams have inflicted upon the other, this one had to be a killer.

"And the Dodgers do the unbelievable, but then again, they're the Dodgers."

46 Pedro and A-Rod

Close your eyes, and you can almost see it.

Pedro Martinez. Mike Piazza. Alex Rodriguez.

Hall of Famers. Teammates. Dodgers.

It really could have happened.

In a parallel universe so close and yet so far, future Cooperstown colleagues Martinez, Rodriguez, and Piazza led the Dodgers of the 1990s to a World Series dynasty. But in a six-month period in 1993, two of the pieces fell away, and their absence indirectly led to parting ways with the third.

In 1992, the Dodgers ended a streak of 86 consecutive seasons without finishing in last place, losing 99 games to end up at the bottom of the NL West. It was a miserable year, punctuated by rioting following the Rodney King verdicts in April. But if there was an upside, it was that the Dodgers would have their highest position ever in baseball's amateur draft. They'd have the second pick behind Seattle. And there were two clear top players: Rodriguez and Darren Dreifort.

In fact, it was only a fluke of the AL and NL alternating the No. 1 pick each year in that era that kept the Dodgers from having the first choice overall (they actually had one more loss than the Mariners). But maybe that didn't matter. For the longest time, it looked like Rodriguez would fall in L.A.'s lap. Seattle had signability concerns with the 17-year-old high school phenom. Dreifort, a college pitcher closer to the big leagues, began to emerge as the more responsible pick.

"Dodgertown. Tom Lasorda. Dodger blue. I fell in love with the whole mystique about being a Dodger," Rodriguez told Ross Newhan of the *Los Angeles Times*. "I mean, I didn't know anything about Seattle except that the Seahawks played there. I barely knew where it was or who the Mariners were.

"I told them not to draft me. I told them I wanted to play for the Dodgers and I wanted play in the National League so that I could get home a couple times a year."

But in the end, Seattle—which had enjoyed recent success drafting Ken Griffey, Jr. No. 1 and distress drafting pitcher Roger Salkeld in the first round, couldn't resist A-Rod's potential. He went to Seattle. The Dodgers picked Dreifort.

While the Dodgers lost out on Rodriguez, they had already begun reloading. As of that day in June 1993, the 21-year-old Martinez had an ERA of 1.89 in his first full major league season, a year he would finish at 2.61 (147 ERA+) with 119 strikeouts in 107 innings. The Dodgers were rebounding to an 81–81 record, thanks in no small part to their unanimous Rookie of the Year Mike Piazza, who slugged 35 home runs with a .370 OBP and .561 slugging (.317 EQA). That being said, the looming threat of a players' strike or owners lockout further complicated the Dodgers' future. Furthermore, it would take still another leap to pass the Giants, coming off a 103–59 season in 1994's realigned NL West (Atlanta and Houston were moving to different divisions.)

Part of the leap forward was supposed to include second baseman Jody Reed, who wasn't much of an offensive threat after joining the Dodgers in 1993 but who helped reduced the team's defensive failings. General manager Fred Claire made what might have been an overindulgent offer to Reed of $7.8 million for three years—a raise for a player who had already been earning the fifth-highest salary in baseball for a second baseman. But Reed still turned it down, a decision that might have been the most shocking in the entire history of Dodgers contract negotiations. In the book *My 30 Years in Dodger Blue*, Claire wrote that Reed asked for $11.25 million for three years.

Claire turned to the Montreal Expos and Delino DeShields, who, like Martinez, could boast a strong rookie season at the age of 21. DeShields was 24 now, and coming off a year in which he had batted .295 with 43 stolen bases and only 11 errors. But DeShields was not a free agent. He would have to come in a trade, and Martinez was whom Montreal wanted.

Claire discussed the future of Martinez with Tommy Lasorda, head of Dominican Republic baseball operations Ralph Avila, and

Dr. Frank Jobe, who later told Newhan, "His shoulder had come out once, and once an injury of that type occurs, you can't say it won't reoccur. He had kind of a delicate stature to start with and there were already questions about his stamina. It's a judgment call, but you had to kind of wonder, 'Golly, is this kid going to break down?'"

If Rodriguez had been in the organization, the chances of the Dodgers investing in another young middle infielder would have shrunk. But A-Rod was two states to the north. Claire pulled the trigger and got DeShields.

Martinez would become one of the most dominant pitchers of all time (his 291 ERA+ in 2000 is a major league record), striking out more than 3,000 batters with a career ERA below 3.00. Rodriguez would become among the greatest hitting infielders of all time and a likely home run king. And Piazza would establish himself as the greatest hitting catcher of all time even before being traded away in 1998, a trade that might not have ever happened if he had been part of a trio of stars with Pedro and A-Rod.

DeShields would suffer through three miserable seasons with the Dodgers before salvaging something of his career with St. Louis and Baltimore. As for Reed, he ended up settling for a one-year deal with Milwaukee that failed to net him even $1 million, and for the rest of his career combined, earned almost exactly what the Dodgers offered him for 1994 alone.

Having three future Hall of Famers on your roster doesn't guarantee success. The Mariners, with Rodriguez, Griffey, and Randy Johnson, who incidentally was another rumored Dodgers trade target in the '90s, never reached the World Series.

But better to have had them and lost, then not to have had them at all.

47 The First High Five

As much as George Washington is the father of our country, Glenn Burke is the father of the high five. Which is to say that he was involved, and he gets most of the credit—but it isn't quite that simple.

Here's the cherry tree version of the story: At the end of the 1977 season, when Dusty Baker circled the bases after joining teammates Steve Garvey, Reggie Smith, and Ron Cey to form the first quartet of 30-homer hitters in MLB history, the on-deck hitter, Burke, was there to greet him.

"When Baker crossed home plate, the first man to congratulate him was the exuberant rookie center fielder, who had been in the on-deck circle," Randy Harvey wrote five years later in the *Los Angeles Times*. "Glenn Burke raised his right hand high above his head. Baker did not know what would happen next, but he did the same. They slapped palms. It was the first high five.

"'You think about the feeling you get when you give the high five,' Burke says. 'I had that feeling before everybody else did.'"

Burke then went up to bat and homered himself, and according to the story, got a return high five from Baker. In the passing years, Dodgers fans have not only assumed but taken pride in the fact that this timeless form of celebration, the long-running successor to the handshake and the low five, was brought to life on their home field, by one of their own.

"When the legend becomes fact, print the legend," says the newspaper editor in *The Man Who Shot Liberty Valence*. It's a time-tested strategy. Except sometimes, people can't help themselves. In 1995, *Village Voice* writer Gersh Kuntzman found footage of the legendary moment and started pointing out some facts. "Our analysis of the videotape of the Baker home run is inconclusive," Kuntzman wrote. "It does show Burke raising his arms [yes, plural] above his head, but Baker winds up hugging his teammate rather than smacking Burke's upraised palms."

While granting Burke a place on the evolutionary path of the high five, Kuntzman's research brought him 2,000 miles from Dodger Stadium to Kentucky, where an entirely different origin story for the high five resides. This version starts with the Louisville University basketball team in the fall of 1979.

"One afternoon, I was just sitting there trying to think of something crazy," Louisville's Darryl Cleveland told Kuntzman. "I met a group of players at center court, held my hand up high and just said, 'Gimme five up high!' and it worked."

Though this event went unwitnessed by the public, Kuntzman concluded that the popularity of the Louisville team, which defeated UCLA to win the NCAA title, constitutes the true origin of the high five.

Perhaps Kuntzman is too hasty to take credit from Burke. After all, two years passed between these two invention stories. Even if Burke's high five wasn't fully executed, it almost seems too improbable that it was the last time a Dodger raised his arms in celebration.

However, another source claims to knock both the Dodgers and Louisville out of the inventors' chair. In 2002, students at the University of Virginia staged what they called the first National High Five Day. Compelled to research the true origin story, they came upon former Murray State basketball player Lamont (Mont) Sleets, Jr., who claims he adopted a gesture based on what members of his father's Vietnam battalion used to greet each other.

"It was the Bobcat division," Sleets wrote, "but my dad and his friends always called it 'The Five.' When they'd later reunite at the Sleets household, they continued to extend their right hands up in the air, saying the name of their division. They'd walk in the door, and a three-year-old kid, he doesn't know the difference between all these grown-ups. But they're all sayin' 'Five' with their hand up like this, so I just start saying to them, 'Hi, Five!' like it was their name." This, Sleets says, evolved into the high five that Mont Sleets brought to his high school and college basketball teams in the late 1970s and early 1980s.

Veritable? Apocryphal? Who knows? Maybe the truest story of the high five is that, like the United States, it has many forebears. This much is certain: You can't tell the story of the high five without talking about Glenn Burke, who passed away of AIDS-related illness in 1995. A high-five to his memory.

48 Chief Noc-a-Homa and Joe Morgan

The two leading hitters for the 1982 Dodgers were named Topsy and Turvy. The ping-ponging jolts of that season, even more than in years like 1951 and 1962, left Dodger fans virtually seasick.

Defending their 1981 World Series title with much of that team's core intact, the '82 Dodgers found themselves blindsided by the Atlanta Braves, who had an MLB-record 13 consecutive wins to start the season and held a 7½ -game NL West lead over the fourth-place Dodgers half a month into the season. By the last day of May, Los Angeles closed within three games of the Braves, only to get swept in Atlanta in early June. When the third-place Dodgers returned to Atlanta on July 30, they trailed the Braves by 10½ games in the standings and 8–3 in the sixth inning of the first game of a doubleheader.

In those days, the Braves had a mascot named Chief Noc-a-Homa, who held court from a teepee placed in the outfield stands. In the 21st century, he would have struggled against the test of political correctness, but the bigger issue back in the '80s was that when Atlanta was doing well, the Chief's teepee occupied some very saleable seating real estate. With the Braves' red-hot start bringing pennant fever to Atlanta by summertime, owner Ted Turner had the teepee removed so that more seats could be sold.

For those who lived through it, it was an unforgettable decision. Starting by rallying for two runs in the sixth and five in the seventh to beat the Braves 10–9, the Dodgers saw their fortunes shoot upward just as those of the Braves collapsed. Los Angeles won 12 of its next 13 and 17 of 22, while Atlanta lost an astonishing 19 of 21. Within three weeks of Noc-a-Homa's banishment, the Dodgers had gone from a double-digit deficit to a four-game lead.

Responding to the panic of Braves fans who certainly were going to be less likely to buy tickets if the team's collapse continued, Turner reinstated the teepee. Atlanta promptly went on a 13–2 binge and, just like that, the Dodgers were looking up at the Braves in the standings again.

The teams would jockey for position for the remainder of the hold-your-breath season. Meanwhile, the San Francisco Giants lurked. The descendants of Bobby Thomson's miracle workers were a fourth-place 66–67 on September 1, nine games out of first. But their own 18–4 spurt, capped by a three consecutive one-run victories in Los Angeles, created a logjam in the West with one week to go: the Dodgers at 85–70; the Braves and Giants each at 84–71.

Heading into enemy territory on the final weekend of the season, the Dodgers eliminated the Giants with 4–0 and 15–2 victories Friday and Saturday. But the Dodgers had stumbled earlier in the week, and trailed Atlanta entering the final day by one game. For the second time in three years, the Dodgers would be playing on the final day to extend their regular season into a tiebreaker game.

Fernando Valenzuela would be the starting pitcher, but he was gone for a pinch-hitter in the top of the seventh with the bases loaded in a 2–2 tie, a decision that stood in contrast to manager Tommy Lasorda's do-or-die approach with Valenzuela in his final start the year before during the 1981 World Series. The game was then turned over to two pitchers: Tom Niedenfuer and Terry Forster. If only the Dodgers had had a crystal ball.

Niedenfuer gave up a single and a double, prompting Lasorda to send in Forster with one out in the seventh. Giants pinch-hitter Jim Wohlford struck out, bringing up left-handed hitting second baseman Joe Morgan.

Through the Dodgers' first 161$\frac{2}{3}$ games of the season, Forster had not allowed a home run to a left-handed batter. After the game, an inconsolable Forster, who had missed most of the previous three seasons because of two surgeries, told Mike Littwin of the *Los Angeles Times* that he wanted to run and grab the 1–2 slider to Morgan as soon as he let go of it. But Morgan's bat got there first, blasting it over the right-field fence for a three-run homer.

"I live for those kind of moments," Forster said. "That's what I've worked for. What's the use of working hard when you go out and make a bleeping pitch like that?"

The Dodgers got doubles from Dusty Baker and Ken Landreaux with one out in the eighth to bring the tying run to the plate. But none of the team's remaining five batters—including Steve Garvey and Ron Cey, in what would turn out to be the final at-bats of their historic Dodgers careers—could reach base. Bill Russell grounded out to end the game, thereby handing the division over to Atlanta. Chief Noc-a-Homa would get a seat for the playoffs and, in a coin-toss of a season, the Dodgers had landed on their heads.

49 Coliseum Carnival

Old news became news again in 2008. A stroke of genius 50 years after the team's arrival from Brooklyn inspired the Dodgers to stage an exhibition game at the Los Angeles Memorial Coliseum, their original home that fit them like a half-tailored suit.

Back in the '50s, while waiting for Dodger Stadium to be built, Dodgers owner Walter O'Malley had the option of playing in the home of the Pacific Coast League's Los Angeles Angels: a 22,500-seat Wrigley Field, an actual, albeit cozy, venue for baseball. Too cozy, it was decided, for major league baseball. Instead, O'Malley chose the historic but inflexible Coliseum to host the Dodgers for what would turn out to be their first four years.

Baseball stadiums had a history of catering their dimensions to fit the sub-ideal public spaces they were thrust into, but the Coliseum broke new ground in contorting the game. The left-field fence could not extend more than 251 feet from home plate. To mitigate this, a 42-foot tall screen substituted for the fence itself, preventing stubby fly balls from becoming home runs, but not stopping arcing ones. Wally Moon, the player most famous for taking advantage of the screen, slugged .543 with 37 homers in 217 career Coliseum games. The setup prominently altered the game of baseball 77 times a season, not much less significantly than if the Dodgers abruptly decided to turn the sport's hallowed diamond into a pentagon. It left Los Angeles fans with two choices: chagrin that their first taste of baseball was subverted, or gratitude to get any kind of bat-and-ball game at all.

They chose gratitude.

The first major league game played in Los Angeles was on April 18, 1958, as the Dodgers beat the San Francisco Giants 6–5 at the Los Angeles Memorial Coliseum. 78,672 fans were in attendance—the largest Opening Day crowd in major league history. Photo courtesy of University of Southern California, on behalf of the USC Specialized Libraries and Archival Collections.

What's unmistakably important about the Dodgers' Coliseum legacy is the fondness that it engendered. Rather than castigate O'Malley, who had become detested by some in Brooklyn for high-tailing the Dodgers out of town, Dodgers fans don't seem to have been offended in the slightest that their first taste of major league baseball had a distended configuration—at least no more than they were offended by the team's first Los Angeles season producing a 71–83 seventh-place finish.

The Dodgers, or the fates, rewarded the fans' generosity of spirit with a stunning World Series victory in 1959, a year in which the Coliseum established itself as a record-setting facility. An exhibition tribute to fallen legend Roy Campenella drew a record 93,103 fans. Three World Series games against the White Sox broke 92,000 or more as well.

Yet team attendance that year was 2.1 million, a figure the modern-day Dodgers achieve by August (though in the 21st century, the measuring stick is tickets sold rather than tickets used). For all those football-size crowds, the Coliseum could be a barren place, especially during its numerous day games in the summer. The second home game of the 1959 season drew fewer than 15,000. On June 22 and August 2 games against the Phillies, the crowd barely broke 10 grand. A year earlier, a game against the Cubs booked 6,195 fans—the stadium was 6 percent full.

The final regular-season baseball game at the Coliseum was Wednesday, September 20, 1961. Five games behind the Cincinnati Reds with 10 to play, the Dodgers sent 25-year-old Sandy Koufax (17–11, 3.73 ERA) against Barney Schultz of the Cubs. The game went 13 innings and Koufax pitched all of them, allowing two runs on seven hits (Ron Santo hit a two-run homer in the fourth), three walks, and a hit batter, while striking out 15. He threw *205* pitches, yet did not allow a hit from the ninth through the 13th. Moon, appropriately enough, scored the winning run. The attendance was 12,068.

It was entirely possible that Los Angeles could have greeted the idea of tripping down Memory Lane back to the Coliseum in March 2008 with similar lack of commitment, especially when traffic on Memory Lane figured to be backed up for an hour or

Opening Day for L.A.

The Los Angeles Dodgers actually made their official debut in San Francisco, playing their fellow New York expatriates the Giants on April 15, 1958—with 21-year-old Don Drysdale taking an 8–0 drubbing. The team split its next two games, then headed south for its new homecoming.

On April 18, the team paraded in the morning from City Hall to the Coliseum, where 78,672 customers greeted them. Carl Erskine, whose best years were behind him by his own admission, got the start.

"I was kind of surprised [Walter] Alston had selected me to pitch the opener," Erskine recalled, 50 years later. "But I think he wanted an experienced pitcher. That was a wild day, man. There were 80,000 people coming into this football stadium to see a baseball game, in a new city, playing before a crowd that had sort of heard about us and didn't really know about us. It was a curious crowd."

Staked to a 5–2 lead by the fifth, Erskine went eight innings, allowing four runs, to get the win. But as far as game details go, Erskine's recollections again harked back to the crowd.

"I remember in the second or third inning I looked over at the Dodgers dugout, and about five or six guys were looking back over the dugout at the movies stars we were seeing. Bing Crosby, Danny Kaye, Lana Turner—you could name about a dozen of them."

more. (The Sig Alert, the label defined as an unplanned stoppage of traffic for 30 minutes or more, was born in Los Angeles not long before the Dodgers' arrived.) But the pull of that particular, peculiar Coliseum era was simply too powerful to be ignored. As a one-time-only opportunity, rarer than a World Series game, to see or re-see what it was like to play under such un-pristine circumstances, the Coliseum game allowed Dodgers fans to travel through time, and a record 115,000 people decided to take advantage. It was a true celebration of baseball in Los Angeles.

50 Chaos at Candlestick

"This was the worst I've seen since I've been born. And I've been in World War II."

— San Francisco Giants president Al Rosen,
quoted by Sam McManis in the *Los Angeles Times*

It was the afternoon, and the night, and the morning...that the heated Giants-Dodgers rivalry boiled over into a *Lord of the Flies* remake.

You could blame it on Bruce Springsteen if you want. According to Ray Ratto of the *San Francisco Chronicle*, after the Dodgers were rained out at Candlestick Park on April 22, 1988, they voted against making up the game on an open date three days later, because a number of players had tickets to see the Boss that night at the Los Angeles Sports Arena. So instead, the teams scheduled a doubleheader for 5:30 PM on a midweek summer day, July 26.

They might as well have penciled mayhem into their calendars. As the day began, the Dodgers had a 5½-game lead over Houston, but the feisty Giants—the defending NL West champs—were six back after beating Los Angeles the night before and looking to make a move.

Tensions began building as the teams entered the seventh inning of the first game tied 1–1. Dodger catcher Rick Dempsey hit a two-run homer in the top of the seventh, though San Francisco kept it close in the bottom of the eighth with a trio of singles producing a run. In the ninth inning, a homer by Jeff Hamilton and a two-run triple by Steve Sax built the Dodgers lead up to 6–2.

For years inside the multipurpose stadium at Candlestick Point, there was a gap between the front row of the left-field seats and the chain-link outfield fence, and after home runs, fans would bound into the area in pursuit of the ball. With the heat of the rivalry and copious amounts of alcohol being consumed on a summer's day-turned-night, the pursuit splintered into something particularly zealous. Regardless of whether there was a home-run ball to retrieve, fans began climbing the chain-link fence to throw objects at Dodgers left fielder Kirk Gibson and, as the *Chronicle* recalls, trying to shake the fence from its moorings.

And as if the drunken behavior needed a chaser, this was baseball's Year of the Balk. Baseball's rules committee had asked umpires that year to strictly enforce baseball's arcane "discernable stop" rule requiring pitchers to come to the set position, which led to record numbers of violations (924 balks in 1988, compared to 356 the previous year) and endless aggravation for the victims.

So when Scott Garrelts balked Sax in for the Dodgers' seventh run, the call seemed to twist the knife in the Giants and the Candlestick crowd (even though home-plate umpire Jerry Crawford called one earlier on Dodgers winning pitcher Orel Hershiser and later on closer Jay Howell). The Giants clawed for a run in the bottom of the ninth, but with two runners on, Howell struck out Robby Thompson and Will Clark to end the game.

Amazingly, that was only the prelude. The second game was the doozy. In the nightcap, which began at 9:08 PM, San Francisco struck first on a third-inning Chris Speier homer off Tim Belcher, but the Dodgers quickly trumped that with a four-run fourth, capped by Belcher's two-run double.

Back-to-back doubles by Mike Aldrete and Ernest Riles knocked out Belcher in the sixth and cut the Giants' deficit to 4–2. Howell entered the game in the bottom of the eighth bidding for his second save of the day, but instead gave up a game-tying two-run triple to Bob Melvin. Sax put the Dodgers back in front in the ninth with an RBI single, but the Giants tied it yet again. They even loaded the bases for a chance to win the game, but Kevin Mitchell grounded out.

Past midnight and into extra innings went the teams; past midnight and into havoc went the fans. The *Chronicle* later tallied 30 arrests and more than 100 fan ejections at the park that night. At one point, crew chief Doug Harvey was going to order the Dodgers off the field for their protection. Gibson, amid a minefield of bottles and batteries, was cowed enough after the game not to comment. "I've got to go out there again," Gibson said. "I'm not saying anything."

In the top of the eleventh with the score still 5–5, Franklin Stubbs led off with a double and advanced to third on a Tracy Woodson groundout. Dave Anderson stood at the plate against Garrelts.

Balk.

Stubbs was waved home. Candlestick went berserk. Giants manager (and former Dodgers pitcher) Roger Craig and pitcher Mike Krukow—then on the disabled list—were ejected for arguing. A fan was arrested for nearly beaning umpire Greg Bonin with a baseball, and more debris rained on the field.

When Brian Holton struck out Candy Maldonado to end the game at 1:21 AM, what was left of a bitter, strung-out Giants crowd stumbled out into the night.

The Dodgers needed every inch of that doubleheader sweep. The Giants extracted some revenge with an extra-inning victory the next night, sending the Dodgers into a 3–9 spin that would cut their lead in the NL West to half a game over the Astros and 3½ games over San Francisco, before Los Angeles recovered to win the division and more.

As a footnote, the doubleheader also might have been a flashpoint in baseball's decision to abandon its attempt to enforce the balk rule so strictly in following years. "It's a tough way [for the Giants] to lose," the level-headed Hershiser told McManis. "But I have no gripe with the umpiring crews on balk calls. My gripe is with the National League office for telling them how to call it."

But most of all, the doubleheader remains vivid for how it changed Candlestick and the nature of Dodger-Giant games forever. The events of July 26-turned-27 compelled officials to finally lay down stricter rules for the ballpark.

"I talked to Bart Giamatti because it's frightening," Dodger general manager Fred Claire told McManis. "That's the only word for it. The Giants and Al assured us they'd take all the steps they can. There's a problem that's here. I called upon the National League to put a stop to it."

Rosen didn't argue. "The beach at Okinawa was safer," he said in the *Chronicle*. Before the next game, in addition to adding security, the Giants put an end to the fans' scramble for home run balls, lining the area with protective steel barriers. The distinctive sight of fan participation, which was part of the fun of Candlestick on calmer days, was gone.

The Dodger-Giant rivalry, egged on by September pennant-race clashes and hot feelings toward Barry Bonds, burns brightly today. But since the witching hour July 27, it hasn't been the same.

51 Don Sutton

In the 2008 Dodger media guide, the Los Angeles Dodgers career pitching records could be found on page 330. On that page, the name "Sutton, Don" is listed atop the categories for wins, losses, games, games started, strikeouts, innings pitched, hits, walks, and shutouts. Accompanying the section is a photo with the caption,

Don Drysdale's name can be found throughout the Los Angeles Dodgers' Career Top 10 lists.

And therein lies the invisibility of Don Sutton.

It's not as if Sutton toiled in obscurity or faded into reclusiveness. He pitched more than 15 years in the media center that is Los Angeles, and then became a major league announcer the year after his 1988 retirement, mostly before a national cable TV audience for the Atlanta Braves. The Hall of Fame welcomed him after only a bit of hesitation in 1998. Yet you get a sinking feeling that Sutton is becoming more and more obscure in Dodger history.

So let's refresh some memories. Those record-setting numbers for Los Angeles include 3,814 innings, 533 starts, 233 victories, 156 complete games (tied with Drysdale, who tops the list thanks only to the biases of alphabetical order), and 52 shutouts. For his major league career, which after 15 seasons with the Dodgers also included stops at Houston, Milwaukee, Oakland, and with the Angels, Sutton collected 5,282⅓ innings and 3,574 strikeouts—seventh all-time in each category. His 58 shutouts rank him 10th in major league history.

Sutton and left-handed contemporary Steve Carlton became eligible for Hall of Fame balloting in the same year, 1994. Carlton was elected with 436 votes (95.8 percent of total ballots), nearly twice as many as Sutton—even though, as Bill James pointed out in 1994's *The Politics of Glory*, they had almost identical career innings pitched, wins, and ERA. Carlton struck out more but also walked more. Similarly to Carlton, Sutton's more-than-respectable career ERA of 3.26 would have been lower if not for the 1,000-odd innings he threw in his late 30s and 40s.

What Sutton never seemed to have was the legendary season of someone like Carlton, who memorably won 27 games for a 59-win Phillies team in 1972 with a 1.97 ERA (182 ERA+). Sutton's best year wasn't anything to sneeze at, but his 2.08 ERA (161 ERA+) in

Pitcher Don Sutton's 15-year career with the Dodgers puts him at the top of several "Best of" lists in Dodgers history. His record-setting 156 complete games is tied with Don Drysdale, yet Sutton gets less recognition as a major league pitcher.

'72 was overshadowed by Carlton's campaign and earned him only a fifth-place tie in the Cy Young voting, and his quest to win 20 games in a season seemed to take forever, partly because he was an established big-leaguer at age 21 and didn't top the mark until 10 years later. Sutton had the kind of career that never had a no-hitter—merely five one-hitters and nine two-hitters. It's possible that some remember Sutton more for his 1978 clubhouse fight with Steve Garvey or his rumored scuffing of the baseball than appreciate the overwhelming totality of his accomplishments. Though Sutton's longtime reliability shouldn't be undervalued, his greatness isn't a byproduct of mere endurance.

As a rookie on a team that already featured Sandy Koufax at the height of his powers, Sutton immediately made himself a candidate for the Cooperstown pantheon. He struck out 209 batters, the most by a National League rookie in more than half a century. If the rest of Sutton's career somehow seemed less than godlike, he nevertheless needs to be remembered as a Dodger immortal.

52 Boom Boom Boom Boom

Gil Hodges and Shawn Green each played the game with dignity, but try telling that to the pitchers they humbled and the baseballs they smashed.

A 49-homer hitter the year before, Green had gone 24 games and more than 100 plate appearances without hitting that little white ball over that big outfield fence when he snapped out of it on May 21, 2002, and hit two home runs that night in Milwaukee. Was it a fleeting glimpse of success for the Dodgers right fielder, or a sign of things to come?

Well, there were no home runs the next night, but he did triple in the only run of a 1–0 Dodgers victory. Green was starting to feel it.

"The first night here, after my first home run, I thought, 'I finally got one,'" Green told Mike DiGiovanna of the *Los Angeles Times*. "Then I hit another one and thought, 'OK, maybe I'm starting to catch on, and that first one wasn't a fluke.' I felt my swing was where I wanted it to be, which is something I hadn't felt all season.

"Then I hit that triple on the kind of inside pitch that was eating me up all season. Little signs like that help you realize that things are right."

May 23, 2002, found the Dodgers playing a getaway day game. To say that Green bought a first-class ticket home was an understatement. He hit an RBI double in the first inning, a three-run homer in the second, a solo home run in the fourth, a solo homer in the fifth. Five innings in, and he had three homers and 14 total bases.

When Green came up in the eighth inning for what figured to be his last at-bat, he faced an opportunity to tie the major league record of four home runs in a single game, shared in part by his Dodgers predecessor Hodges. On August 31, 1950, Hodges faced future Hall of Famer Warren Spahn and the Boston Braves in Brooklyn. He hit a two-run homer in the second inning, and by the time he got up again, Spahn had already waved the white flag, knocked out of the game with none out in the third. Normie Roy, a 21-year-old in his only major league season before arm troubles ended his career, surrendered a three-run shot.

Hodges grounded out in his next at-bat, but in the sixth he homered off Bob Hall with a man aboard. He settled for a single in the seventh, but the Dodgers offense gave Hodges one more shot in the eighth. He hit his fourth home run off his fourth Braves pitcher Johnny Antonelli to cap a 19–3 Dodgers victory. His nine RBI were also a franchise record (later equaled by James Loney).

Kevin Elster

The inaugural Opening Day at San Francisco's long-awaited, beautiful new ballpark, had finally arrived. A day for celebration. But it was a Dodger who put the first imprint on the Giants' new home in a bold but unlikely way.

Kevin Elster hadn't even played in the majors in 1999. The Dodgers signed him as a backup to help plug a gap in their middle infield. But getting the start on April 11, 2000, Elster hit the first home run at what was called Pacific Bell Park in the third inning, tying the score at 1–1. Then, after Barry Bonds hit the Giants' first homer in the bottom of the inning, Elster answered with a two-run shot to put the Dodgers ahead 3–2. And in the top of the eighth, Elster hit a third homer, giving the Dodgers an insurance run they would cash in for a 6–5, festivities-spoiling victory.

This would be Elster's only season with the Dodgers and his last in the majors, but he still became an enduring talking point in Giants-Dodgers history.

Green stepped in against Jose Cabrera of the Brewers in the top of the eighth and hit a grounder up the middle for a single. And that would have been it, except that Cabrera embarked upon a four-homer quest of his own.

Little-known Hiram Bocachica drove in Green with a homer. Cabrera closed out the eighth by getting the next two batters, and then, after allowing a double, got two outs in the ninth. But with Green in the on-deck circle uncertain whether he'd get another shot, Adrian Beltre hit the Dodgers' sixth homer of the game and third off Cabrera, thus allowing Green to bat.

Green would leave no doubt about it. He blasted the ball approximately 450 feet, giving him his four homers, a Dodger record-tying six hits, a Dodger-record six runs, and a major league record 19 total bases, breaking Joe Adcock's 48-year-old record of 18.

"That was awesome—it was like slow-motion when that last ball went out," Dodgers third-base coach (and future manager)

Glenn Hoffman said. "I had goose bumps. It gave me chills...I was like a kid watching him."

DiGiovanna wrote that "Green made history in blue-collar fashion, showing the same kind of emotion that he did throughout his 1½ -month struggle. That is, none."

"He didn't showboat or anything," Milwaukee coach Cecil Cooper said. "He hit that last one, dropped his head, and that was it. He's a classy kid."

Dave Hansen followed with yet another home run to help the Dodgers set a team record of eight in their 16–3 win. When the Dodgers moved on to Arizona, the spotlight didn't leave Green. He homered once the next night and twice more on May 25, setting yet another record with seven home runs in three days. He capped his hot streak with a circuit clout on May 27—10 home runs in seven games—and managed to save enough magic to homer in four consecutive at-bats in June, spread over two games.

A labrum injury in 2003 hastened the decline of Green's power and his Dodgers career, but he left an indelible mark—a shorter-term version of Hodges, who finished his Dodger tenure with 361 career homers, second in team history only to Duke Snider.

53 4 x 30 x 2

On October 1, 1977, one day before the end of the regular season, Dusty Baker drove a pitch within a few feet of the right-field fence.

"I thought I had it," Baker told Ross Newhan of the *Los Angeles Times*. "I'll be taking another shot tomorrow. It's definitely been on my mind and has probably affected my swing. I'm going to try and think in terms of line drives tomorrow. [But] being sharp for Philadelphia [and the 1977 NLCS] is more important than hitting the 30th."

Baker was probably right to temper his expectations, at least publicly. On the final day of the season, the Dodgers were facing a tormentor in Houston Astros pitcher James Rodney Richard. In 24 career starts against Los Angeles, Richard pitched at least nine innings while allowing one run or less 10 times, and his career ERA against the Dodgers in 208 innings was 1.86.

But in the sixth inning of the final game, in his penultimate at-bat, Baker cleared the left-center field corner of the Dodgers bleachers, joining Steve Garvey (33), Reggie Smith (32), and Ron Cey (30) to give the Dodgers the first foursome of players in baseball history with 30 or more home runs.

And lest you think Baker didn't care, he told Newhan the next day that hitting the homer made him "the happiest man on Earth."

It's hard to know what was more unlikely—that it took baseball until 1977 to achieve this feat, or that these four were the ones to do it. Subsequently, in home-run-happier times, several teams would repeat the deed—including the Dodgers 20 years later with Mike Piazza (40), Eric Karros (31), Todd Zeile (31), and, by hitting two on the second-to-last day of the season, Raul Mondesi (30).

But this crew? Once in his life, Smith had hit 30 home runs. Cey's career high in homers was 25. Both Baker's and Garvey's career high in homers was 21, and the year before, they had *combined* for 17.

But setting the stage for the accomplishment in his first full season as Dodgers manager, Lasorda urged Garvey before the 1977 season to try to aim for the fences, saying that "the home run is the most important part of the offense." Garvey agreed to try, even though, according to Bob Oates of the *Times*, he disagreed with the premise.

Entering the season thinking that 20 was a realistic goal, Garvey reached that number before the All-Star break thanks to a 12-homer June. He hit his 30th on September 14. Cey got off to a ferociously hot start in April, hitting nine home runs and driving in 29 runs (a team record at the time) before reaching 30 on September 18, five innings before Smith did the same. All members of the Dodger quartet homered in that game, in fact.

But it was Baker who completed the most remarkable journey, a year after he hit only four home runs in a miserable first Dodgers season following his acquisition from Atlanta. As late as September 2, Baker was stuck on 20 homers for the year, reinforcing how unlikely it was for the Dodgers to complete this task. But Baker homered in seven of his next 11 games to get within striking distance before hitting his 29th on September 25. Then came 5½ agonizing days before finally came No. 30.

"The only thing I told him," Tommy Lasorda related to Newhan, "was that the Lord didn't intend to strand him on 29."

54 1941: Three Strikes, You're Not Out

On January 22, 1857, 11 years and four months after Alexander Cartwright published a set of *Rules & Regulations of the Recently Invented Game of Base Ball*, a convention was held in New York to entertain revisions. There, according to 19cBaseball.com, it was decided that if a batter swung at a third strike that was not caught on the fly or on the first bounce, he could attempt to "make his first," that is, run to first base before the catcher threw him out.

Those gents in the Civil War era could have fairly decided that, regardless of the disposition of the ball, a swing and a miss for a

The First Playoff

Four years after Brooklyn's gut-wrenching loss of the 1942 NL pennant to St. Louis, the two teams—Branch Rickey's former and current organizations—were at it again. Once more, the Dodgers had the lead for most of the season—though it was a narrow one—before a hard-charging Cardinals squad passed them. This time, however, the Cardinals couldn't put the Dodgers away quite so easily, losing three of their final four games, and for the first time since the NL was founded in 1876, the scheduled regular season had ended in a tie.

That set up a best-of-three playoff. A coin toss determined that St. Louis would host the first game, with Brooklyn being the home team for the second and third, if necessary. Turns out, Game 3 wasn't necessary. St. Louis scored three runs in the first three innings off Ralph Branca to give pitcher Howie Pollet all he would need for a complete-game 4–2 victory in the first contest. Two days later, the Dodgers were held hitless from the second inning through the eighth and fell behind 8–1 heading into the bottom of the ninth, then nearly staged a comeback that would have dwarfed 1951 or 1962. They scored three runs and loaded the bases with one out, but potential tying runs Eddie Stanky and Howie Schultz struck out to finally end Brooklyn's season.

third strike was an out the moment the bat cut its arc through the plane of home plate. Instead, this baseball congress sought a more emphatic resolution, setting the stage, more than 84 years later, for the most memorable pitch in the first half of 20th-century Dodgers history.

By 1941, it had been 21 years since the Dodgers won the NL pennant; it had been nearly that long since they had even won as many as 90 games. With five games to go in the '41 season, they led the NL, but their margin over the St. Louis Cardinals was down to one game. However, a three-game winning streak, two by shutout, clinched the flag for Brooklyn and presented an opportunity for the Flatbush fans to celebrate their first World Series title.

On the first day of October in '41, that team from the Bronx hosted the Dodgers in their first World Series game ever against each other. Joe DiMaggio's crew won that inaugural contest 3–2, but Brooklyn tied the Series the next day with Dodger catcher Mickey Owen knocking a key RBI single in the fifth inning. After a day off, the reunion at Ebbets Field for Game 3 found the tightly matched squads scoreless into the eighth.

Dodgers righty Hugh Casey, who had just entered the game in relief, allowed a single to Red Rolfe before inducing a grounder to first from Tommy Henrich. As baseball writer Rob Neyer notes, Casey failed to cover first base, allowing Henrich to reach. Joe DiMaggio and Charlie Keller followed with RBI singles, with Henrich's run the difference as the Yankees held on for a 2–1 victory.

Game 4 found the Dodgers down by a 3–0 score before they rallied with two runs in the fourth and two in the fifth to take a 4–3 lead. Meanwhile, Casey was redeeming himself. As the Brooklyn offense went silent, Casey retired 12 of the next 14 batters. There was one batter to go, an ever-so-appropriate one: Henrich. Time to turn the tables.

On a full count pitch, Henrich swung—and missed. For a split second, a Game 4 victory dipped into the small space between Henrich's bat and Owen's glove.

"Casey had two kinds of curveballs," Owen recalled in a 1988 interview alongside Henrich with Dave Anderson of the *New York Times*. "One was an overhand curve that broke big. The other one was like a slider, it broke sharp and quick. But we had the same sign for either one. He just threw whichever one was working best. When we got to 3 and 2 on Tommy, I called for the curveball. I was looking for the quick curve he had been throwing all along. But he threw the overhand curve, and it really broke big, in and down. Tommy missed it by six inches."

Added Henrich: "As soon as I missed it, I looked around to see where the ball was. It fooled me so much, I figured maybe it fooled Mickey, too. And it did."

The ball found its way to the backstop, and once more Henrich had sneaked onto first base. And a flood like Brooklyn had never laid eyes on before rushed through.

"I couldn't believe what happened; none of us could," Owen said. "Then Joe DiMaggio hit a fastball, a screaming line drive over Pee Wee Reese's head into left field, then Charlie Keller hit a quick curve high off the right-field screen."

DiMaggio's hit was a single; Keller's a double.

"That was a soft screen above that angled wall," Henrich said. "The ball came straight down off that soft screen, hit the wall, bounced up in the air to give DiMaggio another two seconds and he slid across with the go-ahead run."

"That was as good a play," Owen said, "as Enos Slaughter scoring from first base for the Cardinals in the 1946 Series."

After a Bill Dickey walk, a two-run double by Joe Gordon added two more runs to pad the lead 7–4. The Dodgers went down meekly in the bottom of the ninth, then mustered only a single run in a 3–1 Game 5 loss that ended the Series. It was this defeat that prompted the legendary *Brooklyn Eagle* headline, "Wait 'Til Next Year," a mantra that would hang over Brooklyn for the next 14.

It's worth remembering that in the immediate aftermath of the defeat in '41, as Richard Goldstein recalled in his 2005 obituary for Owen, Brooklyn forgave. "I got about 4,000 wires and letters," Owen said in an interview with W. C. Heinz for the *Saturday Evening Post* on the 25th anniversary of his error (in that era, those plays were not scored as passed balls). "I had offers of jobs and proposals of marriage. Some girls sent their pictures in bathing suits, and my wife tore them up."

Decades after the pitch, historians have debated whether Casey really threw a curveball or whether, as many came to speculate, it was a spitball—an illegal pitch that brought Casey and the Dodgers what they deserved. But the conjecture might just as easily be spent on those men in 1857, and why they couldn't be satisfied that a swing and a miss on strike three could result in the batter being out. They could have done their Brooklyn neighbors a huge favor.

55 Branch Rickey

It took a Branch Rickey to push integration forward in major league baseball. If Jackie Robinson was Chuck Yeager (the man to bust the sound barrier), then Rickey was the aircraft engineer whose unique combination of idealism and pragmatism put Robinson in position to soar.

Integration was not Branch Rickey's life's work. Fundamentally, he was a man of religion—two religions, really, because baseball stood along side his faith, and God was in the details in both. He lived and breathed the sport meticulously as a player, as a manager, and ultimately as an executive—except on Sundays when he would piously shut it out. But though it was not as much of a preoccupation, he had an instinctive conviction about racial equality at a time such beliefs could not be taken for granted. There is a story mythical in its drama but true at its core: Coaching Ohio Wesleyan's baseball team, Rickey checked into a hotel on a road trip to Notre Dame, but his black catcher Charles Thomas was denied a room. Rickey entered to find Thomas sobbing and tearing at his own skin. Thomas ended up sleeping on a cot in Rickey's room. The experience never left Rickey;

indeed, according to biographer Lee Lowenfish, Rickey and Thomas remained friends for life.

This incident happened more than four decades before Rickey met Jackie Robinson. Rickey made his name as a remarkably savvy general manager, building a pioneering farm system for the St. Louis Cardinals organization that helped make them the envy of any team that didn't have Babe Ruth—the Cards won five NL pennants and three World Series in nine seasons. As historian Steven Goldman notes, Rickey started to pursue integration while with St. Louis, but found the opposition too overwhelming. Coming to the Dodgers in 1942, however, he lost none of his thirst for success and innovation. When the opportunity finally came to marry his morality with his work, he calculated exactly how he would succeed.

"In 1945, the New York state legislature passed the Quinn-Ives Act, a ban on discrimination in hiring," Jonathan Eig wrote in *Opening Day: The Story of Jackie Robinson's First Game*. "The same year, New York City's mayor, Fiorello LaGuardia, appointed a commission to investigate discrimination in hiring and appointed the sociologist Dan Dodson chairman. When Dodson turned his investigation to baseball and interviewed Branch Rickey, the Dodger boss was thrilled. He believed the public pressure and the commission's investigation would make it easier for him to integrate the team, and he quickly shared the details of his secret plan with Dodson. What's more, he asked Dodson for his help. Rickey told the sociologist he wanted to learn the politics and psychology of integration. He wanted to study the track records of institutions that had already integrated. He also wanted Dodson to help him stall. With a little more time, Rickey knew, he would have the chance to corner the market on black players, select just the right black man to break the color line, and prepare his white players for the new man's arrival. Dodson, thoroughly charmed, agreed to do whatever Rickey asked of him."

And so began the final steps that led Rickey to invite Robinson to his office on August 28, 1945, where they had perhaps the most important baseball meeting since the sport was born.

"Thus was born one of baseball's favorite legends," writes Eig. "But in one important way, the accounts are misleading. Rickey didn't want Robinson for his ability to turn the other cheek. Had Rickey wanted a pacifist, he might have selected any one of half a dozen men with milder constitutions than Jack Roosevelt Robinson's.

"Rickey wanted an angry black man. He wanted someone big enough and strong enough to intimidate, and someone intelligent enough to understand the historic nature of his role. Perhaps he even wanted a dark-skinned man whose presence would be more strongly felt, more plainly obvious, although on this point Rickey was uncharacteristically silent. Clearly, the Dodger boss sought a man who would not just raise the issue of equal rights but would press it.

"It is testament to Rickey's sophistication and foresight that he chose a ballplayer who would become a symbol of strength rather than assimilation."

Rickey was not a beloved figure. Many thought him pompous and beyond self-righteous. And the man who made it a mantra to trade a player a year too early rather than a year too late would alienate his fan base more than once. "When he arrived in Brooklyn and dealt the beloved Dolph Camilli to the hated Giants," Eig comments, "it was indisputably the right move, but it infuriated fans, who hung Rickey in effigy from Brooklyn's Borough Hall." But the man had nothing less than the courage of his convictions, and in his case, that was plainly significant, even long after integration was complete.

"For Robinson," wrote Arnold Rampersad in *Jackie Robinson: A Biography*, "absorbing Rickey's death [in 1965] was a trial to

Dodgers president Branch Rickey swings a bat at West Point during Dodgers spring training at Bear Mountain, New York, circa 1943. Photo by Barney Stein.

compare to his 1947 ordeal: 'I tried to prepare myself emotionally the same way I had for that first year.' His deep feeling for Rickey, Jack made clear, was only in part owing to the fact that Rickey had chosen him to be the first black player. Far more, he loved Rickey because Rickey had been loyal to him. He had been loyal during their four tumultuous years in the Dodger organization, but, more important to Jack, loyal when the cheering had died down, and especially after Jack retired from the game."

56 Larry MacPhail

Over three weeks in August 1959, *Sports Illustrated* published more than 15,000 words by writer Gerald Holland about a former major league general manager who had been out of work for a dozen years. "Warts and all" is a phrase that could have been invented for Larry MacPhail, an explosive character and front office rebel—not to mention rogue would-be kidnapper of Germany's Kaiser Wilhelm near the end of World War I—who nonetheless gave birth to the Dodgers as a competitive franchise leading into the Boys of Summer years.

MacPhail came to Brooklyn during the 1937–38 off-season after helping introduce several innovations to the major leagues while with Cincinnati, including (against fierce resistance) night baseball. His entry into the sport had been as the president of a Columbus, Ohio, minor league team that he convinced a different kind of innovator, Branch Rickey, to purchase for the St. Louis Cardinals. Together, they could have put Oscar and Felix to shame as an odd couple, and not just because of their diametrically opposed feelings about alcohol.

"Whereas Rickey viewed the baseball business from a perspective of containing costs, MacPhail embodied the consumer component of modern capitalism," wrote Jules Tygiel in *Past Time: Baseball as History*. "Revealingly, while MacPhail frequently spoke of 'what the consumers want' and the 'fellow who sits out there in the bleachers,' Rickey, the most quoted man in baseball history, left no remembered adages about fans."

MacPhail's impact in Brooklyn was instant and multifaceted: immediate renovations for Ebbets Field, the import of Red Barber to the broadcast booth, the introduction of batting

Dodgers president Larry MacPhail (left) and Branch Rickey (right) are all smiles at the 125th Street train station in New York City, circa 1942. MacPhail left the Dodgers to serve in World War II after the 1942 season and the Dodgers hired Rickey to replace him. Photo by Barney Stein.

helmets following a frightening Joe Medwick beaning, and on the roster, transactions that shook the Dodgers out a generation of doldrums. First baseman Dolph Camilli and future Hall of Famer Leo Durocher (who didn't hit at shortstop but would become player-manager at age 33 in 1939) brought an initial dose of credibility to the team, soon complemented by a pair of 21-year-olds breaking in with Brooklyn in 1940—Pee Wee Reese and Pete Reiser. After finishing 62–91 the season before his arrival, the Dodgers improved to 69 wins in 1938, 84 in 1939, 88 in 1940, and 100 in 1941—the last season before World War II took its toll on baseball and the country.

His temper and drinking, as well as his disintegrating relationship with Rickey who later replaced MacPhail as Dodgers GM following the '42 season, are intrinsic to MacPhail's legend. But most disheartening of all was his stance in 1945–46 against the impending promotion of Jackie Robinson and other Negro Leaguers to the major leagues.

"He condemned 'political and social-minded drum-beaters for their efforts on behalf of integration," Tygiel wrote. "Tellingly, MacPhail questioned the ultimate consequences of increased black attendance at the ballparks. Noting that Robinson's presence in the International League had attracted thousands of black fans, MacPhail worried that 'a situation might be presented...in which the preponderance of Negro attendance...could conceivably threaten the value of Major League franchises.'"

Though the demerits remain on his record, MacPhail's pull on the game remains indisputable.

"If MacPhail came to me tomorrow," former Dodgers board member James Mulvey told Holland, "with a proposition he had dreamed up, I'd be tempted to chuck everything and go in with him. I'd just like to be around him, to watch him work. MacPhail can make a success of anything he puts his mind to."

57 The Head-Spinning, Allegiance-Shifting, Authority-Defying Leo Durocher

At the end of the 1938 season, Larry MacPhail named the team's 33-year-old shortstop Leo Durocher the Dodgers' new field boss. "Nobody but MacPhail would ever have thought to make Durocher a manager," Bill James wrote.

"There were managers before Durocher who drank, swore, chased women, bet horses, and screamed at umpires—but they were, in some fundamental way, 'responsible' men. They were men who obeyed the rules and asked the world for respect. Durocher didn't give a—what you thought of him. He didn't make any pretense to being a nice person.

"Durocher, who grew up essentially fatherless, once said that he had spent his life looking for father images. In a sense, all managers in the generation before Durocher (and most managers after) were *paternal* managers, surrogate fathers for their players. Durocher was more like an older brother, not all that much older, and certainly not much more responsible. Other managers did bed checks. Durocher, in effect, gave his players permission to hit the bars and woo the women until all hours, so long as they were ready to play ball at game time. And if you weren't ready to play ball at game time, God help you."

Durocher was still at the job in March 1947, when a handful of Dodgers, including their most popular player Dixie Walker, two top pitchers, Kirby Higbe and Hugh Casey, and a rising young outfielder named Carl Furillo declared their objection to playing on the same team with Jackie Robinson. They had a big problem, though—more than just the will of Robinson or Branch Rickey. Durocher had just seen Robinson play, and he liked what he saw.

Dodgers player-manager Leo Durocher jumps high in the air during spring training exercises at Clearwater, Florida, circa 1940. Durocher's career with the Dodgers was volatile; however it did help land him in the Hall of Fame. Photo by Barney Stein.

"The Dodgers hopped around Central America for exhibition games throughout spring training, and they were in Panama when Leo Durocher heard about the players' uprising," wrote Jonathan Eig in *Opening Day*. "He roused the team from bed one night for a meeting in the team's dining room. The players came in various states of undress. Durocher wore a yellow bathrobe atop his pajamas. No one writing of the meeting bothered to mention the color of the pajamas, but even if they had been pink with purple bunnies Durocher's authority would have been undiminished and unquestioned. The manager had a cinderblock jaw and a piercing stare, which he likely used to full effect in this instance. 'I don't care if a guy is yellow or black, or if he has stripes like a...zebra,' he told the team, according to one eyewitness account. 'I'm the manager of this team, and I say he plays.' Robinson was going to put money in all their pockets by helping the team get to the World Series, Durocher said, and anyone who didn't like it would be traded or released as soon as the details could be arranged."

Robinson stayed and led the Dodgers to the World Series. But without Durocher.

Less than a month after laying down the law, Durocher was suspended for the season by major league commissioner Happy Chandler. It had nothing to do with Jackie. Durocher had been under fire on multiple fronts: from Chandler for associating with gamblers, and from the holier-than-thou contingent of the public for marrying actress Laraine Day while her divorce was barely ripe.

Pettiest of all—yet most significant—Durocher (and even more so, his current benefactor, Rickey) had gotten on the wrong side of the mercurial MacPhail, now co-owner of the Yankees. Rickey and MacPhail had been feuding for years by this point; Durocher became entangled when he and MacPhail had a public, he-said/he-said disagreement over the Yankees managerial vacancy, with

Durocher either turning down MacPhail's offer or lying that it had even been made.

When a fed-up-with-it-all Durocher pointedly told the press that MacPhail had been consorting with gamblers as well, MacPhail erupted. He called in a favor with Chandler, whom he had helped win election to the commissioner's office two years earlier after Kenesaw Mountain Landis died—ironically, according to Red Barber in *1947–When All Hell Broke Loose in Baseball* (which spends more than 100 fascinating pages detailing the origins of Durocher's suspension), because MacPhail had often clashed with NL president and Chandler rival Ford C. Frick over the league's unfair treatment of Durocher.

"Commissioner Chandler released his statement in Cincinnati just before he telephoned Rickey," Barber recalled. "From then on it was bedlam. Phones rang until…all phone lines were jammed. Radio programs were interrupted with bulletins on Durocher's suspension. Headlines screamed the suspension. I can't recall a sports story so suddenly dominating all the media. It seemed, certainly in Brooklyn, as though there was no other topic of conversation. The borough was stunned.... Manager Leo Durocher was suspended for a year!"

Burt Shotton guided the Robinson Dodgers to the Series, and by the time Durocher took back reins in 1948, even Rickey had soured on him. On July 11, Durocher's Dodgers lost to their NL archrivals the New York Giants 3–2. The next game Durocher managed was the All-Star Game, and the next one after that was for the Giants. Their owner, Horace Stoneham, had called Rickey to inquire about hiring Shotton—and came away with Durocher instead. The manager cheering Bobby Thomson's "Shot Heard 'Round the World in '51" was the ex-Dodgers skipper.

In 1961, Durocher returned to the Dodgers as a coach under Walter Alston, and inside of two seasons was accused of plotting to take Alston's job after the Dodgers' 1962 collapse against, of course, the Giants. Instead, Durocher later found work managing the Cubs and the Astros. He won his 2,000th career game September 11, 1973, and helmed his final contest September 30—34 years after his first.

Talk about the volatility of the modern Dodgers all you want, but they never had anyone like this. His memoir, published in 1975, carried his defining title: *Nice Guys Finish Last.* Leo Durocher? He finished in the Hall of Fame.

58 Zack Wheat

For all the nostalgia that floats like gossamer from the Brooklyn Dodgers era, memories of Zack Wheat have tumbled off the currents. Yet a century after making his Dodgers debut, Wheat remains worthy of attention, not only as the franchise's all-time leader in several major categories, but as someone much more modern than the timing of his playing days would suggest.

Wheat, who played all but the final season of his career with the Dodgers, tops the team in career hits (2,804), games (2,322), at-bats (8,859), doubles (464), triples (171), and total bases (4,003). In 1916, his on-base percentage of .366 and slugging percentage of .461 (150 OPS+) helped lead Brooklyn to its first World Series.

"Wheat was far ahead of his time in many aspects of hitting, adopting strategies that wouldn't be widely accepted until decades later," wrote baseball historian Eric Enders, whose definitive biographical sketch of Wheat can be found online with the SABR

Baseball Biography Project. "He was sometimes criticized for his reluctance to bunt, but he argued that he was more valuable to the team by swinging away."

"I was young and inexperienced [in the minors]," Wheat himself said. "The fellows that I played with encouraged me to bunt and beat the ball out. I was anxious to make good and did as I was told. When I came to Brooklyn I adopted an altogether different style of hitting. I stood flat-footed at the plate and slugged. That was my natural style."

When baseball transitioned to the lively ball era, Wheat was readier than most to take advantage—a big-ball player waiting to emerge from a small-ball age. His performance not only remained steady well into his 30s, but in 1924, when he was one of the 10 oldest players in the game at 36, Wheat had his finest year: a .375 batting average, .428 on-base percentage and .549 slugging percentage (163 OPS+). Even allowing for the overall growth in offense in baseball starting in the 1920s, Wheat, who also had an exceedingly high defensive reputation, only seemed to get better.

The other way Wheat presaged the modern ballplayer was in salary negotiations. Decades before players had the right to become free agents, Wheat was a perennial holdout. A farmer in his home state of Missouri, Wheat made it clear to Brooklyn's owners, according to Enders, that as much as he loved the game, he was more than willing to live off the more traditional field of dreams. Not surprisingly, his show of backbone paid off in raises.

After his retirement in 1927, the tables turned in an unfortunate way for Wheat. The Great Depression sapped the value of his farm, and in-fighting among Dodgers brass helped keep him from remaining in the organization in a managerial post. He survived and even thrived, but though he was inducted into the Hall of Fame in 1959, right after the Dodgers moved to Los Angeles, the full dimension of Wheat's accomplishments have fought an uphill struggle with time. Though seeing his name rest undisturbed atop the Dodgers record book for so long is impressive enough, it's important we remember he was more than just a name, more than an obscurity from another epoch.

59 The Ballplayer

Day after day, for 24 days, the Dodgers and their fans kept vigil for Jim Gilliam. Day after day, they awaited word of his improvement, and day after day, the only update was no update.

"Dodgers coach Jim Gilliam remained unconscious Sunday in Daniel Freeman Hospital where he was admitted last month following a massive brain hemorrhage," a typical September 1978 report in the *Los Angeles Times* stated. "A spokesman for the hospital said his condition has not changed since the surgery."

The team soldiered on under this cloud while wrapping up its second consecutive NL West title. Gilliam had been a Dodger for nearly 30 consecutive years, in many ways a model Dodger for his dedication and acumen. He thrived upon being underestimated. Though his public nickname was "Junior," close friends and teammates knew him as—"The Devil"—after a cheeky, daring challenge at a pool hall.

"Every year we'd go to spring training and some hotshot was going to take his job away," former Dodgers manager Walter Alston told Milton Richman of United Press International. "Jim would start the season on the bench and never bitch or moan, and after a while he would have the job back again."

Artist of the Stolen Base

Davey Lopes was the first of the Dodgers' long-running infield to depart, and so even after he left following the 1981 season, it was hard not to keep an eye on how he was doing. Lopes was with the Chicago Cubs when he turned 40 on May 3, 1985. For the remainder of that season, Lopes stole 42 bases and was thrown out only four times. Dodgers fans still took pride, because Lopes had been one of theirs for so long.

It was the third time that the 5'9" sparkplug with the thick mustache had stolen more than 40 bases in a season and been caught four times. He went 45 for 49 in 1978, and the following year, he not only went 44 for 48, he blasted 28 home runs from the leadoff spot and walked 97 times. Aside from Jackie Robinson, Lopes probably had the greatest season ever for a Dodger second baseman.

But most of all, Lopes was always a precision base-stealer. In 1975, just after turning 30, he set what was then a major league record by stealing 38 consecutive bases without being caught. Even though he didn't reach the majors until he was 27, when his fastest years were behind him, Lopes was successful on 83 percent of his stolen-base attempts—both as a Dodger and for his entire career. Caught stealing records are sketchy for much of the Brooklyn era, but Lopes was very likely the best base runner in Dodgers history. He retired with 557 stolen bases, 418 of them as a Dodger, second behind Maury Wills' 490—but in 158 fewer attempts.

For that reason, perhaps—no matter how bleak it seemed—people couldn't quite believe that Gilliam, a young 49 when stricken, wouldn't make it back. He was tenacious to the point that he could seemingly slow down time.

"My first recollection of him goes all the way back to when he was playing for Montreal [the Dodgers' minor league team], and I was managing the club," Alston recalled. "We were playing in Toronto and I was on the lines, coaching third, when I put on the hit-and-run with him at bat and a runner on first.

"The runner didn't go and Jim didn't swing.... When we got back to the dugout, we talked about it, and Jim told me he could see the runner wasn't going to go out of the corner of his eyes and that was why he didn't swing at the ball. I was in baseball quite a long time but Jim was the only man I ever saw who could do that."

As Gilliam transitioned to coaching (though the Dodgers kept pulling him from the sidelines back to the active roster in 1965 and 1966), he became in every sense of the word a mentor, one whose absence would be keenly felt. The Dodgers dedicated their 1978 division title and then their league title to Gilliam.

"It seems like all the things he preached and practiced to us became more vivid when he was no longer there to see us do those things," reserve infielder Lee Lacy told Scott Ostler of the *Times*. "We utilized the knowledge and skills learned from him at a time when we had to be at our best. He was just a helping hand that made us strong."

The Dodgers earned their trip to the World Series on October 7. The next night, at 10:55 PM, Gilliam passed away. "It's going to be very difficult not to keep thinking about him," said second baseman Davey Lopes, another Gilliam protégé.

On October 10, the franchise ensured that he would never be forgotten and retired his No. 19. Taking the field that night with his number on the shoulders of their uniforms, the Dodgers opened Game 1 of the Fall Classic with an 11–5 victory, with a distraught but galvanized Lopes blasting two homers and driving in five runs.

On the afternoon of October 11, with Game 2's first pitch hours away, baseball paused and gathered at Trinity Baptist Church to pay their respects—2,000 strong—at Gilliam's funeral. A memorable photo from that day shows Dodgers tormentor Reggie Jackson of the Yankees standing solemnly between Lopes and Tommy Lasorda. All three delivered eulogies.

Jim Gilliam was NL Rookie of the Year in 1953, a two-time All-Star, and one of the best in team history at drawing a walk, but finished his career with lesser stats than many Dodgers whose uniform numbers won't ever be retired by the team. Every other retired Dodgers jersey was worn by someone in the Hall of Fame. If Gilliam was the team's greatest citizen, even that by itself wouldn't have been enough to forever hang up his No. 19.

His death just hurt that much. It was a Hall of Fame hurt. If future generations aren't meant to realize it, his retired number will have to do as a reminder.

60 See the Dodgers on the Road

You ready to live a little? As definitive as the Dodger Stadium experience is, you can't ignore the reward of seeing the Dodgers at another team's ballpark. Away from Los Angeles' own friendly confines, you're impelled to root a little harder for a win and die a little harder over a loss. Emotions are more naked when you're in the minority. But there are several ways to go about this, and it's worth considering the differences.

Though times have changed since the Giants moved from Candlestick Park to AT&T Park, situated beautifully at water's edge and offering something of a pacifying effect, the most intense ride for a Dodgers fan on the road remains San Francisco. Giants fans continue to despise the Dodgers more than Dodgers fans hate the Giants, which is saying something. Showing up in neutral colors will sufficiently expose you to the loathing, but an appearance in Dodgers paraphernalia or even just some pro-Dodgers cheering will give you the added jolt of being a target of a Bay Area barrage. There may be no sweeter victory than walking out of a Giants home game wearing the colors of a victorious Dodgers team.

San Diego's PETCO Park can offer a slimmed-down version of the San Francisco challenge. The Padres are also in a 21st-century facility, though not quite as breathtaking as the Giants', and the town detests the Dodgers, though not quite as venomously as San Francisco. But one thing to consider is that over the years, the Dodgers have fought more of an uphill battle down south than up north. In the past 31 seasons (1978 through 2008), the Dodgers have had a winning record in San Diego only 11 times.

Trips to the Dodgers' other NL West rivals, Arizona and Colorado, are only about as intense as the pennant race in that given moment, though Colorado's Coors Field offers a sensational skyline as a backdrop. Once you leave California's NL cities, a Dodgers road game becomes less an exercise in traditional rivalry and much more of an excuse to simply view more of the best baseball has to offer. Wrigley Field in Chicago, the only remaining NL park still older than Dodger Stadium (by a lot—48 years), is a must-see for fans of all stripes—not just for the nostalgia, but also because it really is a fun, intimate spot to take in a game. If there's any ballpark to visit when the Dodgers *aren't* playing so that you can soak in the atmosphere without mitigating loyalties, it might be Wrigley. Otherwise, most of the rest of the National League presents a tour of new construction, as nearly every other NL city has something fresh. New York opened two parks in 2009: the Mets' Citi Field (modeled after Ebbets Field and featuring a Jackie Robinson rotunda) and a new Yankee Stadium for the Bronx Bombers.

Ah, the American League. Nearly the entire 20th century was played without the Dodgers visiting an AL park during the regular season, but interleague play created all kinds of possibilities. Again, modern facilities dominate, with only Fenway Park in Boston providing an Old School locale. Of course, the not-really-in-Los Angeles Angels of Anaheim offer the closest shot at accompanying the Dodgers on the road, but that's a rivalry that hasn't really ignited.

Ultimately, the Dodgers road experience *nonpareil* belongs to fans of the team who live in other cities. A pilgrimage to Dodger Stadium from afar, a prodigal son finding home—that's a win-win. And if the Dodgers win, a win-win-win.

61 Take the Field

You don't have to suit up for the Dodgers to roam the Dodger Stadium outfield—nor do you need to make the mad dash in the middle of a game with security guards tackling you and hauling you off to the cops. Fans have more ways than ever of treading the thriving Stadium grass. Here are some recent popular examples:

- At least twice a year, including an evening on or around July 4, Fireworks Night lets you lay a blanket out on the grass, lean back, and watch the colorful explosions above the stadium.
- Before every game, eight children are picked to meet and get autographs from the Dodgers starting position players as they take their warmups—moments before the first pitch. Another slot is open for kids to grab a microphone and say to the crowd, just like Vin Scully, "It's time for Dodger baseball."
- Every year for Father's Day, the Dodgers invite parents and kids on to the field to play catch.
- Photo Day allows you to come onto the field to snap pictures of the Dodgers as they parade by, but get there early if you want to stake out a good position.
- Bring your glove and shag balls on the warning track during live Dodgers batting practice, which also features an

Beach Balls: Fun or Folly?

What is it about the beach ball? What is it that is so addictive, so beguiling that a child's toy can draw the attention of so many fans of all ages away from the actual baseball contest they theoretically came to see at Dodger Stadium?

Though they're the bane of the hardcore Dodgers fans who find them a distraction, beach balls nevertheless delight a majority of those they bounce to, near, or even off of. They're a sign of how much people really want to get in the game, admittedly at the most remedial level possible.

Beach ball fans should recognize that the annoyance beach ball foes feel for the bounding orbs is legitimate, and shouldn't be offended if one were to fall victim to the sharp poke of a car key or ballpoint pen. But perhaps some tolerance for beach balls is deserved. After all, the umpire isn't utterly specific when he calls out, "Play ball!"

"Autograph Alley" with different past and present Dodgers stopping by.

- Concerts at Dodger Stadium—past performers have included the Rolling Stones, Elton John, Bruce Springsteen, and Madonna—turn the field into baseball's biggest mosh pit.
- At the annual Hollywood Stars game, seating is available in the grass behind the shortened outfield fence. Apparently, no one thinks Jimmy Kimmel can clear the 395 mark.
- Your company or organization can arrange a sponsored batting-practice event that allows you to take a few swings in the same spot where Gibby hit his home run in '88.
- Sing the National Anthem before the game. You can submit your rendition of "The Star-Spangled Banner" any time to the Dodgers' Special Events Department.
- Attend a four-day youth baseball camp, where current and past Dodgers guide your child with instruction on fundamentals of the game, four hours per day. Scholarships to the camp are available.

- Sign up for a Dodger Stadium tour, which not only includes field access but visits to the dugouts, press box, and other hidden areas of the ballpark.

If you've got your wallet and future wife aligned, you can even rent Dodger Stadium for your wedding. Whether you can get Vin Scully to pronounce you man and wife is another matter.

62 When Were the Dodgers Born?

If you want to ski the black-diamond runs of Dodgers expertise, one useful tidbit to know is that the roots of the franchise predate Brooklyn's entrance into the National League. Just make sure you don't get lost among the several other baseball clubs calling Brooklyn their home.

In *The Dodgers*, Glenn Stout traces organized baseball in Brooklyn back to the mid–1850s:

"By 1857," Stout writes, "Brooklyn sported no fewer than four well-organized, formal baseball clubs. One year later they were invited to join an association of clubs in Manhattan to create what can be considered the first baseball league, the National Association of Base Ball Players."

Brooklyn was the home of the man generally acknowledged to be baseball's first star player, Jim Creighton, who brought the wrist snap to pitching and began its transformation into an art form. Creighton was also the game's first martyr, dying at age 21 of internal injuries said to have been suffered during a game.

But it's between then and Brooklyn's 1890 NL debut that the Dodgers franchise as it's known today was born. The 1890

Touchdown, Dodgers!

More than half a century before the NFL almost came to Chavez Ravine, pigskins flew at Pigtown. From 1930–43, the Brooklyn Dodgers football team gave the borough's World Series-starved fans something to root for in the fall. In those 14 seasons, unfortunately, the team never finished in first place.

However, like their baseball counterparts who hosted Cincinnati for major league baseball's first telecast on August 26, 1939, the football Dodgers also have the distinction of playing in their league's first televised game, which they won 23–14, on October 22 that same year.

After changing its name to the Tigers before a 1944 season in which it went 0–10, Brooklyn football merged with a team whose name must have been very difficult for the city's baseball fans to swallow: the Boston Yanks. Football briefly left Ebbets Field, but in 1946, a new Brooklyn Dodgers team began play in the All-American Football Conference. In the winter of 1947–48, Branch Rickey, John L. Smith, and Walter O'Malley purchased the squad.

"Rickey told O'Malley and Smith that operating a pro football team in Ebbets Field would be both a good community gesture and, ultimately, a money-making proposition," Lee Lowenfish wrote in his Rickey biography. Peter O'Malley recalls going as a child to the games with Rickey. But the team went 2–12 and was in the red by about $300,000 at the end of 1948, and once again, it merged into oblivion.

Brooklyn Bridegrooms, who won the NL pennant in their first season, were brought over by co-owner Charles Byrne from the American Association, which was foundering with the establishment of a rival confederation, the Players' League. Previously, the same franchise had spent the 1884–89 seasons in the AA, using such other official and unofficial nicknames as the Grays (1885–88) and the Atlantics (1884). The AA, though a bit inferior to the NL in strength was nonetheless considered a major league—the top echelon of professional baseball.

And the journey back in time goes back yet one step further. Brooklyn's arrival in the AA came after it won—under the same ownership and in the same locale—the 1883 Interstate Association title. That team came into being when, Stout writes, *New York Herald* night editor George Taylor, ex-journalist/real estate investor Byrne, Byrne's brother-in-law and business partner Joseph Doyle, and Rhode Island casino operator Frederick Abell applied for an IA franchise, found a place near the Gowanus Canal to build a ballpark, and recruited 40 ballplayers from which to form a squad. That group took the first step as the franchise that today operates nearly 3,000 miles and more than 100 years away in the splendor of Dodger Stadium.

63 Hercules

Charles Ebbets' middle name was Hercules, befitting a man who undertook prodigious labors in the big leagues. He had formidable ideas and great passions: He loved money, baseball, and Brooklyn, and though those devotions sometimes clashed titanically, they also gave birth to the Dodgers of the 20th century.

Born in 1859, at the end of the decade in which baseball in Brooklyn came to life, Ebbets made careers for himself in architecture, publishing, and politics but found his true calling in a job with the local ballclub in 1892. Understand that whatever zeal for the Dodgers you might ante up, Ebbets could probably see you and raise you—at least as far as trying to build up the overall organization. At first, he worked mainly in accounting and sales, but there were few tasks he wasn't compelled to pursue, including manager. Often accepting stock in the franchise as compensation, Ebbets rose to become club president in 1898.

From that point on, Ebbets was frequently mortgaging his entire financial well-being to fulfill his Brooklyn fantasies. He entered into a syndicate agreement with Baltimore, a popular method of the time that allowed one franchise to plunder another for talent, and won pennants in 1899 and 1900. He emptied his bank account to buy out minority owner Ferdinand Abell in 1902, according to John Saccoman's biographical sketch of Ebbets at the SABR Biography Project, and soon borrowed even more money so he could become majority owner. As if that weren't enough, Ebbets then prioritized the building of a state-of-the-art ballpark, which stretched his financial situation even further.

Not surprisingly, as Glenn Stout points out in *The Dodgers*, this made Ebbets less than generous with player payroll, allowing the newly forming American League to make off with many of his players to an extent that undermined his end-of-the-century Baltimore talent heist and sapped the on-field product in Brooklyn for years to come. And, of course, for all the financial deep-sea diving he took, for all the aggressive ticket pricing he instituted (including raising World Series grandstand tickets to a record $5 in 1916), for all his ambitions regarding the ballpark that would eventually be named for him, he couldn't muster the resources to create a facility that would stand the test of time. But that didn't stop the borough of Brooklyn from finding a special connection with the team in large part through his efforts.

Ebbets passed away in April 1925—destitute neither in money nor spirit. "The Dodgers were scheduled to open a three-game series against the Giants at Ebbets Field later that day," Saccoman writes. "'Charlie wouldn't want anybody to miss a Giant-Brooklyn series just because he died,' said Wilbert Robinson. The game went on, with the crowd standing for a moment of silence beforehand and both teams' players wearing black mourning bands on the left sleeves of their uniforms. NL president John Heydler ordered all

NL games postponed on the day of the funeral, which was attended by most of the league's magnates."

At the funeral, acting team president Ed McKeever caught pneumonia and died days later, setting the stage for the next chapter of Brooklyn history. Replacing Ebbets would be a Herculean task.

64 Wes Parker and the Cycle

Ritual is a part of sports that can sometimes be simultaneously soothing and annoying. For the Dodgers, this is easily illustrated by "The Ballad of Wes Parker."

Any time—*every* time—a Dodger player would get three different types of hits in a game, in that player's next at-bat the broadcaster of the moment would point out that the player's chance to become the first Dodger to hit for the cycle since Parker did so on May 7, 1970. The historical anecdote pushed the limit of diminishing returns; many Dodgers fans eventually learn it by rote like their times tables or their ATM code.

Parker rode his cycle against the defending World Series Champion New York "Miracle" Mets at Shea Stadium, and it was one of the brighter moments in a season that quickly found the Dodgers seven games behind Cincinnati—Los Angeles would finish 14½ back. Only 16,552 saw the game, and one thing they don't usually tell you about Parker's cycle is how dramatic it was. Through six innings, the last anyone would have expected was that he was going to achieve the feat.

Parker doubled to lead off a scoreless second inning for the Dodgers, then grounded out to end the fourth. Given a run in the

Dodgers first baseman Wes Parker (shown here with Ted Williams) was voted the all-time best fielding baseman in major league history. Parker also became the first Los Angeles Dodger to hit for the cycle on May 7, 1970. Photo courtesy of www.walteromalley.com.

first inning, Mets starter Ray Sadecki was making it hold up, leading 1–0 entering the seventh when Parker led off with a home run to tie the game. A double by Billy Grabarkewitz then chased Sadecki, but the Dodgers ended up tallying three more runs off reliever Tug McGraw.

In the eighth, Parker led off again and singled, but the Dodgers got no other men aboard in the inning. Manny Mota forced Parker, then Mota was caught stealing. By this point, Parker was only one hit away from the cycle, but when you need a triple with a 4–1 lead and one inning to go, and you're due up sixth, frankly, it wasn't even worth mentioning that the last time a Dodger hit for the cycle before Parker was Gil Hodges, June 25, 1949. [Note: Hodges was watching Parker in the opposing dugout as Mets manager.]

But in the bottom of the eighth, the Mets got three singles and a walk to pull within 4–3 while loading the bases. Joe Foy struck out, and then Duffy Dyer hit a fly ball to right fielder Von Joshua, who mishandled it for an error, allowing the tying run to score. The Dodger victory was in jeopardy, but Parker's attempt at the cycle was very much alive.

The Mets loaded the bases again in the bottom of the ninth with one out, threatening to end the game before Parker could bat, but against Ray Lamb, Ken Boswell grounded into a double play.

When Parker came up for the fifth time in the game, Ted Sizemore was on third base and Willie Davis on first. With everything on the line, Parker nailed it. He hit a triple to center field, a low line drive that zoomed over Tommie Agee's head, bringing home the go-ahead runs and the cycle. Parker later scored, and

Double Triple Plays

The Dodgers had gone 38 years in Los Angeles and 47 years overall without turning a triple play before shortstop Juan Castro ran back and made an over-the-shoulder catch of Chipper Jones' pop fly in Atlanta on June 16, 1996. Braves base runners Marquis Grissom and Mark Lemke had both assumed the ball would drop in for a hit, so Castro was able to turn and fling the ball to Delino DeShields to double up Grissom, and then DeShields threw to Eric Karros at first base to triple up Lemke.

The wait for another triple play wasn't nearly as long, ending almost exactly two years later, on June 13, 1998. Kurt Abbott of Colorado popped up a bunt attempt—enough to freeze teammates Jamey Wright and Neifi Perez on first and second base (the infield fly rule can't be called on bunts). Pitcher Darrren Dreifort let the ball drop, and then the throws went from Dreifort to shortstop Jose Vizcaino to force Perez, then to Eric Young at first base to retire Abbott, and finally across the diamond to Bobby Bonilla at third base to tag out Wright. The ol' 1–6–4–5.

Lamb made the 7–4 lead stand up, allowing Parker's celebration to go undeterred.

"Really, I'm so thrilled," Parker said on the radio postgame show after the game, "I really hardly know what to say, because it's been a long uphill climb. You know, for seven years now I've been playing and I've always felt I've been a good hitter, and tonight I finally felt like I arrived finally as a big-league hitter.

"I turned to Harry Wendelstedt, the first-base umpire, in the bottom of the 10th inning after there were two outs and said, 'Harry, you just saw me have the greatest night I've ever had in baseball.' And he looked at me and just kind of shook his head."

Since then, the Dodgers have had numerous close calls: more than 300 games in which a batter got three of the four hits he needed for a cycle. By nearly 20 years, it's the longest cycle drought of any major league team (except the three that have never had one: San Diego, Florida and Tampa Bay). Willie Crawford, Steve Garvey, Gary Sheffield, and Marquis Grissom each had games in which they were missing the easiest hit of all, a single. Garvey, in fact, had three-fourths of a cycle 21 times in his Dodgers career. Marlon Anderson, who already had two singles, a triple, and a homer, could have gotten a cycle if he had stopped at second base when hit the Dodgers' fourth consecutive homer in the ninth inning of 2006's 4+1 game, but that wasn't gonna happen.

The absolute nearest misses since Parker's cycle were by Cesar Izturis on September 8, 2003, and Andre Ethier on September 5, 2008. Needing a double, Izturis lined one to center field and trying to stretch it, slid in safely at second base (according to replays) but was called out. In his game, Ethier needed a triple and laced a ball into the gap in right-center, but hesitated between second and third base and was thrown out. The wait continues.

65 Two Infields

In the 1960s and again in the 1970s, the Dodgers unveiled two remarkable infield combinations that people would talk about into the next century. One was a novelty act, while the other was the real deal.

The Dodgers' all-switch-hitting infield is one of the classic Dodgers stories of the '60s, and the way people talk about it, you'd think it was a regular feature at the ballpark. Certainly, it was a renowned foursome: Wes Parker won Gold Gloves year after year, Jim Gilliam was royalty from Brooklyn, Maury Wills a base-stealing legend, and Jim Lefebvre an NL rookie of the year. Yet the four never even played a full season together.

Wills and Gilliam had been Dodgers since the 1950s, while Parker made his debut in '64. Lefebvre graduated to the majors the following year, but newly acquired John Kennedy (coming from Washington with Claude Osteen) made the Opening Day start, not Gilliam, who had retired after the 1964 season to become a coach. But May 28, less than a month after Tommy Davis broke his ankle, Gilliam rejoined the active roster, and in the second game of a doubleheader on May 31, 1965, the four switch-hitters finally made their first ensemble start.

It wasn't a rousing beginning, not with the quartet combining to go 2 for 13 in a 6–1 loss to the Reds. Though the four did make key contributions toward the Dodgers' World Series title, they only made 69 starts that season as a unit. And by '66, the phenomenon was already petering out. Nate Oliver opened the season at third base, leaving the switch-hitting group to start only 25 more games together, scattered throughout the year. Their final bow came in

Game 2 of the Dodgers' 1966 World Series drowning, when they went 1-for-13 with two walks in a 6–0 loss to Baltimore.

Gilliam retired from playing for good following the '66 season, Wills went in trade to Montreal, and the Dodgers went into what was at the time a postseason drought.

By 1973, the Dodger infield didn't have the switch-hitters but was no more stable, as second and third bases became revolving doors and shortstop only temporarily solidified after Wills came back to the team. But before fans even could realize it, the most steadfast baseball infield of all time was being born. When the Dodgers took the field in the second game of a June 23 doubleheader with Steve Garvey at first, Davey Lopes at second, Bill Russell at short and Ron Cey at third, it was a grouping that came together almost as if by alchemy.

Russell was the first to establish himself—but only after he was converted from the outfield—by becoming a regular in 1972 and an All-Star game participant in '73. Cey hadn't even had 50 major league plate appearances before 1973 when he nailed down the job, while Lopes was already 27 when he made his major league debut the year before, an age that most players have either hit their prime or their ceiling.

The key change was Garvey. Bill Buckner had been getting the bulk of starts at first base, but Buckner could play left, while it was becoming most apparent that Garvey couldn't play third—he made 28 errors in 85 games in 1972.

"I had always had a strong arm," Garvey told Steve Delsohn for the latter's oral history of the Dodgers, *True Blue*. "And then my freshman year at Michigan State, I separated my shoulder playing football. It was enough of a separation that I never threw quite the same again after that.

"But it may have been partly psychological, too. Because if I had to make a quick throw, if it was a quick play, boy, it would be on the money. Give me time and who knows where it would be going."

Barely a year after moving from the trading block to first base, Garvey became the 1974 NL MVP and a perennial All-Star, giving the Dodgers solid and at times exceptional starters at all four infield positions, and for the rest of the decade, management could focus its energies elsewhere. This was no disparate bunch linked only by a rare confluence of ambidextrous ability. This was an *infield*—an infield that helped the Dodgers to three NL pennants in their first five full seasons together (1974–78), a period in which Dodger fortunes looked better than they had at any time since Sandy Koufax's climactic press conference.

After a trashbin of a first half sunk the team in 1979, the team rallied in 1980, only to fall short in the season's 163rd game. And then, all of a sudden it seemed, the ninth inning was arriving. By the time the infield returned from the 1981 players' strike, it had passed the eight-year mark together, starting more than 1,000 games side-by-side-by-side-by-side. The game was finally close to ending. Lopes was now 36, and there was new blood in line to replace him in the form of prized prospect Steve Sax. Short of major reversal of fortune, this would be the infield's last shot together.

The good news was that, thanks to MLB's decision to split the season after the strike and award first-half NL West championship to the Dodgers, the team was guaranteed a playoff spot earlier than ever. Starting in July, the focus was October. And though it took a then-record 16 postseason games, they did it—Garvey, Cey, Lopes, and Russell could finally taste World Series champagne.

On February 8, 1982, 14 years after they drafted him, the Dodgers traded Lopes to Oakland for minor leaguer Lance Hudson, who never rose above Class AA ball. Though Lopes would remain productive into his 40s, Sax performed so ably that it helped convince the Dodgers to let Garvey go as a free agent and allow Albuquerque slugger Greg Brock to replace him after the 1982 season. Cey went to the Chicago Cubs in a trade for minor leaguers Vance Lovelace (who years later became a special assistant to the general manager with the Dodgers) and Dan Cataline the following month.

At the end, the last man standing was the first man standing: Bill Russell, the all-time Los Angeles Dodgers leader in games played, a future coach, and a future manager. An era, however, was over.

66 Eric Gagné—Fact or Fiction

If, in the end, *The Eric Gagné Story* became at least in part a novel, a memoir rooted in more fantasy than we had been led to believe, than what a novel it was.

And if it wasn't a novel, then...wow. Just wow.

Welcome to the jungle! We got fun 'n' games! Electric. Dodgers fans weren't just swept up by the result, they were taken with the show, a show that evolved into Gagné emerging from the bullpen to piercing sounds of Guns 'n' Roses. After beginning his career as a starting pitcher with strikeout potential but inconsistent performance, Gagné was thrust into the role of bullpen closer mainly because no more obvious alternatives existed for the Dodgers in 2002. And just like that, Clark Kent turned into Superman.

With a fastball that approached 100 miles per hour, setting up a changeup that could break your wrists, and a curve that dropped down from heaven, Gagné left hitters like cats flailing at a piece of string. "Oh, yes!" the usually collected Vin Scully exclaimed after one Gagné close-out. "Oh my gosh, what a pitch! That's amazing! That's not fair."

It wasn't just pitching. We're talking sensory overload. A rock concert in a bullet train. The first eight innings were the warmup act. Gagné was the main event. And yes, it's true: Dodgers fans stayed in their seats—or rather stood up in front of them—until the very end of the game to see it.

For three seasons—each of them coincidentally totaling 82⅓ innings—Gagné struck out 13.3 batters per nine innings while allowing barely half that many base runners. His ERA those years was 1.79. In 2003, when he won the Cy Young Award, he allowed 12 runs the entire season. He set a major league record with 84 consecutive saves, though that almost makes him sound too robotic. The force was with him.

It was too good to last forever, that much you knew, though it ended all too soon. Starting in 2004, injuries began to sideline him. He pitched 15⅓ innings total for two remaining years of his Dodger career. In 2007, he had something of a renaissance with the Texas Rangers, but then fell apart following a trade to Boston.

And then, as some suspected, Gagné was too good to be true, or entirely true, anyway. Following the 2007 season, the Mitchell

Mike Marshall

Though he was a pitcher, Mike Marshall practically became an everyday player for the Dodgers in 1974. He went to the mound for a major league record 106 games, averaging nearly two innings per outing. At one point, he appeared in 13 consecutive contests, picking up victories in six of them along with two saves, pitching 26⅔ innings in those two weeks with a 1.69 ERA. Marshall finished the season with a 2.42 ERA (141 ERA+) and won the NL Cy Young Award.

Marshall later completed his doctorate in exercise physiology (in fact, he once said that he played professional baseball to pay for his college expenses) and insisted that he had methods that would increase the durability and resiliency of pitchers, but his approach has been found too extreme for the mainstream.

Report investigating the use of performance-enhancing substances by major league players named Gagné as a recipient of two shipments of human growth hormone. For many fans, this rendered Gagné's accomplishments null and void, on the theory that they rested on artificial and illegal stimulants. On the other hand, despite the general refrain in the media, several studies have shown that HGH does not help improve an athlete's performance—and, of course, if Gagné were using HGH, so were some of the batters he was facing.

Different minds will review *The Eric Gagné Story* in different ways. For those who experienced him, the memories still exist. When you close your eyes, you can still feel them. It's your choice what you do with them.

67 Team Trolley

The story that explains the origins of the Dodgers team name usually leaves out one important detail: why the name stuck.

First, here's the story…

"Trolley lines crisscrossed Brooklyn with little plan or forethought," Glenn Stout writes in *The Dodgers*. "An elevated train line dumped fans near the park, but to reach the stands they were forced to cross several sets of railroad tracks that sent electric trolley cars from Greenpoint to Coney Island.

"The newfangled contraptions proved a challenge for both drivers and pedestrians, neither of whom seemed to realize that the added weight of the mechanized cars made them much more difficult to stop than the horse-drawn variety. The result was carnage. Accidents became daily occurrences. Barely a week went by without one or more Brooklyn residents meeting his or her demise by trolley, and countless more were maimed. As such, surviving Brooklynites began to be known as 'trolley dodgers' for their skill at cheating death."

But as we also know, about a dozen nicknames have been associated with the team since it began play in the 19th century. That's because teams didn't set their nicknames in stone in the early decades of baseball—in fact, they didn't even always choose them, leaving the labels to the whim of the press covering the team. Often, the press simply played off the name of Brooklyn's manager at the time. Almost from the moment Wilbert Robinson took the helm of the team, for example, the *Brooklyn Eagle* began calling the team the Robins, and did so through the end of his tenure in 1931, although Stout notes *New York Sun* editor Joe Vila banned the name in 1926 over a spat with Robinson.

The pattern had been set back in the 1800s, when fans might know the team at any given moment as Ward's Wonders (after John Montgomery Ward, 1891–92), Foutz's Fillies (Dave Foutz, 1893–96) and even more prominently, the Superbas, because manager Ned Hanlon had the same last name as a group of performing brothers whose crowning production was titled "Superba." Superbas actually stuck for years after Hanlon left the scene (managers Patsy Donovan, Harry Lumley, and Bill Dahlen apparently lacking sufficient cachet).

Use of the Dodger name overlapped some of these, as did a nickname that was popular throughout the 1890s: the Bridegrooms (or Grooms), which actually came into use in 1889 after a winter that saw several Brooklyn players find wedded bliss. And still more names popped up during the infancy of Brooklyn baseball—Infants, for one, along with Grays (after the color of their uniforms), Kings (after Brooklyn's home in Kings County), and even one that appropriated a nickname for Brooklyn itself, the Church City Nines.

"Dodgers" survived all these alternatives to become the official choice, appearing on team jerseys by 1933, in time for it to fend off what might have been a Brogdingnagian challenge by "Bums," inspired by Willard Mullin's unforgettable series of cartoons about a mythical, hoboesque Brooklyn fan. Players and managers would come and go, but the trolleys hung around, making it hard for the Dodgers moniker to lose its appeal even if Brooklyn's denizens side-stepped the streetcars with more success.

The Los Angeles Grooms or Superbas might have been fun to root for—those Brooklyn newlyweds or multitalented Hanlon brothers are worth remembering fondly. But there's just something irresistible about being linked over a span of more than 100 years with fans who put their lives at risk just to see a ballgame, who invested their well-being in a team, as Vin Scully might say, destined to break your heart.

68 Ode to Joy

The next best thing to witnessing a no-hitter is reading what people had to say about it. Here are some joyful quips and eloquencies culled from the 10 Los Angeles Dodgers no-hitters.

"One time, after the eighth inning, John Roseboro said something about throwing a curve when I get behind a batter. I said, 'Heck with the no-hitter, let's get the game over.' And Gabby said, 'Let's get it.'

"I was almost sure I'd lose it. I figured a ball would fall in or something like that. Richie Ashburn's foul down the left-field line in the ninth really put a lump in my stomach."

—Sandy Koufax, June 30, 1962

June 30, 1962
Sandy Koufax
No-hitter—0 for 4

—Blackboard writing from Dodger teammates in front of Koufax's locker, teasing that he was a no-hit pitcher on the mound and at the plate.

"Speaking of O'Malley, it is Walter's custom to tear up a no-hit pitcher's contract and give him a new one calling for a $400 raise. That bonus will keep Sandy in alpaca sweaters until at least the Christmas holidays."

—*Los Angeles Times* sportswriter Frank Finch, May 11, 1963

"I was supposed to leave [my parents] tickets for the game. But I forgot."

—Koufax, May 11, 1963

"I was in Washington on business and hadn't heard anything about it. So I turned on the radio for the 11 o'clock news. The announcer said, 'Sandy Koufax has done it again. He's just pitched the third no-hitter of his career.' Right away, I just had one question: Did he win it?"

—Dodgers pitcher Don Drysdale, the day after Koufax's third no-hitter (June 4, 1964)

"I never saw him throw as hard as he did the last time I was up. He threw one ball right past me, and I was waiting for it.... This guy could drive you to drink."

—Cubs third baseman Ron Santo on Koufax, September 9, 1965

"He lay in a hospital bed 10 weeks ago, looking up at a bottle that dripped glycerine into his veins. He stood on the pitchers' mound at Dodger Stadium Monday afternoon, staring out of the shadows, and there was ice water in his veins."

—*Times* writer John Wiebusch on Bill Singer, who pitched a no-hitter July 20, 1970, less than two months after being hospitalized for hepatitis

"In the first inning. Any time I get the side out, I think no-hitter."

—Jerry Reuss, June 27, 1980

"That's great, now maybe we'll see another no-hitter."

—Fernando Valenzuela, after seeing on TV that former teammate Dave Stewart had thrown a no-hitter for Oakland earlier that day, June 29, 1990

"It was the first time [Kevin] Gross, 31, has allowed fewer than three hits in a game in his nine-year major league career. It was the first time he has won a game in five weeks.... The only thing more improbable was that his magical night was saved by shortstop Jose

Brooklyn no-hitters

Tom Lovett	June 22, 1891	Brooklyn 4, New York 0
Ed Stein	June 2, 1894	Brooklyn 1, Chicago 0 (6 innings)
Mal Eason	July 20, 1906	Brooklyn 2, St. Louis 0
Nap Rucker	September 5, 1908	Brooklyn 6, Boston 0
Dazzy Vance	September 13, 1925	Brooklyn 10, Philadelphia 1
Fred Frankhouse	August 27, 1937	Brooklyn 5, Cincinnati 0 (8)
Tex Carleton	April 30, 1940	Brooklyn 3, Cincinnati 0
Ed Head	April 23, 1946	Brooklyn 5, Boston 0
Rex Barney	September 9, 1948	Brooklyn 2, New York 0
Carl Erskine	June 19, 1952	Brooklyn 5, Chicago 0
Carl Erskine	May 12, 1956	Brooklyn 3, New York 0
Sal Maglie	September 25, 1956	Brooklyn 5, Philadelphia 0

Offerman, who leads the majors with 32 errors but did not miss either of two tough chances in the late innings."

—*Times* sportswriter Bill Plaschke, August 17, 1992

"We were trying to be cool about it, acting as if nothing was happening. I thought we were home free until Rocket [pitcher Ismael Valdes] couldn't control his enthusiasm. Finally, I just said, 'Rocket, shut up, will you?' "

—Dodgers outfielder Chris Gwynn,
July 14, 1995, on the bench during
Ramon Martinez's no-hitter

"You kidding me, there was no way I was going to let the ball drop. I was going to run that ball down. I would have dove on the ground. Leaped against the fence. Jumped over the wall. That ball wasn't dropping on me."

—Dodgers outfielder Todd Hollandsworth,
who made his first career start July 14, 1995

"Throwing a no-hitter at this place, he should be canonized on the spot."

—Dodgers catcher Mike Piazza, on Hideo Nomo's no-hitter
at hitters paradise Coors Field in Colorado, September 17, 1996

69 Dodgertown

On July 1, 1954, Dodgertown Camp for Boys opened at the team's six-year-old training facility in Vero Beach. As vice president of O'Malley Seidler Partners and former Dodger director of broadcasting and publications Brent Shyer notes, nearly 200 kids came from all over the country—some of them guided by 16-year-old camp counselor Peter O'Malley—not just for baseball, but also tennis, basketball, swimming, and fishing, before going to sleep at night in the very barracks where Brooklyn heroes like Pee Wee Reese and Jackie Robinson had slept earlier that year.

You could make a case that in those early years of Dodgertown, when the organization's roster reported for duty in March's precocious Florida warmth, the place had a decidedly summer camp feel. No doubt, more than one player wrote home outlining their sufferings.

"It wasn't too pleasant," outfielder Duke Snider once recalled to Shyer, who conducted a series of interviews with former Dodgers about the facility. "You had to walk through these vacant lots and there were paths, but there would be snakes. You'd always take a bat with you just in case you needed it. I went after a ball when the main ballpark was over by the airport, and there was sort of a ditch in left and right field and it had all grass, big bladed grass, and a ball got in between the left fielder and myself and we went over for it. I started down the ditch to get the ball, because it was in play, and there was a snake down there right by the ball. The guy got an inside-the-park home run! I wasn't going to go down and get that ball."

At the same time, the precedent-setting facility, which prioritized training a ballclub like no other, also became a full-fledged home away from home.

"All the minor leaguers dressed in the minor league clubhouse, which was very small," first baseman Wes Parker said. "It was partitioned off into separate rooms that were extremely small. We all dressed together maybe 15–20 of us, shoulder to shoulder. You hardly had enough room to stretch and put your arms up to put on your jersey. It was cold in there. They had I think electric heaters, but it didn't matter, it was cold, very cold. Air didn't circulate well.

The "Dodgertown Camp for Boys" in Vero Beach, Florida, was a popular summer all-sports camp, inaugurated in the summer of 1954, as a way to further utilize their spring training site and fulfill Walter O'Malley's desire for year-round activities. For $500, each boy aged 12-16 was instructed in baseball and many other recreational activities while living on base where the Dodgers players normally resided during training.

Photos courtesy of
www.walteromalley.com

DODGERTOWN CAMP FOR BOYS
VERO BEACH, FLORIDA
JULY and AUGUST

No activity in the year-'round calendar of the Brooklyn Dodgers brings more pleasure to officials of the club than our Dodgertown Camp for Boys at Vero Beach, Florida. A two-months, all-sports program for boys between the ages of 10 and 16 is conducted on the spacious Spring Training grounds of the Brooklyn Dodgers.

At Dodgertown your son sleeps in the same rooms, dresses in the same lockers, plays on the same ball fields, swims in the same pool and fishes in the same private lake enjoyed by Pee Wee Reese, Duke Snider, Gil Hodges, Carl Furillo and all the Dodgers.

At Dodgertown, under the supervision of a staff of men expert in their sports, your son will improve his ability in baseball, basketball, football, tennis, badminton, volleyball, track and field, swimming, fishing, archery and many other sports. He will be offered a well-rounded program set up on a pattern designed for the healthy entertainment of the growing boy. Whatever his favorite sport, he will play it better after he returns from Dodgertown.

At Dodgertown, too, your son will find other interests—craftsmanship, visits to scenic Florida spots, and the fellowship of meeting youngsters from many parts of our country.

At Dodgertown your son will be fed in the large dining hall where more than five hundred ball players eat their meals each Spring. He will have the round-the-clock call on a Camp doctor and a Camp nurse. He will be encouraged to enjoy an active, wholesome, healthy Summer.

At Dodgertown he will have the "Summer of his life."

Date..........
Camper's Name.......... Age..........
Address..........
City.......... State..........
Home Phone..........
Name of Parents..........
Employed by..........
Business Address..........
City.......... State..........
Business Phone..........
Activities of special interest to prospective camper:

We fly to Dodgertown on chartered Eastern Airlines Planes — some class!

Baseball every day at Dodgertown and plenty of action, too.

The Dodgers' stars use OUR lockers in the Spring.

We've got two outdoor basketball courts and indoor courts, too.

THE DODGERTOWN STAFF

Bill Cecroni, a member of the faculty of Wooster School, Danbury, Conn., is Camp Director. He is ably assisted by a staff which includes Fresco Thompson, Al Campanis, Buck Lai, Tex Warrington, Pete O'Malley, Steve Lembo, Don Schwartz, Ted Schettel and others. The Camp is under the over-all supervision of Edgar Allen, the "Mayor of Dodgertown." Individual as well as team instruction is provided. All competition is within definite age groups so as to assure each Dodgertown boy a fair chance to excel. The groups, to add to the competitive zest, are named after Dodger minor league teams—Montreal, St. Paul, Forth Worth, Mobile and Elmira. The older boys, of course, comprise the Brooklyn group.

THE AIMS

Our first aim at Dodgertown is to assure your boy a Summer full of clean, wholesome fun. With our excellent staff of instructors we definitely feel we can improve the playing ability of each boy. We know we can add to his healthy interest in all sports. He will be offered a well-coordinated, well-disciplined, well-rounded all-sports program.

THE COST

The two-months tuition, including board, lodging and laundry service, is $800. A Camp Canteen is operated at specified hours and your boy should carry a Canteen Account of about $25. We do not encourage excessive spending. Camp clothing is available at low cost at the Vero Beach department store. This includes royal blue Camp shorts, white T shirts with the Dodgertown script in blue across the front, and a Dodger baseball cap.

TRANSPORTATION

For boys living in and around New York we arrange chartered flights by Eastern Airlines, non-stop between New York and Vero Beach. The round-trip fare is less than $100. Train accommodations can also be obtained.

VISITORS

We encourage visitors to Dodgertown and there are ample hotel and motor courts in the Vero Beach area to accommodate parents.

ENROLLMENT

We are now interviewing applicants for the camping season ahead. If you are interested in receiving a formal Dodgertown Camp Application or want to arrange an interview, please fill in the form and mail to:

Dodgertown Camp, 215 Montague Street, Brooklyn 2, New York.

A swell pool is always ready for that cool dip—and expert swimming instruction.

Ted Schettel teaches us how to play tennis—some of the boys are pretty good.

towels.
MOBILE and ELMIRA—Pick up clean sheets and pillow cases.

8:30 - 11:30	BROOKLYN—Intra-squad game at Holman Stadium. MONTREAL—Basketball in the Auditorium. ST. PAUL—Riflery at the Range. FORT WORTH—Batting cages, one hour—Pitching strings, 1 hour. MOBILE—Track, one hour—Tennis, one hour. ELMIRA—Intra-squad game—Field No. 1.
11:30 - 12:30	SWIM in Lake or Pool 12:30 - 1:00 SICK CALL
12:30 - 1:15	LUNCH 1:15 - 1:30 CANTEEN
1:30 - 2:30	REST HOUR—Today is Write-a-Letter-Home-Day. This letter is your ticket to Dinner. Camp Barber will be available during Rest Hour.
2:30 - 4:30	The following activities will be available: Ocean Swimming, Life Saving Instruction—Pool, Boating and Canoeing—Lake, Horseback Riding, Trip to McKee Jungle Gardens, Fishing in the Indian River, Outdoor Basketball. BASEBALL: Pitching instruction at the String area, Infielders clinic on Field No. 2, Batting Cages.
4:30 - 5:30	SWIM in Lake or Pool 5:55 COLORS
6:00 - 6:30	DINNER 6:30 - 7:30 SICK CALL
7:00 - 7:30	The following activities will be available: Badminton, Volley Ball, La Crosse, Golf, Touch Football, Batting Cages, Bamboo Shop, Ping Pong, Horseshoes, Croquet.
7:30 - 9:30	BASEBALL GAME under the lights at Holman Stadium. MONTREAL vs. ST. PAUL. Both teams report in uniform at the Stadium at 7:15 for short infield drill and the game will begin shortly after. No inning will start after 9:30. Since this game will not be televised, everyone will want to be at the Stadium at 7:30. No admission—plenty of choice seats available.
9:30	CANTEEN 10:00 LIGHTS OUT

Ocean bathing in the surf at Vero Beach—the best! While New York suffers in 90 plus heat, youngsters at Dodgertown enjoy weather ten degrees cooler.

And fishing, too. You bet. Big ones!

And, of course, we all enjoy—Chow time! We eat in the big dining room where the Dodgers feed more than 500 players during Spring Training.

DODGERTOWN CAMP FOR BOYS
VERO BEACH, FLORIDA
BROOKLYN DODGERS 215 MONTAGUE STREET, BROOKLYN, N. Y. Tel.: MAin 4-5091

"The funny thing is, you started to love it.... I think it was a beautiful setup that there weren't distractions because guys would have gone out. As it was, we had our focus completely on baseball because there was nothing else to do, nothing else to think about."

Added former Dodger traveling secretary Bill DeLury: "Years ago, after dinner, we had what looked like a huge hotel lobby, and it had a canteen in it for soda pop and ice cream. It had a pool table and players would go in there and play pool and ping pong. It had a juke box. That's all they had. There were no TVs in the rooms. There was no heat in the rooms. You stayed in this huge lobby with 300, 400 or 500 people. You told stories and it was very interesting.... I listened to stories from Roy Campanella, (Don) Drysdale, Carl Furillo, Duke Snider; you can go on and on."

Born through the initiative of Bud Holman, who sought the Dodgers as a post-World War II occupant of the former U.S. Naval Air base, the frequently upgraded Dodgertown evolved into spring training's paradise, an unsurpassed locale for players to gear up for the coming season and for fans to kick back and soak in their team along with the Florida sunshine. There are countless Dodgers fans for whom the quintessential Dodger experience was not in Chavez Ravine, but following Manny Mota on his bicycle from the corner of Vero Beach's Don Drysdale Avenue and Vin Scully Way to a game at Holman Stadium. From business conferences to fantasy camps, Dodgertown was a destination in and of itself.

In March 2008, the Dodgers bid Dodgertown a somewhat acrimonious farewell, playing a truncated schedule there while gearing up to move to a new spring training home in Glendale, Arizona. It will be a ritzier complex, and perhaps most importantly, much easier for Los Angeles fans to visit than the cross-country flight and hours-long drive for a trip to Vero. There's little reason to think that the change won't be good for the Dodgers and their fans on many levels. Nonetheless, there's something a little sad, even heartbreaking, about leaving summer camp behind, snakes and all.

"Basically when I look back, it is as if I stood in one place and thousands of players, coaches, managers and newspapermen went through and I was there watching this big parade," Vin Scully said. "And so, in all honesty, there is no single other place in the world that holds more memories for me than Vero Beach."

70 Cool

Russell Nathan Jeanson Coltrane Martin, Jr: son of a saxophone player, middle-namesake of the legendary John Coltrane, spiritual descendant of Roy Campanella and Mike Piazza. Russell Martin, cool.

Russell Martin, plays the game the right way, *and* Russell Martin, puts up the numbers for substance to go with his style. Makes his big-league debut in 2006 at age 23 with the spirit of a kid but the composure of an old soul, and posts an on-base percentage of .355 with 10 homers and 10 steals. He homers in the 10th inning to end what had been a scoreless game in August, then hits the third of the four ninth-inning homers in September's 4+1 epic. He establishes immediately that he will play all night, catching 17 innings in Oakland in June (going 3 for 7 at the plate) and an NL-high 1,015 innings from the time he arrives through the end of the season.

In 2007, he goes platinum. A promising artist's second album can have its pitfalls, but Martin only refines his repertoire: 19 homers and 21 steals (a Dodger record for a catcher), .374 on-base percentage, .469 slugging percentage. Wins the Silver Slugger and Gold Glove awards, joining Gary Carter and Benito Santiago as the only catchers to do so. And he won't stop playing; he plays so

'Legs' Gibson

Though Kirk Gibson had all but lost the use of his lower extremities by the time he hit his homer for the ages in the 1988 World Series, his legs had already provided one of the more inspirational, indelible memories of that season.

With the Dodgers trailing Montreal, 3–2, in the bottom of the ninth at Dodger Stadium on August 20, Gibson singled in the tying run. Mike Marshall fouled out to first base for the second out. But with John Shelby up, Gibson stole second base. And then, pitcher Joe Hesketh threw a 1–1 pitch in the dirt.

Gibson took off for third base, saw the ball still being retrieved near the backstop screen, and kept on chugging for home, sliding in without the Expos even being able to make a tag. In a precursor to his classic arm pump of October, Gibson leaped up and exulted with his left arm.

"I knew it would be close," Gibson told Ross Newhan of the *Los Angeles Times*, "and I said, 'Here I come.' If I make it, we win; if I don't, we're in extra innings. We had tied the game and I was in the mood to be aggressive.

"It went through my mind what I would do (after he had stole second). I hesitated when I got to third and saw the ball near the backstop. My adrenaline was pumping with every stride. I mean, once I got going, there was no way I was going to stop. I just pumped my arms and my legs followed."

often it scares people, catching 1,254 innings, 1⅔ off Piazza's franchise record.

In 2008, he hits his first bum note, a 3-for-29 start to the season. Even then, he walks six times, finding a way to make music with one bat tied behind his back. After that, another solid season—he's old reliable now at age 25, the no-fuss, lots-of-muss, down-and-dirty leader of a crazy-quilt team. Every other hitter on the team has some issue, but Martin, the fair Canadian, finds his groove and hangs there. He even plays some third base in a pinch—his original position in the minors—just to show off his versatility.

Still maybe plays too much for his own good, but it's so hard to resist.

Russell Martin on vinyl. Indispensible to the Dodger collection. Just don't wear him out.

71 Manny Mota Mota Mota Mota Mota...

Some performers aren't destined to be leading men. Some are meant to be character actors, who live beneath the marquee but steal the show at every opportunity. Though he spent his most memorable years on the Dodger bench, Manny Mota was such a stealth star. The Dodger Stadium cheers, grander than any baseball backup ever received, still echo through the years: "Mo-ta! Mo-ta! Mo-ta!"

More than a quarter of a century after he finally retired as a player, he remains the ultimate pinch-hitter in Dodgers history. Not that there hasn't been competition—Dave Hansen smacked a record seven pinch-hit homers one year, and Lenny Harris wore a Dodger uniform for 4½ seasons on the way to surpassing Mota to become the majors' all-time leader in pinch-hits. But Mota almost made you look forward to the Dodgers needing a rally, such was the excitement when he came up to bat—and so often was the reward.

"Manny Mota was a bigger bargain than Alaska, or the Louisiana Territory," Jim Murray wrote. "He has the most amazing talent in the history of baseball for getting wood on a ball. He could do it if he had just spent the previous 12 months on the moon. He can recognize a strike in the dark."

In his Dodger pinch-hitting career, Mota went 106 for 330 with 43 walks, two hit-by-pitch and six sacrifice flies: a .396

'Bats' Leary

The last thing Dodger pitcher Tim Leary expected to do in the bottom of the 11th inning on August 13, 1988, was pinch-hit. But with the Dodgers and Giants tied 1–1, Pedro Guerrero was ejected (followed by Tommy Lasorda) for arguing for a balk call after his leadoff single. Franklin Stubbs pinch-ran for Guerrero, and Mike Marshall walked, but then the lone remaining position player on the Dodger bench, Mike Davis, also got himself kicked out for too much lip.

The Giants walked Alfredo Griffin intentionally, even though he was batting .168 at the time, to get to the pitcher's spot. That meant Leary had to grab a bat. But he wasn't unfamiliar with the equipment—he was 15 for 49 on the season (.306). Leary ran the count to 3–2, then lined a no-doubter single up the middle, driving home Stubbs with an unforgettable victory.

on-base percentage. In 1977, at age 39, he reached base in more than half his at-bats. In 1980, after he had become a Dodger coach at age 42, he was activated out of retirement for the stretch run in September and went 3 for 7.

"The trick is, Manny doesn't get his hits in the fourth inning of a so-what game against Houston on the 19th of August," Murray added. "Manny gets his hits when the game is on the line and the other guys have their craftiest or swiftest pitcher in that spot, the infield is pulled around towards right, the game—or the pennant—is on the line."

"Manny's role is, keep the rally going. He usually does this with as neat a trick as a bear on roller skates. He steps into the pitch, adjusts his hands at the last minute to the slightest blur of daylight in the defense and rockets a swift 'bleeder' to right field that is uncatchable. He moves the pennant into scoring position."

Mota remained a Dodger coach past his 70th birthday, putting on his Dodger uniform in 2008 for an unmatched 40th consecutive season, serving as an active link to glorious memories. In addition, the Manny Mota International Foundation has directly aided thousands of children in his native Dominican Republic. Perhaps the most remarkable part about Mota is that his dedication to community service exceeds his contributions to the Dodgers.

72 Jobe and John

It wasn't the operation that was unprecedented. It was the patient.

Recalling his 1974 surgery to replace the ruptured medial collateral ligament in Dodger pitcher Tommy John's left elbow, Dr. Frank Jobe pointed out to UPI's Jim Cour that it had been performed "many times before with people with any kind of paralysis," such as polio. This time, however, success would depend on it satisfying the demands of a pitcher, someone who would put overwhelming stress on the affected area.

And that's what made it revolutionary.

On the afternoon of July 17, 1974, John complained to reporters about being left off the NL All-Star team despite a 2.50 ERA. But that night, as he faced Hal Breeden of Montreal with two on and none out in the top of the third inning, his only concern was to try to induce a double play. So on a 1–1 pitch, he threw a sinking fastball.

"Right at the point where I put force on the pitch, the point where my arm is back and bent, something happened," John told Ron Fimrite of *Sports Illustrated*. "It felt as if I had left my arm someplace else. It was as if my body continued to go forward and my left arm had just flown out to right field, independent of the rest of me. I heard this thudding sound in my elbow, then I felt a sharp pain. My fingers started to tingle. The ball got to the plate somehow, high and away. I threw one more pitch, at about half speed, and felt the same sensation. That pitch was even higher and farther away. I walked off the mound and met Walter Alston coming out of the dugout. 'You better get somebody,' I told him. 'I just hurt my arm.'"

Jobe, who had been treating Dodgers and other athletes for about a decade, initially prescribed rest while he monitored the injury. But in a very quiet, one sentence September announcement in the *Los Angeles Times*, readers were told that John would have surgery that day. Jobe removed a tendon of about seven inches from John's right arm and wound it into John's left elbow.

"The thing we hoped was that by placing the tendon in a part of the body where there's a good blood supply," Jobe said, "blood vessels grow into it, and it remains a live piece of tissue and then permanently supports the elbow. But not every transfer works that way. We have done them where they become a dead piece of tissue. In other words, like a piece of string in there. Then in a couple of years down the road, the string breaks."

That didn't happen, but another complication developed. There was nerve deterioration in the traumatized part of the elbow, and on December 18, Jobe operated again on John to reposition the nerve. Whatever optimism there was for John's recovery was similarly jostled.

"Dr. Jobe advised me to look for something to do outside of baseball," John recalls. "He told me he didn't think I'd ever pitch again."

"With a withered arm and a clawlike hand," wrote Fimrite, "John reported to the Dodgers' spring training camp in 1975. His teammates were staggered by his appearance. 'He couldn't throw a ball from here to that chair,' says Don Sutton, gesturing to a folding chair in the Dodger clubhouse no more than 15 feet away." On the anniversary of the surgery, Jeff Prugh of the *Los Angeles Times* reported that John had regained strength but still lacked complete dexterity. "His ring finger, for example, is slightly crooked and his thumb is not fully maneuverable, thus preventing him from throwing breaking pitches effectively."

But suddenly that month, things turned. "I was preparing to throw when I discovered I could bend my fingers," John recalled to Fimrite. "I hadn't been able to do that since the first operation in September. I knew then it was just a matter of time. I had cleared the biggest hurdle."

John still missed the rest of the 1975 season, but he was ready for spring training in 1976. That year, he threw 207 innings, and the next, 220⅓ with a 2.78 ERA (138 ERA+), pitching a pennant-clinching complete game victory at Philadelphia and finishing second in the NL Cy Young balloting. Instead of his career ending, John pitched 2,544⅔ more innings in the majors with a 3.66 ERA, retiring at age 46. Only seven pitchers in major league history have ever been older.

Tommy John surgery, as the procedure came to be known, not only became routine in baseball, but some actually looked forward to the new life it brought to their pitching arms. Jobe performed about 1,000 Tommy John surgeries himself, and in 1989 pioneered a new procedure used on Dodger great Orel Hershiser that also extended the life of major league pitchers. John became a borderline Hall of Fame candidate, but surely Jobe should be in.

73 Sing, Sing a Song

Sure, a Dodger fan knows to expect "Take Me Out to the Ballgame" during the seventh-inning stretch at Dodger Stadium, and anyone who has listened to the team on the radio for any length of time knows the first verse to "It's a Beautiful Day for a Ballgame." There's

And Now a Word About Farmer John

"Braunschweiger"

—Vin Scully

also music that's uniquely special to the team's Brooklyn past—plenty of it, in fact, such as "Follow the Dodgers," performed by original Ebbets Field organist Gladys Goodding. A master class in the Dodger songbook certainly includes the Woodrow Buddy Johnson & Count Basie number, "Did You See Jackie Robinson Hit That Ball?"

But to be a real cut above the crowd, you've got to know "The D-O-D-G-E-R-S Song (Oh, Really? No, O'Malley)," an epic composition recorded by Danny Kaye and co-written by his wife, Sylvia Fine, with Herbert Baker. The jaunty opening is the part most fans encounter:

So I say D,
I say D-O,
D-O-D,
D-O-D-G,
D-O-D-G-E-R-S, team, team, team, team

Near the climax, however, as the action heats up in the imaginary Giants-Dodgers game depicted in the lyrics, the turns of phrase spin you like a whirligig:

Gilliam up
Miller grunts
Miller throws
Gilliam bunts

Cepeda runs to field the ball and Hiller covers first
Haller runs to back up Hiller, Hiller crashes into Miller

Miller falls, drops the ball and Conlan calls "safe!" Yeah Conlan!
Willie Davis gets a hit and Tommy does the same
Here comes Mr. Howard with a chance to win the game
Hit it once
Big Frank...bunts?

Cepeda runs to field the ball, so does Hiller, so does Miller
Miller hollers Hiller
Hiller hollers Miller
Haller hollers Hiller points to Miller with his fist
And that's the Miller-Hiller-Haller hallelujah twist!

The five-minute song really is the Dodgers' *Odyssey.* It'll cheer you up when you are down, and when you're up, it'll pump you upper. It is, in so many ways, the embodiment of the spiritual craziness of this team.

74 Burleigh Grimes

The very last legal spitball in the major leagues took root at the end of a 12-year-old boy's train ride in 1906 to help his family sell some livestock.

"My father and uncle were sending four carloads of cattle to St. Paul," Burleigh Grimes recollected at age 73 to Herman Weiskopf of *Sports Illustrated.* "When you sent a carload or more you were allowed to ride in the caboose, and that's how I got to go along on the trip with my uncle. When he had taken care of his business in St. Paul, he said, 'How'd you like to go to a ball game?' and he takes me out to the ballpark. I saw this guy—his name was Hank

After retiring, spitballer Burleigh Grimes spent a couple of years managing the Dodgers. In June 1938, Grimes (left) is shown in the Ebbets Field dugout with his first-base coach, Babe Ruth (center), and shortstop, Leo Durocher.

Gehring—using a spitball that day. When I got home, I cut some basswood—some people call it chokeberry—and put it in my mouth to make me salivate. As school kids we used to chew it all the time. Well, I got a catcher and I'd work out with him at noon at school and I'd practice on throwing the spitter. From then on I was a spitball pitcher."

When Grimes reached the major leagues in 1916, there was nothing particularly unusual about his mouth-watering moundswork—or at least about doctoring the baseball in some fashion. As historian Rob Neyer has written, "if a pitcher did *not* do something to the baseball, at least occasionally, it was cause for mention." In February 1920, to help inject some dignity in a game that was hearing scuttlebutt about players from the Chicago White Sox losing World Series games on purpose, as well as beginning to appreciate the Babe Ruth-led potential of an emphasis on offense in general and home runs in particular, major league baseball barred pitchers from using any foreign substance on the ball, such as, the *New York Times* wrote, "resin, salice, talcum powder, paraffine, and like aids to the shine ball."

But the new measures were anything but draconian. A great deal of sympathy existed for "moist ball pitchers" whose livelihood was put at risk. Within months, a one-year grandfather clause designed to protect two spitballers per club was extended to lifetime grace for 17 whose effectiveness depended on the wet weapon. (According to the *Times*, team owners were also none too eager to search for wholescale replacements for their best hurlers.) Grimes, who had an ERA of 2.22 (145 ERA+) in his third season with Brooklyn in 1920, was considered a definitive spitballer worthy of practicing the dark art as long as he liked. "The big right-hander was at his best yesterday and even the Pirates, who have been known to wield a wicked ash on occasions, were paled into submission before his spitball assortment," the *Times* wrote about a 1921 game.

For his part, Grimes considered himself anything but dependent on the gimmick. "It wasn't necessarily my number one pitch—the fastball generally was," he said in Donald Honig's *The Man in the Dugout.* "People meet me today and they say, 'Oh, Burleigh Grimes? You were the spitball pitcher.' Well, hell, I threw a fastball, curve, slider, change, screwball. One time I pitched 18 innings against the Cubs, beating Hippo Vaughn 3–2, and I threw only three slow spitballs in the ball game. The rest were all fastballs.

"It was a wonderful pitch for me some days," he added to Weiskopf. "Other days it would make me weep. Just couldn't make it work at times. There are a lot of untruths about the spitball, like about how hard it was to control, about how it used to be so wet that the infielders had a hard time picking up ground balls and about how hard it was on the arm. I'll tell you, I never had trouble controlling it and only once hit a man with it. That was Mel Ott. Hit him in the neck."

Grimes, who would go on to manage the Dodgers in 1937–38 before being inducted into the Hall of Fame on the basis of his 270 career wins and 3.53 ERA (107 ERA+) in 4,180 innings, outlasted the other 16 spit doctors, presumably throwing the last sanctioned spitball in his final start for his original team, Pittsburgh, against the Brooklyn franchise that made him famous.

"I like to sit in this easy chair by the window here," he told Weiskopf at his Missouri farm. "That way I can look out at the birds and animals that come right up on the back lawn—foxes and rabbits. The quail come in the morning. At night the deer show up. I sit here and look out at it all, and I think to myself that everything I've got I owe to the spitball. Yes, sir, I owe it all to the spitball.

"I remember my baseball days fondly, and there has been many a night when I've sat by the window looking out at the sunset or the stars and then looked down and noticed that my right hand was wrapped around my left as though I were gripping my spitball. I haven't pitched in more than 30 years, but I guess I'll never stop throwing my spitter."

75 Dip Into Philippe's

When it comes to mouthwatering eats and the Dodgers, it isn't always about hot dogs, nor the other concessions inside Dodger Stadium. A host of ballpark regulars plan their chow from the outside looking in—and leading off the alternative Dodger menu is Philippe's.

Alternative Alternatives

In addition to Philippe's, a major dining spot for Dodgers fans (and employees) is Yang Chow (819 N. Broadway), famous across the city for both its slippery shrimp and its collection of business cards from more than 100 past and present Dodger executives. Here are some other pregame dining choices to consider, as suggested by Dodger Stadium regulars Martin Leadman and Craig Minami:

Leadman Loves:

- Langer's Deli (7th and Alvarado): "In my opinion, the best sandwich in town is Langers' No. 1," Leadman says. "It's a pastrami on rye with coleslaw and Russian dressing in the sandwich. Best pastrami in the country. They have great crinkle-cut fries too." (Closed after 4 pm and on Sundays, Langer's is a pregame option for any day games Monday through Saturday.)
- Yum Cha Café (Broadway and Alpine): "I usually don't recommend Chinese restaurants in Chinatown, but this is a relatively new branch of a place in Monterey Park. Terrific dim sum. I like the pork shu mai and shrimp hargow. The steamed pork buns are also good."
- Tacos Baja Ensenada (Whittier east of Atlantic): "This is the only place I've found that makes fish tacos just like you get at the stands in Baja Mexico."
- East Side Italian Deli (1013 Alpine Street): "This is probably the closest place to Dodger Stadium. It's practically on Stadium Way. Good sandwiches. The combo beef and pastrami is a gutbuster."
- Grand Central Market (Broadway). "Terrific place for fruits and vegetables. But I also go there for Ana Maria's Mexican food. Huge burritos, gorditas and tortas."

Minami Morsels:

- Suehiro Café (337 E. 1st St.): "Good selection of Japanese dishes (grilled fish, chicken katsu—think Chick-fil-A on a plate—and noodles)."
- Koraku (314 E. 2nd St): "Ramen and fried rice served here until 3 AM, so a good place for after the game, too. Get one of the many types of ramen, and you will be happy."

- Empress Pavilion (988 N. Hill Street): "Large dining rooms filled with dim sum carts starting at 8:30 am on Sundays and 9:00 am on Saturdays. Still a good value and a great place for kids and adults."
- Pho 79 (727 N. Broadway, Suite 120): "Sure, Vietnamese food in Chinatown, only the best pho I have ever had. Pho is a rice noodle soup, normally served with beef in a broth cooked all day. Pho 79 has been serving it up for a while now and they do a great job. A little hard to find as it sits in the middle of shopping court between Hill and Broadway; you can get there before day games, but you'll have to get there quick before heading over at night since they close at 6:30."

Philippe's is nothing less than the global home of the French dip sandwich. Established in 1908 in the lost-to-history Frenchtown section of downtown Los Angeles, Philippe's (or officially, Philippe the Original) moved to its present location at the corner of Alameda and Ord, up the street from Union Station, 11 years before Dodger Stadium opened. Though the details are disputed, the consensus is that founder Philippe Mathieu invented the French dip, intentionally or accidentally dipping a roll in his delicious gravy. Whatever the truth, the savory beef, pork, lamb or turkey inside the dipped rolls, with Philippe's own hot mustard a side option, can hardly be topped. In 2008, the restaurant's 100th-anniversary year, sandwiches were between $5.35 and $6.50, with lemonade 70 cents a glass and a cup of coffee $.09. That's right: nine cents. If French dips aren't your style, the Philippe's menu is actually quite expansive, with customers topping off their meal by choosing one of the many pie options.

From Philippe's, you need only take a short drive up Ord to Broadway, then north a few blocks to College Street, then west a few blocks to Chavez Ravine Place, and from there you're primed to join the lineup of cars to Dodger Stadium. So a number of Dodgers fans will get their Philippe's to go; the sandwiches becoming a little soggier in transit but no less tasty. However, the downtown institution has a character all its own, and it's worth budgeting the time to eat in house. Either way, Philippe's is popular with baseball fans in the know, so allow yourself 20–30 minutes just to get your order completed. The wait will be worth it.

76 Capture the Flag

What it would have meant, had 37-year-old William Errol Thomas, his 11-year-old son, their lighter fluid, their matches and their willful intentions succeeded in setting an American flag on fire in the outfield grass of Dodger Stadium in the fourth inning on April 25, 1976, is left to your imagination.

One thing that is clear that when Cubs centerfielder and future Dodger Rick Monday snatched the flag from the Thomases and carried it to safety fewer than three months before the nation's 200th birthday, the action did more to make baseball feel like a national pastime to many people than anything since, at least until the resumption of games following the tragedies of September 11, 2001.

"It was a moment that brought more emotion to a crowd of spectators than I have ever witnessed in a half-century of following the game of baseball," wrote Fred Claire, who at the time was the Dodgers vice president of public relations and promotions and would later become general manager.

Claire instructed the operator of the old Dodger Stadium message board in left field to write, "Rick Monday...you made a great play." And spontaneously, first in one part of the Stadium and then another, soon melding into one giant voice among the 25,167 in attendance, the crowd broke into a rendition of "God Bless America."

As word of the event spread, aided by a Pulitzer Prize-winning photo by James Roark of the *Los Angeles Herald-Examiner*, Monday arguably became the most popular person in America. He would be honored in ceremonies wherever the Cubs next road trip took him.

Without discounting in the slightest the honor Monday brought to the flag, it is hard to reflect on the scene without acknowledging its poignancy. Thomas and his son weren't immediately swarmed upon by stadium security. A photo taken moments later shows the pair standing forlornly in the outfield, not attempting to flee. Cubs leftfielder Jose Cardenal, another ballplayer obscured from view and an umpire (probably second-base umpire Andy Olsen) look on as Tommy Lasorda, then the Dodgers' third-base coach, is by his own admission cursing them—in fact, baiting them.

"When I got there," Lasorda recalled, "I see these two guys and I told them, 'Why don't one of you guys take a swing at me?' because there were (thousands of) people in the ballpark and I only wanted them to swing at me, so I could defend myself and do a job on them."

Following up on the case days later, the *Los Angeles Times* found that "the man who tried to burn the American Flag at Dodger Stadium was attempting to draw attention to what he claims is his wife's imprisonment in a Missouri mental institution, authorities say." It paints the attempt to burn the flag as something less than viciously anti-American. The elder Thomas served three days in jail and received a year's probation, then disappeared from the public record. His son was never prosecuted, and no news ever emerged about Thomas' wife.

Decades later, Monday's rescue of the flag remains a rallying point at the nexus of baseball and patriotism. Lurking beneath the surface was a cry for help, however inappropriately expressed. We know what happened to Monday. We can only hope that somehow, the Thomas family found rescue before putting themselves in further jeopardy.

77 Willie Davis

"I would say to myself, 'This is the year,' then every time I would go back to my old way of doing things."

Inside and outside the Dodgers organization, they never seemed to stop psychoanalyzing Willie Davis. No matter what he did—whether it was hitting 21 homers while stealing 32 bases in 1962, or moving up the franchise leaderboard (he remains first all-time in Los Angeles history in plate appearances, hits, total bases, triples and extra-base hits)—second-guessing was ongoing, acceptance grudging. The focus inevitably turned to Davis' internal struggle as a ballplayer, his identity crisis.

"People have been saying for several years that if Willie Davis ever put all his talents together he would be an outstanding ballplayer," Dan Hafner of the *Los Angeles Times* wrote just before the 1968 season. "The trouble is nobody could ever convince Willie."

Around the time he first came up as a 20-year-old in 1960, some called Davis the second coming of Willie Mays. Those who saw him run insisted that he was faster than basestealing king Maury Wills. But the combination of Davis' underwhelming offensive numbers following that '62 season and his endless tinkering with his batting stance kept him under scrutiny for the entire decade.

"Willie, you see, did imitations," wrote Jim Murray. "The only way you could tell it wasn't Stan Musial was when he popped up. But Willie's repertoire included Ted Williams, Billy Williams, Babe Ruth, Babe Herman (usually it came out more like Babe Phelps). He had more shticks than a Catskill comic. He wasn't a ballplayer, he was a chameleon. Sometimes, he imitated three different guys in one night. None of them was Willie Davis. 'Willie,' Buzzie Bavasi used to ask him, 'Why don't you arrange it so that somebody imitates you?'"

Even when Davis rolled out a 31-game hitting streak in the late summer of 1969—the longest streak in baseball since Stan Musial in 1950—baseball held its breath.

"First he tried to be Stan Musial and then Ernie Banks and he would imitate every hot hitter that came along," Montreal manager Gene Mauch told Ross Newhan of the *Times*. "Now he's simply Willie Davis and he's damn exciting. If he goes 0-for-10 and changes, he'll be a darn fool."

Even his teammates, the guys he won two World Series titles with, were left unsatisfied.

153

Tommy Davis once held a major league record he has mixed feelings about: most teams in a career. After spending nearly 12 years in the Dodgers organization (including the minor leagues), the Dodgers traded Davis to the Mets in December 1966. Davis ended up playing for eight teams in nine seasons before retiring. (Todd Zeile later shattered his record with 11 teams).

None of that can overshadow the astonishing 1962 campaign that Davis had as a Dodger, in which he collected 230 hits, 120 runs and a franchise-record 153 runs batted in. He had 374 plate appearances with men on base that season and batted .348. RBI are a function of opportunity, but it's safe to say that no Dodger answered opportunity's knock as often as Davis did.

"Willie Davis, throughout the 1960s, was regarded as a huge disappointment, a player who never played up to his perceived ability," historian Bill James wrote. "As John Roseboro said, 'He has never hit .330 in his career. But he should have.'"

But James goes on to make the point that however vexing Davis was, he was judged too harshly, with contemporaries not appreciating the difficult hitting conditions he played in. The mid–1960s in general, and Dodger Stadium in particular, depressed offense considerably.

"Davis was a terrific player," James said. "True, he didn't walk, and he was not particularly consistent—but his good years, in context, are quite impressive.... He should not be regarded as a failure, merely because he had to play his prime seasons in such difficult hitting conditions."

After the 1973 season, Davis still had enough value to be traded to Montreal for reliever Mike Marshall, who would win the NL Cy Young Award for the Dodgers in '74. But Davis played for seven teams (including two in Japan) in his final six seasons, stability having left his baseball life forever.

78 The Penguin

Ron Cey played in a couple of giant shadows, one across the diamond in the form of Steve Garvey, the other across the country by the name of Mike Schmidt. With the 5'9", 185-pound, short-striding stature that inspired his "Penguin" nickname, Cey couldn't help being underestimated. He was the comfy chair in the living room, not the *Better Homes & Gardens* centerpiece. But so, so valuable.

Many consider Schmidt, who set third baseman records with 548 home runs, a 147 OPS+ and 10 Gold Gloves in his career, the best in history at the position, so it's understandable that Cey couldn't compete for headlines on that level. But Cey was too accomplished to be as ignored as he was. He ranks 17th all-time among third baseman with a 121 OPS+. Cey had underrated range defensively, reaching more balls than the league average year for a third baseman after year while at one point setting a record for consecutive errorless games.

Garvey, of course, was first and foremost in people's minds when it came to the Dodger lineup, wowing Los Angeles with his MVP season in 1974. Yet Cey, while cooling off the more challenging hot corner, was essentially Garvey's equal offensively, edging him for his Dodger career in OPS+ and EQA. Cey just didn't have the glamour. He had thick legs instead of thick arms, he lacked the prime-time haircut—but most of all, Cey didn't have the cachet that 200 hits a year provided Garvey. Cey had more power and more plate discipline—walking more than 1,000 times, but that didn't matter.

Every so often, though, Cey would shine unencumbered. In June 1974, he drove in seven runs in a game, and on July 31, he topped himself with eight. In April 1977, he set a major league record for the month with 29 RBI (on-base percentage of .543, slugging percentage of .890), igniting the Dodgers' 22–4 start. That October, he hit an NLCS Game 1 grand slam and outplayed Schmidt, who went 1 for 16 with two walks in the series.

In the 1981 World Series, nearing the culmination of his Dodger career, Cey's profile took off when he twice hit the dirt. In Game 3, Cey made a diving catch of a sacrifice attempt in foul territory and doubled the runner off first base to protect the Dodgers' 5–4 lead. In the eighth inning of Game 5, Cey was slammed in the head by a screaming Rich Gossage fastball, yet he came back to play in Game 6, drove in the Dodgers' go-ahead run

Frank Howard

At the time, he was the tallest player in Dodgers history. He was the heaviest player in Dodgers history. But Frank Howard, listed at 6'7", 255 pounds, was more than just someone you could spot from the moon, more than a candidate for the oddities chapter in the Guinness Book of Dodger Records. As the franchise entered a decade in which they would be starved for runs, Howard was almost the entire power source.

After cups of coffee in 1958 and 1959, Howard became a starting outfielder in May 1960, three months before his 24th birthday. By the end of 1964, he would be gone, traded by the Dodgers to the Washington Senators in the deal that yielded pitcher Claude Osteen. In those five seasons, Howard homered 121 times, more than twice as many as any other Dodger during that run-challenged period except Tommy Davis (83). During Dodger Stadium's first two seasons, he hit 52 of the team's 189 homers—28 percent. And Howard, predictably a below-average fielder, didn't even play every day for the Dodgers (even after winning the 1960 NL Rookie of the Year award), peaking at 141 games in 1962 and averaging 121 per year.

Howard's on-field legacy really remains in the nation's capital, where he ended up hitting 237 of his 382 career homers, including more than 40 per year from 1968 to 1970. From Los Angeles' perspective, Howard's size was usually the biggest part of his story. "Ever since he first showed up, baseball has taken the position Frank's real name was 'Frankenstein' Howard, that he had been concocted out of a test tube and a machine that shot blue sparks by a mad scientist in bottle-bottom glasses," wrote Jim Murray after the trade to the Senators, adding that Howard had become "Washington's second monument."

in their title-clinching victory and shared series MVP honors with Steve Yeager and Pedro Guerrero thanks to a 7-for-20, three-walk performance. (Surprisingly left off the official thank-yous was Garvey, despite reaching base in nearly half his at-bats.)

Cey once attributed his major league career to ignorance. "If I'd known the circumstances I'd have to overcome, I probably wouldn't have felt so strongly about it," he told *Sports Illustrated* writer Larry Keith about his wish to become a ballplayer while a lad in Tacoma, Washington. "I'm not from a good baseball area, and I don't have the size or speed of a lot of players. But baseball is all I ever wanted to do, and I was fortunate to make it, even though a lot of people said I never would." There might have been reason to underestimate Cey as a kid, but there's no reason to do so now.

79 (Re)read *The Boys of Summer*

The names form such a pantheon of gods—Robinson, Reese, Campanella, Snider, Hodges, Furillo, Erskine, Labine—that it's too easy to forget that they were human. Not just human in the way some fought racism or a catastrophic injury, but human in the way of immature rivalries, witching-hour confessions, barstool wise-crack perfection, overarching family worries and cherished private memories. *The Boys of Summer* brings that home.

Roger Kahn grew up as a boyhood fan of the Brooklyn Dodgers, and grew up again as a beat writer covering the team for the *New York Herald-Tribune*, and grew up once more when he revisited those select ballplayers a decade after the team had left for Los Angeles. As his initial idolization of those who roamed Ebbets Field in his youth dissolves into a first tenuous, then collegial, then warm bond with them, as he guides us back to and inside that celebrated era of Dodgers history, his wonder and insecurity as traveling companions, Kahn lets his readers simply *be* with the Brooklyn Dodgers of the 1950s.

If, in the years since its 1972 publication, *The Boys of Summer* has almost drowned in the same kind of unadulterated praise that

Dodgers greats Jackie Robinson (left) and Pee Wee Reese (right) share a light moment with teammate Ralph Branca. Robinson and Reese, among others, were elevated to god-like status in Roger Kahn's tribute to his beloved Dodgers, The Boys of Summer. Photo courtesy of www.walteromalley.com.

made the Boys of Summer themselves seem unreal—it's not a perfect book, lagging in certain parts—it is still unique in its clear-headed facility to bring this peak period of Dodgers history to life. For Dodgers fans who have never read it, it's essential. For those who did read it but a generation ago, for those who have been growing up themselves and seen baseball and the world become at once more simple and more complex, it's exactly the type of literature worth revisiting, a treasure trove of experiences meant to be shared and shared again. It's better the second time around.

Dynasty Challenged

In their entire history through 2008, which includes two NL Wild Card appearances, 10 division titles, 21 NL pennants (not to mention the 1889 American Association crown) and six World Series championships, the Dodgers have never played postseason ball more than two seasons in a row. Close calls? Before consecutive playoff appearances in 1995–96, the Dodgers were in first place in the NL West in '94 when the players' union strike shut down the season. But the real chance for even a mini-dynasty was broken in 1954. A five-game deficit to the Giants interrupted what could have been five NL pennants in a row—six if it weren't for Bobby Thomson in '51.

80 Bill Russell

Who thought the skinny kid from Pittsburg, Kansas, would wear a Dodgers uniform for more games than anyone else in Los Angeles history? The Dodgers certainly had some amount of faith in Bill Russell, even after he posted batting averages of .226, .259, and .227 playing mostly right field (and experimenting with switch-hitting) as a reserve from 1969–71. During that '71 season, they started moving him to second base, and then on April 27, 1972, with 39-year-old Maury Wills off to a 5-for-47, two-walk, no-steals start, Russell replaced Wills in the seventh inning at shortstop. He went 2 for 2, earning the start the next day—the third of his career at that position. Over the next week, Russell went 13 for 23 with three walks, three doubles and two home runs—you'd have thought that a Hall of Famer had been born.

Inside of three months, Russell was making enough errors that even he admitted that the team might be relieved to see him depart for two weeks of Army Reserve duty. But overall, the Dodgers liked what they had. For the next 12 seasons, he owned shortstop in Los Angeles—the first member of the team's record-setting Garvey-Lopes-Russell-Cey infield in, and the last one out.

Russell was Wonder Bread: clean, almost bland, yet a strangely agreeable staple, especially if you weren't accustomed to something more exotic. He tended to blend into the background behind his Dodgers teammates and NL West shortstops like Cincinnati's Davey Concepcion. He wasn't particularly rangy, yet he made at least 28 errors in eight different years. His highest EQA was .270 (in 1982), and some seasons he struggled just to be mediocre at the plate.

But he had his moments. On August 2, 1972, he walked, singled twice, tripled and—in the bottom of the ninth—homered to give the Dodgers a 12–11 victory over San Francisco. Three times an NL All-Star, Russell had the game-winning hit in the Dodgers' miraculous ninth-inning comeback at Philadelphia in Game 3 of the 1977 NLCS. The next year, he won the NL pennant for the Dodgers with his 10th-inning single to center against the Phillies, then registered a .464 on-base percentage in the World Series.

By the time he retired, after the 1986 season, the soft-spoken shortstop had appeared in a city record 2,181 games, playing for six division winners. And he wasn't done with Los Angeles. For the next five seasons, he became a Dodgers coach, then followed in Tommy Lasorda's footsteps by managing in Albuquerque before returning to the majors as Lasorda's bench coach. When Lasorda suffered his heart attack in July 1996, Russell became only the third manager in Los Angeles history. He guided the Dodgers to a wild-card berth that season, though the team lost its final four games of the regular season and all three in the playoffs. In 1997, the team finished two games out in the NL West.

Russell joined the list of casualties of Fox's purchase of the Dodgers the next year when he was fired at midseason with a 36–38 record. On June 22, 1998—for the first time since the Dodgers drafted him 42 years before—Russell was gone.

81 Was Brooklyn Still in the League?

In 1920, the Brooklyn Robins won their second NL pennant in five seasons and reached Game 5 of a best-of-nine World Series with Cleveland, all square at 2–2. In the next five innings, Brooklyn ace Burleigh Grimes allowed a grand slam, and Clarence Mitchell gave up a three-run homer to opposing pitcher Jim Bagby before coming to the plate and lining to Indians second baseman Bill Wambsganss for the only unassisted triple play in World Series history.

Over the next 20 years, Brooklyn's fortunes hardly improved upon those five frames. Brooklyn finished the 1920 Series with one run in its final 32 innings and did not win another NL pennant until 1941, landing as high as second place only once. From 1922–1929, whether you called them the Dodgers, Robins or Superbas, Brooklyn finished in sixth place in the eight-team NL every year but one.

Having played in October during the previous two presidential campaigns, the Robins did bid for re-election to the World Series in 1924. Twenty-seven years before the New York Giants would succeed in the comeback for the ages, the Robins (as the Dodgers

'The Dodgers Have Three Runners on Base'—'Which Base?'

The Dodgers have never had a .400 hitter, but Babe Herman came closest, batting .393 in 1930. You'd think that might be what Herman is remembered for, but when the legend next to your name says "doubled into a double play," that tends to trump all (although admittedly, Russell Martin escaped this fate in the 2006 playoffs).

On August 15, 1926, Brooklyn had the bases loaded (Chick Fewster on first, Dazzy Vance on second and Hank DeBerry on third) when Herman drove one toward the right-field wall. The base runners had different reads on whether the ball would be caught—and no read on what their teammates were reading—so that when Herman raced to third base, he found Chick Fewster at the base and Dazzy Vance abandoning his attempt to score and retreating there as well.

Sorting through the confusion, the umpires ruled Herman and Fewster out. Though Vance was the primary cause of the roadblock and Fewster also should have been able to score, for decades baseball storytellers remembered Herman as the culprit. Great story, but too bad for the Dodgers' Babe.

were then known, under manager Wilbert Robinson) tried their own. After losing to St. Louis on August 9, Brooklyn sat in fourth place with a 56–50 record, 13 games back of New York. What followed was as remarkable a stretch of baseball rallying as Brooklyn ever saw.

Led by Dazzy Vance, a rookie two years earlier at age 31 but now in the midst of posting a 2.16 ERA (174 ERA+) and 262 strikeouts in 308⅓ innings, the Robins started their rally by winning 11 of their next 13 games to pull within seven of the Giants. When St. Louis swept Brooklyn in a doubleheader, the second game by the score of 17–0, one could easily have concluded the Robins were spent. Instead, they won the last two games of the series at Sportsman's Park, then swept three from the Giants at Ebbets Field to draw within four games of first.

"I recently saw the Robins win three straight from the Giants at Ebbets Field, and I formed one conclusion, that Uncle Robby's men would come out on top," wrote *Sporting News* columnist Joe Vila. "McGraw's team was clearly outplayed and outclassed in those games which, by the way, drew 63,000 paid admissions, averaging 80 cents each."

Rather unbelievably, because of makeup games, Brooklyn now faced four consecutive doubleheaders. Even more unbelievably, the Robins swept them all, scoring 57 runs in four days. At the end of play September 4, the Giants were 78–52, .003 ahead of 80–54 Brooklyn. Wins in their next two games extended the Robin streak to 15 in a row and, for a couple of hours in between a September 6 doubleheader, the Robins could claim they were in first place.

However, Brooklyn couldn't complete the comeback. Though the Robins won 10 of their final 18 games to complete a season-ending 36–12 run, and were .001 back with four games to play, the Giants clinched the pennant on the second-to-last day of the season with a 3–2 victory over Brooklyn. No miracle here.

Charles Ebbets died the following April, and with him seemingly any semblance of competitiveness for his team. Brooklyn had no greater achievement for the next 10 years than responding to Giants manager Bill Terry's rhetorical wondering if Brooklyn "were still in the league" in 1934 by spoiling the Giants' postseason chances with a two-game sweep at season's end. The Dodgers' record that year: 71–81. A Pyrrhic victory, to say the least.

When the Dodgers finally returned to the World Series in 1941, they were the only NL team besides the Phillies that had never won it. That drought continued for 14 more years, but at least in that latter stretch they eliminated any doubters over what league they belonged in.

82 Attend Dodgers Adult Baseball Camp

You can't kill someone's fantasy, and for that matter, you can't really kill camp. Dreaming and escaping...these are imperatives. They hit at different times, in different ways. But they surely hit, as sure as Duke Snider hit.

So it isn't any wonder that the Los Angeles Dodgers Adult Baseball Camp has had perennial popularity for decades, making into reality the dream of putting on a Dodgers uniform on the same field as legends like Snider, Carl Erskine, Maury Wills, or Reggie Smith. Yes, a reality with more bruises and hamstring pulls than your worst nightmare—camp always had its ugly side, no matter how pristine the wilderness—but a blessed reality nonetheless. Those Dodgers greats tutor attendees as if they were the young ruffians trying to make an impression at spring training. And if it's any consolation, the official Dodgers training staff is there to treat the inevitable aches and pains.

For a week, you're a Dodger. That's a serious thrill we're talking about. It's Little League in reverse—time for the kids to cheer Dad and Grandpa (or even Grandma). You do the drills, you play the games, you live the life. You bond with your teammates, and you take home eternal memories.

"Each camper had his own reasons for coming, expectations as to what he will or will not receive," attendee Mark Stone said. "It is true that this is, generally speaking, not the 'vacation of a lifetime' that the whole family might enjoy. I know my wife would definitely prefer a trip to Europe, the middle or far East, or even a cruise of the Caribbean. But in listening to the others talk about their childhood dreams and memories, previous camp experiences, whether here or at other pro camps, there was no doubt that this experience,

Good Times

Dodgers Adult Baseball Camp Top–10 List (according to camp veteran Joe Bernadello):

1. Everybody is really great. Everybody.
2. You get to hang with Dodgers greats. (I have an e-mail from Maury Wills in my inbox today!)
3. Steve Yeager, if he is there, is salty and funny and right out of central casting. He was my manager, and there is nothing I wouldn't do for him.
4. Your job is to play baseball. You have time for nothing else but baseball. All the thoughts of day-to-day life—poof—gone.
5. You are treated like a baseball player. Batting practice with white balls, well-groomed fields, a training staff to keep you playing, good food and lots of it.
6. Your teammates. Being on a real team again, not some quasi-corporate team, but a real team—need I say more?
7. The tired feeling as you crawl into bed. That honest feeling you had as a kid knowing that you exhausted yourself playing ball.
8. The minor league coaches and trainers. These guys love the game and it is infectious. They don't make big bucks, but boy do they love baseball.
9. Winning! We won a key game in the eleventh inning—I still find myself remembering my hit in the rally inning.
10. I love baseball again as I loved it as a kid. I can't explain it other than that.

from a baseball lover's point of view, was one that has had no equal and will never be forgotten.

"We had our lawyers and doctors, investment consultants and insurance types, contractors and cops. We had guys who could play, former college or minor league players, and guys who could barely swing a bat. But we all had one thing in common, the love of baseball and the love of the Dodgers. I can only hope that I get the opportunity to return again someday."

Maybe this is something to know, or maybe it's something to

repress, but as the camp moves away from Florida, there are things it will leave behind. The team's Arizona facility won't unite dining, housing, golf, and swimming on the same campus as the playing fields, the way Dodgertown did. It will be more like a day camp than a sleepaway camp.

In addition, though this was inevitable as time passed, the camp leaves behind the Dodgers' most intimate remaining connection to Brooklyn. When Snider, Clem Labine, or Ralph Branca participated, well into the 21st century, the Brooklyn Dodgers were alive and well. But those days are passing.

Still, there's plenty of reason to try to stop time, or at least slow it down, by stepping into the box and taking one's Dodgers fantasy head on.

83 Question the Conventional Wisdom

For decades, people were told that Jackie Robinson retired rather than play for the New York Giants, that Walter O'Malley was the ogre in the takeover of Chavez Ravine, that free agency would bring financial ruin to baseball. None of it was true.

Baseball myths, even if they're based on as much fact as George Washington and the cherry tree, have a way of being accepted at face value. It takes some nerve to challenge a story that hits just the right notes. One man's falsehood is another's bond with his father. A .300 batting average served as the standard for success for more than a century—who gets any joy out of suggesting it can be a flawed statistic? Paying attention to on-base percentage or the number of pitches someone throws in a game has been taken in some parts as a form of outright rebellion.

But why? Is baseball sacred? No way—it's too alive to be sacred. Rather, baseball is great, great because it stands *the test* of time.

This is not to say that some conventional wisdom isn't real wisdom, nor that all change is good. You can study the importance of a pitcher getting first strikes and conclude yep, they really do matter. You can take a long look at the revenue generated by increased advertising inside Dodger Stadium and decide whether or not it's not worth the sacrifice in the ballpark's beauty. But it never hurts to test the accepted, and that goes for Dodgers fans, Dodgers beat writers, Dodgers broadcasters, and Dodgers management. Tradition is an argument, sometimes the best argument, but just one argument and not an infallible one. Too often, precedent is used as a crutch for a hollow contention, and an extreme or dogmatic position is held at the expense of a more reasonable middle ground. Too often, a time-honored aphorism blocks a better understanding of the game, even blocks the making of a better team.

Let's face it—we've all been questioning already. It doesn't matter how much Tommy Lasorda insists that pitching to Jack Clark was the right thing to do—countless Dodgers fans feel no compulsion to agree. Second-guessing a manager or general manager with decades of experience is challenging the canon—and it's part of being a baseball fan. There's no reason this approach shouldn't extend to other areas of the game. If you hear "it's always been done that way," alarm bells should go off in your head.

No, you don't have to be a jerk about it. Patience and open-mindedness are true virtues when it comes to challenging the conventional wisdom. But the same goes to those receiving the challenge. No one who cares enough about the Dodgers to study them is out to destroy them. If there's a statistic or a scouting report that shows more than meets the naked eye, that's a good thing.

When Vin Scully called the 4+1 game in 2006 and the

Dodgers' victory while being no-hit in 2008, nearly 60 years into his broadcasting career, he had never seen anything like them before. You *never* know. Baseball is designed to be humbling, and no matter how many years it's been a part of your life, there is always more to learn—just as there's always more to see. As you follow the Dodgers, this old franchise that employed a pioneer in developing the use of advanced statistics, that showed that the West Coast deserved baseball, that performed the game's greatest service by killing the notion that you could only have players of a certain color on your team, let that spirit be your guide even over something as small as whether or not they should bunt. No matter what the facts reveal, the romance will always be there.

84 Rookies, Rookies, Rookies

No team has introduced more Rookies of the Year than the Dodgers: 16. They boast the man the award is named after—Jackie Robinson—cherished figures from Brooklyn like Don Newcombe and Jim Gilliam, early Los Angeles prodigies like Frank Howard, as well as more contemporary names like Fernando Valenzuela, Eric Karros, Mike Piazza, and Hideo Nomo.

Here are the remaining Rookies of the Year—memorable in their own right but at risk of slipping through the cracks.

Rook in his prime: Joe Black (1952) was a 28-year-old veteran of the Negro Leagues when he made his Dodgers debut on the first day of May. By the end of the season, he had won 15 games and saved 15 more, posting a 2.15 ERA (168 ERA+) in 142⅓ innings, enough to legitimately beat out New York Giants pitcher Hoyt Wilhelm. But Black, who was never a strikeout pitcher, was already at his peak. His career in the majors lasted only another 271⅔ mostly subpar innings, and he was traded midway through the Dodgers' championship season in '55.

Quick peak: Another player whose rookie season was his best was Todd Hollandsworth (1996). The longest last name in Dodgers history rode a strong second half (.808 OPS) to overcome the reluctance to give Los Angeles an unprecedented five ROYs in a row. But Hollandsworth would play 100 games in a season only four more times in his 12-year career, stretched across eight major league teams.

Hall-of-Famer tamer: Jim Lefebvre (1965) denied Joe Morgan top rookie honors despite posting offensive numbers, even adjusted for Dodger Stadium, nowhere near those of the future Hall of Famer. Lefebvre did belt 24 homers in 1966 and was an offensive asset for most of his career before it ended abruptly following the 1972 season, when he was 30.

Trade bait: After knocking 160 hits in 159 games to win the vote over, among others, an arguably more deserving Al Oliver of Pittsburgh, Ted Sizemore (1969) lasted 12 years in the bigs, providing competent defense though not once generating an OPS+ over 100. He was the player so nice the Dodgers traded him twice, in 1970 with Bob Stinson for Dick Allen and in 1976 for Johnny Oates.

Better early and late than never: The Dodgers used Rick Sutcliffe (1979) so sparingly at the outset of his career that he didn't allow a major league run for more than two years after his 1976 debut. Finally, in his first full season, he pitched 242 innings with a 3.46 ERA (106 ERA+) and easily started a four-year run on the award for the Dodgers. Sutcliffe then almost completely lost it in 1980, his ERA swelling to 5.56 (64 ERA+), and the Dodgers dumped him to the Indians in December 1981. But the 6'7" righty ended up winning the 1984 NL Cy Young Award after becoming one of the greatest midseason acquisitions of all time, going 16–1

Sax Recovers

Steve Sax had already established himself as a big leaguer, winning the 1982 Rookie of the Year award, when he made throwing errors in two consecutive games in April 1983. "Pretty soon it just stuck in my head," Sax later told Steve Delsohn in *True Blue*. "I lost my confidence. I'd wake up in the night sweating. It was the worst thing I ever went through in my life besides losing my parents."

By the All-Star break, Sax made 18 errors, some on simple throws so outrageously awry that Sax's own Dodgers teammates couldn't resist mocking him (at one point, some drafted a phony memo proclaiming Batting Helmet Day for the fans behind the first-base dugout). And then at the All-Star Game, before its national television audience, he made another error on a routine throw. No one was more frustrated than Tommy Lasorda, who also had to contend with the scattershot fielding of Pedro Guerrero at third base, but the Dodgers manager didn't bench Sax. He did offer plenty of tough love, in vintage Lasorda style.

Amid all the teasing, the concerted effort to rebuild Sax's self-assurance ultimately succeeded—much faster than people might remember. During the final two months of the 1983 season, Sax's throws found their target without fail.

(144 ERA+) with the Cubs.

Heir apparent: The first to break into the Dodgers' long-running infield, Steve Sax (1982) weathered the pressure and competition from Johnny Ray, Willie McGee, and Chili Davis to win top rookie honors. Though some remember him mainly for his temporary mental meltdown with regards to throwing to first, Sax would go on to reach base more than 2,500 times in his career. Like his predecessor, Davey Lopes, Sax left the Dodgers right after celebrating a World Series title, in 1988.

Supernovas: As eyepopping an athlete as ever wore a Los Angeles Dodgers uniform, the speedy, powerful, laser-armed Raul Mondesi (1994) broke out with Hall of Fame potential. Slugging

.516 (123 OPS+) in the strike-shortened 1994 season, Mondesi was a unanimous pick for the ROY award. An inability to master the down-and-away pitch separated him from his apparent destiny and washed him out of the game before his 35th birthday, but he still finished his career with 271 homers and 229 stolen bases.

Mondesi was preceded by 1980 Rookie of the Year Steve Howe, whose remarkable effectiveness (2.35 ERA in 328⅔ innings as a Dodger from 1980–84) foundered upon an unending battle with drug addiction. Howe would come back from numerous suspensions to pitch in nearly 500 games for four teams with a 129 ERA+. He died in a single-car accident in 2006, at age 48.

85 The O'Malleys Sell

You don't surrender a half-century of investment in a baseball team lightly, and Peter O'Malley didn't. His decision to sell the Dodgers reflected a confluence of hard realities.

The first was personal—or familial. Between the two of them, O'Malley and his sister Terry O'Malley Seidler had 13 children. Approaching retirement age, the O'Malleys considered what the future held for their descendants. A baseball franchise does not divide easily into a baker's dozen—especially when estate taxes could carve up roughly half the value. The sale parlayed the team into a more fluid, manageable asset.

Though the O'Malleys could have talked themselves into continuing as owners, the changing face of baseball began sapping them of incentive. By 1997, the O'Malleys were the one of a few remaining family owners of a major league baseball team. With salaries rising, they had to compete with corporations for whom baseball was only a part of the whole—teams could be used as loss leaders. Further, baseball's contract with the players' union, following the 1994–95 labor dispute that had shut down the game, called for more extensive revenue sharing, which meant the Dodgers would be further subsidizing other teams. Under Bud Selig, the then-Milwaukee Brewers owner who became acting baseball commissioner in 1992, small-market teams were gaining more power over large-market teams like the Dodgers.

However, even the shifting economic playing field was not a sole determining factor. It took another dose of cold water to push O'Malley into the sale. Los Angeles found itself without a National Football League franchise after the Raiders moved back to Oakland in 1995. That August, Mayor Richard Riordan asked O'Malley to lead the effort to bring the NFL back to the city, and O'Malley was happy to oblige. A football stadium built on the land surrounding Dodger Stadium emerged as a viable possibility to draw a team, diversify the family business and attract new business partners for the O'Malleys.

A year later, after vigorous investment in research, the city asked O'Malley to abandon his efforts and support the Los Angeles Memorial Coliseum's bid to be the home of the team. O'Malley assented reluctantly, but his disappointment by his own admission was palpable. (In a well-researched piece, T.J. Simers of the *Los Angeles Times* wrote that power brokers in Los Angeles had contrived a quid pro quo deal in which they exchanged support for the Coliseum and the proposed downtown basketball arena that would become Staples Center, and O'Malley had been "caught in the middle.")

With the signs discouraging on multiple fronts, O'Malley decided it was time to sell.

There were no illusions about the suitor O'Malley settled on: Rupert Murdoch's News Corp. would use the Dodgers as a means to an end, as a flagship team whose games would be televised by a sports network intended to rival ESPN and boost the Murdoch media empire. Sallie Hofmeister of the *Times* noted that the $311 million outlay "says more about Hollywood than about baseball.... The purchase price, about double the going rate in major league baseball, is so far out of the ballpark that it's highly unlikely the team will make money." That did not suggest a brighter immediate future for the talent on the field at Dodger Stadium.

Of course, when the sale was announced, attention focused not on who was coming in, but who was going out.

"There's a very empty feeling in my house tonight," Vin Scully told Mike DiGiovanna of the *Times,* "and there will be for a long time to come. There's a feeling of a definite loss, almost like a death in the family."

Such harsh realities had entered the lives of every Dodgers player, employee, and fan. Wrote Ross Newhan and Michael Hiltzik of the *Times*: "The vote puts one of baseball's most storied ballclubs in the hands of one of the world's most unsentimental and pragmatic businessmen." Within months, Mike Piazza was traded, and the O'Malley era was long gone.

86 In the Booth: Solo Farewell

On the October night the Dodgers lost the National League Championship Series in 2004, the team's No. 2 announcer, Ross Porter, bid an otherwise uneventful farewell to his radio audience. Bob Keisser of the *Long Beach Press-Telegram* reported a week earlier that the Dodgers had decided not to renew Porter's contract, but team executive Lon Rosen, hired earlier that year, 28 seasons after

Jaime Jarrín

At the start of 1955, the Dodgers were in Brooklyn, and Jaime Jarrín was in Quito, covering the National Congress of Ecuador. Four years later, the Dodgers were in Los Angeles, and Jarrín was broadcasting their games on the radio.

Jarrín arrived in Los Angeles on a permanent resident visa that June, and worked in a factory until a part-time job opened up at the city's only Spanish radio station, KWKW. He made fast progress, and by the time the Dodgers moved to Los Angeles in 1958, Jarrín was KWKW's news and sports director.

They didn't play much baseball in Quito, but Jarrín had become a fan in California, going to see the minor league Hollywood Stars and Los Angeles Angels. Still, when KWKW's owner, William Beaton, announced that the L.A.-bound Dodgers had made a deal to broadcast their games in Spanish, Jarrín didn't consider himself an automatic choice.

"He said they needed two announcers," Jarrín would later tell baseball writer Eric Enders, "and looking at me, he said, 'I want you to be one of the announcers.' I said, 'Mr. Beaton, thank you very much, but I think I'm not ready to be in front of the microphone and call a game.' I was already doing boxing every Thursday night, and I was very successful doing boxing.

"He said, 'You know, you have talent for doing sports,' and I said, 'Yes, I know, but give me some time.' He said, 'Okay, but next year I want you to be with the Dodgers.' So he took me to meet Mr. Walter O'Malley, and by 1959 I was ready, and I was hired."

Half a century later (including a streak of more than 4,000 consecutive games from 1962–1984), nearly two decades after a life-threatening car accident and more than 10 years after the Baseball Hall of Fame honored him with the Ford C. Frick Award for broadcasters, the beloved Jarrín was still broadcasting Dodgers baseball for his fans.

Porter joined the Dodgers, denied the report.

Two weeks later, the team issued a press release: "The English-language broadcast booth for the National League West champion Los Angeles Dodgers will get a makeover for 2005. Announcers Vin

Scully and Rick Monday will return, along with a new play-by-play announcer and a baseball analyst, the Dodgers announced today. The Dodgers also announced that Ross Porter will not rejoin the broadcast team next season."

That, in its entirety, constituted the Dodgers' farewell to Porter. The Oklahoma native debuted in 1977 as the No. 3 play-by-play man behind Scully and Jerry Doggett, and was soon branded as a good-natured announcer who nonetheless relied on arcane statistics as a crutch to get through a broadcast. The label was an exaggeration from the outset, but over time, Porter sincerely endeared himself to numerous fans with his easygoing enthusiasm and fundamentally sound call of the game. And just like that, the Dodgers cast him aside. He deserved a ceremony at Dodger Stadium, and he didn't even get to say goodbye on the air.

That wasn't the only news buried in Dodgers fine print. The team also announced that beginning in 2005, the backup announcers to Scully would work as a two-man team of play-by-play/analyst. Working solo in the booth had been a tradition ever since Red Barber came to Brooklyn in 1939. Barber, Scully, Connie Desmond, Jerry Doggett, Don Drysdale, Monday, and Porter had bonded with listeners by talking directly to them, one-on-one. That setup was going the way of the slide rule long before the Dodgers jettisoned it (with Scully grandfathered as a solo act), but it had lost none of its usefulness. Extra people in the booth have a way of distancing the audience from the game, and the insights of all but a few color commentators rarely amount to much.

Porter, interestingly, was open to sharing the mike. "Don Drysdale joined the Dodgers' broadcasting team in 1988," Porter said in an interview. "Previously, he had announced for the Expos, Rangers, Angels, White Sox, and ABC. On the first day of the '88 exhibition season, Don joined me in the booth at Vero Beach, and shortly before the game began, he said, 'I've not worked alone on the air. I would feel more comfortable if I could chat with you. Is that okay?'

"It was fine with me. I was used to working with an analyst on football and basketball broadcasts and telecasts, and frankly, liked chatting with someone who was knowledgeable about the sport and game. Don and I traded several comments on the air in the top of the first inning. When we went to commercial, the phone in our booth rang. Don was told to pick it up. It was Peter O'Malley. He told Don it was to be a one-voice broadcast. After the game, an irritated Drysdale went to Peter's office at Dodgertown. They were longtime friends so Don didn't hold back. He said, 'Peter, are you telling me that everybody else in baseball is wrong, and you are right about having only one voice on the air at a time?' Peter said, 'Don, that is the way we do it here.' Two Dodgers broadcasters speaking to each other on the air for the first time in 50 years lasted a grand total of...half an inning."

The two-man booth brought the upbeat Charley Steiner in a pairing with either Monday or Steve Lyons on broadcasts, and there's no doubt that plenty of fun is being had. But though nothing could ever compare to Scully's eventual departure, something special was lost in October 2004. A special man, and a special concept.

87 International Goodwill

On the first day of November in 1956, before the start of an exhibition game in Hiroshima, Japan, the visiting Dodgers joined in the commemoration of a plaque at the entrance of the city's baseball stadium. "We dedicate this visit in memory of those baseball fans

Akihiro "Ike" Ikuhara served as assistant to Dodgers president Peter O'Malley and was actively involved in the Dodgers' numerous international, amateur, and professional baseball exchanges. Ikuhara was posthumously inducted into the Japan Baseball Hall of Fame in 2002. Photo courtesy of www.walteromalley.com.

Campo Las Palmas

The Dodgers' relationship with the Dominican Republic dates back to 1948, when the team held spring training there. Numerous players, such as Manny Mota and Pedro Guerrero, later emigrated from the 18,000-square mile country, separated from South America by the Caribbean Sea.

In 1986, after team vice president Ralph Avila purchased 50 acres of land for the Dodgers in the small town of Guerra (east of the capital Santo Domingo) at Peter O'Malley's urging, the Dodgers began construction on Campo Las Palmas, which would open the following year and become one of the top baseball training facilities in the world, featuring multiple baseball fields, batting cages, weight training areas and on-campus dining and housing. As an international baseball academy, it was a pioneer.

Though baseball instruction is obviously a main part of the agenda, players at Campo Las Palmas are classroom students five days a week, studying academic subjects including English as well as how to prepare for cultural situations they might face in the United States. Much of the food they eat is grown on the idyllic property itself. It's not exactly freeway close to Los Angeles, but in many ways, a trip to check out Campo Las Palmas would be an unforgettable experience for a Dodgers fan.

Dodgers manager Leo Durocher and Dodgers president Branch Rickey don oversized hats at Hotel Jaragua in the Dominican Republic during spring training activities in Cuidad Trujillo, D.R. in 1948. Photo by Barney Stein.

and others who died by atomic action on Aug. 6, 1945," it read. "May their souls rest in peace and with God's help and man's resolution peace will prevail forever, amen."

Days earlier on the Dodgers' Japanese voyage, 19-year-old Waseda University student Akihiro Ikuhara had seen the team when they passed through Tokyo. "Gil Hodges, Roy Campanella, Duke Snider—those were awfully big names," he would tell Dwight Chapin of the *Los Angeles Times*. "I couldn't believe I was seeing them."

Ten years later, in the fall of 1966, when the Dodgers returned to Japan for their second team trip, Ikuhara, known as "Ike," was in their employ. Coach of the Asia University baseball team beginning at age 24, Ikuhara had cajoled leading Japanese sportswriter Sotaro Suzuki a couple years earlier into writing Walter O'Malley about the possibility of Ike going to the U.S. In the spring of 1965, Ikuhara found himself in Dodgertown, bereft of any knowledge of English but filled with interest in American baseball. He carved out a place for himself, and at the end of spring training, was invited to join the Dodgers' minor league team in Spokane.

Ike started in the clubhouse but quickly moved up to the front office—after all, that's often the way in the minors, where it's all hands on deck. He worked closely alongside Peter O'Malley, who was Spokane's general manager at the time. After traveling back to Japan with the Dodgers, Ikuhara stayed with O'Malley, who was moving to Dodger Stadium as vice-president of operations, and served in almost every imaginable capacity: scouting, accounting, ticketing, minor league operations, concessions, and public relations. He served as a commentator for Fuji Television's broadcasts of the World Series from 1981–1986.

In the late '80s and early '90s, Ike traveled to Korea, Taiwan, Russia, and Nicaragua on Dodgers goodwill missions. That last phrase can be taken literally. The Dodgers have certainly profited from their relationships with nations on every continent. Their actions paved the way for players like Hideo Nomo, Chan Ho Park, and Hong-Chih Kuo to represent their countries in Major League Baseball. The team's facilities in countries around the globe, particularly in Latin America, created an alternate farm system for young talent that directly fed the Dodgers' success. Dodger Stadium hosted baseball's modern-day entry into the Olympics, as a demonstration sport in 1984. And the team has certainly been known to sell a cap or two overseas with the "LA" insignia embossed in front.

All that being said, many different people outside the borders of the United States have testified to the personal delight and emotional rewards they shared with so many members of the Dodgers family (most notably the O'Malleys and Tommy Lasorda) throughout the decades, rewards that continued in 2008 with the Dodgers' trip to China. At some point, baseball does stop being a commercial or competitive enterprise and becomes...a meeting place, an international haven that encourages real friendship in an age that might seem too cynical for such possibilities. Goodwill, for sure.

Oh, and lots of people around the world just like the game.

Akihiro "Ike" Ikuhara died of cancer in 1992, having spent the final 25 years of his life living in Southern California and working for the Dodgers. Posthumously, he was inducted into the Japan Baseball Hall of Fame.

"No matter where I live or what I do, I want to work for the Dodgers," he told Chapin in 1969. "The main people I have to thank are Mr. Suzuki and the O'Malleys. And as far as the O'Malleys go, I just can never repay them, except to do what I can in whatever way I can for the team."

88 Go to a Minor League Game

If you're invested in the Dodgers, check out the futures market. Attending any minor league game can be great fun, but finding one that features Dodgers farmhands helps get you an early seat on the "I saw him when" bandwagon.

The locations change over time, but the Dodgers began 2009 with affiliates in seven cities:

1. Albuquerque (AAA)
2. Chattanooga (AA)
3. Inland Empire in San Bernadino (High-A)
4. Great Lakes in Midland, Michigan (Low-A)
5. Ogden (Rookie)
6. Arizona League Dodgers (Rookie)
7. Santo Domingo in the Dominican Republic (Rookie)

That puts the Dodgers in a wide variety of longitudes and latitudes, so with any luck you're in striking distance of one of these locations, all of which are intimate enough for you to get a close look at the ballplayers from the cheap seats and maybe even a casual chat if you can catch them before the game. Amateur scouts among you can suss out the kind of work pitchers and hitters need in order to make the leap to Dodger Stadium.

Just imagine if you had seen Jackie Robinson testing the waters in Montreal, or Mike Piazza slamming homers in Vero Beach. Those would be incredible memories to cherish. But you know what? Even seeing a shortstop destined to get only the briefest of careers in the bigs—or a pitcher who will never even set foot on a major league mound, but is fulfilling his destiny in an outpost far from the spotlight—those are moments to remember, too.

89 Free Baseball

Radio reporter: "Good morning."

Tommy Lasorda: "What's so...good about it?"

The 21st-inning stretch is nothing new for the Dodgers. On the first of May in 1920, Brooklyn played in the longest game in major league history, a 26-inning contest that ended in darkness with the score tied, 1–1. The Robins' Leon Cadore and Boston Brave righty Joe Oeschger each threw complete games. As Glenn Stout notes in *The Dodgers*, Cadore allowed two hits over the final 13 innings, while Oeschger finished the final nine innings one walk away from perfection. "It seems reasonable that each man broke the 300(-pitch) barrier.... Even more remarkably, each man would pitch again within the week and finish the season without apparent arm trouble, although Uncle Robbie would later complain that Cadore was nothing more than a 'six-inning pitcher,' and later both men would admit to never being quite the same." Brooklyn then played 13 and 19 innings in its next two games—Burleigh Grimes and Sherry Smith each pitching complete games themselves. All losses.

Six decades later, the Dodgers found the treadmill again. Their struggles actually began on June 1, 1989, with the opening of a four-game series in Houston, when Astros starter Jim Deshaies no-hit the Dodgers for 7⅔ innings on his way to a 7–2 victory. The next night, Houston's Mike Scott shut out Fernando Valenzuela and Los Angeles, 1–0. The lone run scored following an infield grounder that Valenzuela tried in vain to scoop with his glove to Eddie Murray at first base. If it had worked, Valenzuela told Jerry Crowe of the *Los Angeles Times*, "we'd probably still be playing."

Be careful what you wish for. On June 3, the Dodgers led 4–1 going into the bottom of the sixth inning, when three consecutive and excruciating two-out walks, followed by two singles, tied the game. And tied it remained until almost eternity, the innings peeling away without any team scoring. Dodgers centerfielder John Shelby came within one at-bat of a major league record by going 0 for 10. Orel Hershiser, the last remaining Dodgers pitcher that manager Tommy Lasorda could use (short of waking the next day's starter, Tim Belcher, from his hotel-room slumber), entered the game in the 14th and threw seven shutout innings of relief before finally reaching his limit.

Jeff Hamilton, who had played third base for 20 innings, sidled over to pitch for the first time since high school. First baseman Eddie Murray moved over to third base for the first time in more than 11 years, and Valenzuela, who had thrown 114 pitches in his loss the night before, stepped in to play the role of slugging first baseman. Lasorda would later tell Crowe that he had no illusions about his remaining lineup. "It felt to me that we were conceding the game," he said.

Remarkably, Hamilton pitched a one-two-three 21st inning, striking out Billy Hatcher looking while being clocked as high as 91 miles per hour. But after the Dodgers went out in order in the top of the 22nd, Hamilton gave up a leadoff single to Bill Doran. After Doran went to second base on a groundout, Hamilton walked Terry Puhl intentionally—then got Ken Caminiti swinging for the second out.

With Rafael Ramirez as the only remaining hurdle to a 23rd inning, Hamilton quickly got ahead 0–2. He had thrown 20 of his 29 pitches for strikes.

"He was hitting the black," Hershiser later said. "He wasn't just throwing the ball down the middle. He was throwing the ball on the outside corner with movement.

"He just made one bad pitch."

It was the 635th pitch of the game. Ramirez lined a shot over first base. Valenzuela, the athlete in roly-poly disguise, jumped

Suspended Animation

Lest it be forgotten, the Dodgers also tried to burn the midnight oil one time in Chicago—but that was back when Wrigley Field had no midnight oil to burn. On August 16, 1982, the Dodgers and Cubs played 17 innings of a 1–1 tie before umpires suspended the game due to darkness. It resumed the following day with the Dodgers winning 2–1 in 21 innings.

"The guys who had already been in the game were cheering the other guys on," Rick Monday told Mark Heisler of the *Los Angeles Times*. "Someone made the observation that it was like a Pony League game. We were going, 'Hey batter, batter, batter!' all the way to 'Pitcher's got a rubber arm!' Yeah, we were a little nuts."

So was the Dodgers defense. Fernando Valenzuela logged time in the outfield after Ron Cey's ejection in the 20th inning left the team one player short. But in the top of the 21st, Steve Sax scored on a sacrifice fly that saw umpire Eric Gregg raise his arm to call out before switching to the safe sign midway through. Bob Welch entered the game in the bottom of the 21st as, of all things, a defensive replacement for Valenzuela, and Jerry Reuss finished his fourth inning of shutout ball to win in relief—just before throwing five innings in the regularly scheduled game, a 7–4 Dodgers victory, to grab that decision as well.

up, but the ball tipped off his glove and went into right field. Doran rounded third. Rightfielder Mike Davis charged the ball and threw home. Mike Scioscia, who had held on to the ball in home-plate collisions to prevent Houston from scoring the winning run in the eleventh and fifteenth innings, caught this one as well, but it wasn't in time.

"He had Ramirez 0–2 and he could have thrown three balls there and I guarantee you (Ramirez) would swing at one," Hershiser said. "But he threw him a fastball on the outside part of the plate and he got a hit.... But who's going to second-guess a third baseman?"

The Dodgers trudged back to their hotel rooms, only to have to return to the Astrodome hours later for Sunday's day game. As if determined to put the previous night's misery behind them, they scored five runs in the first, capped by a grand slam by Scioscia, who had caught the final 16⅓ innings the night before. But after building the lead to 6–0, Belcher allowed a grand slam in a five-run fifth, Jay Howell allowed a game-tying homer in the ninth and the game went into extras again. Scott, two days after beating Valenzuela as a starter, pitched the top of the thirteenth in relief and then drove in the winning run in the bottom of the inning with a sacrifice fly.

Fifty-three innings in four games, and the Dodgers lost all four—the last three by one run. And even that wasn't all. The next day called for a doubleheader at Atlanta that ended at 1:44 AM, giving the Dodgers 71 innings in five days, including 53 innings of baseball in their last 54 hours. Fortunately for them, the Dodgers swept the twinbill, with 21-year-old callup Ramon Martinez throwing a shutout in the first game.

Fewer than three months later, on August 23, the Dodgers were at it again. Another 22-inning game (kicked off by seven shutout innings by Hershiser as a starter), this one was scoreless until the very end, with the Dodgers poised to set a record by knocking 19 hits without a run before Rick Dempsey hit a leadoff homer off Dennis Martinez. Dempsey then threw out Rex Hudler trying to steal in the bottom of the 22nd to end it.

Not to be forgotten were the feats of broadcasting that accompanied these long affairs. With Don Drysdale unavailable because of laryngitis, Vin Scully called 10 innings in Chicago for NBC on the afternoon of June 3, arrived in Houston as the national anthem was being played and broadcast 22 innings that night, and then returned for Sunday's game, making it 45 innings in 29 hours. And in the August game, with both Scully and Drysdale absent, Ross Porter called all 22 innings by himself.

90 Luck of the Draw

The dream comes true in '68. The dream about the future. You scout the high schools and colleges, driving up and down and through the country, scrounging for ballplayers like a hobo scratching change off the sidewalk. And then, one year—a year so rare that people would still talk about it decades later—there's cash everywhere you look.

You get Davey Lopes. Steve Garvey. Ron Cey. Bill Buckner. Joe Ferguson, who would later be traded for Reggie Smith. Bobby Valentine and Geoff Zahn, who would be flipped for Cy Young Award candidates Andy Messersmith and Burt Hooton. It's a collective haul that has never been topped. Pennies from heaven.

That this is considered the pinnacle of major league drafting shows just how much of a dart-toss the process is. The Dodgers selected 101 players in 1968 over the four phases that used to constitute baseball's amateur drafting process. Fourteen never reached the major leagues, even for a cup of coffee. Only the eight mentioned above earned more than the right just to say they had made The Show. And during their major league careers, the Dodgers won four NL pennants and a single World Series. That's success.

Los Angeles found other gems through the draft in subsequent years, but never the single-year bounty that 1968 provided. To illustrate, the Dodgers only signed five noteworthy players—and just one starting position player—in their next *eight* years of drafting: Lee Lacy (1969), Rick Rhoden (1971), Rick Sutcliffe (1974), Dave Stewart (1975), and Mike Scioscia (1976).

The 1977–79 drafts reversed the recession, with Bob Welch, Mickey Hatcher, Tom Niedenfuer, Mike Marshall, Steve Sax, Brian Holton, Steve Howe, and Orel Hershiser all playing for future

Dodgers World Series champs. But then the bear market really hit. You could take the best of the entire draft roster from 1980 all the way through 2001 and you wouldn't have a group much better than the '68ers by themselves. Yes, Mike Piazza, the courtesy 62nd-round pick in 1988, is the best Dodgers draft pick ever. Eric Karros (1988) holds the Los Angeles career home run record. Todd Hollandsworth (1991) was a Rookie of the Year. But after that, though Franklin Stubbs (1982), Jeff Hamilton (1982), Dave Hansen (1986), Darren Dreifort (1992), Paul Lo Duca (1992), and Alex Cora (1996) all had their moments, the 20-plus years of picks start to look rather enfeebled. (It would have helped if the Dodgers could have stopped donating young talent from that era to other teams in poor trades: Sid Fernandez, John Franco, John Wetteland, Paul Konerko, and Ted Lilly all had fruitful careers after leaving the Dodgers.) The pit was the Dodgers' 1992 draft, which yielded four major league at-bats (by fourth-round pick Keith Johnson, all with the Angels).

During those barren years, international signings of amateur players like Ramon Martinez and Hideo Nomo kept the Dodgers afloat. But with the arrival of scouting director Logan White in 2002 came a revival of the Dodgers draft fortunes. The 2002–2004 crop of James Loney, Jonathan Broxton, Russell Martin, Eric Stults, Chad Billingsley, Matt Kemp, Scott Elbert, Andy LaRoche (included in the trade for Manny Ramirez), Blake DeWitt, and Cory Wade was the team's best since the late '70s, giving the Dodgers the option not to be compelled to chase every free agent around (not that they fully exercised that option). Clayton Kershaw, the seventh overall pick in 2006 and the team's highest since Dreifort, kindled hopes of being a new Sandy Koufax.

No draft can generate a champion by itself. The draft gives you a chance to find good ballplayers to develop. Developing good ballplayers gives you a chance to win the whole magilla. It's not the entire solution, but it's part of it.

91 Resist the Suite

Let's not lie to each other. The luxury suites at Dodger Stadium...they're luxurious. Not in a five-star-hotel way, but a fair piece ahead of a seat in the stands. Food and drink at your fingertips, climate controlled, TVs a-plenty to keep tabs on other games or provide programming to occupy the less enthusiastic baseball fans in your group, even a couch for you or your kids to sack out on. And the dessert cart that rolls by before the end of the game—that actually might be five-star quality. (There's an éclair for you or your kids to snack out on.)

If you want to hang out with a bunch of friends or colleagues—one and the same if you're lucky enough—a suite at Dodger Stadium is a pretty nifty way to do it. And never let it be said that a baseball game had a greater purpose than providing a great setting to hang out.

But suites and the sport really aren't a good fit for each other. There's barely any way to enjoy both at once. To take advantage of what the suite offers is to stuff the ballgame itself into a hall closet, like the toys you hastily hid away when your mom wanted your room clean. The best vantage point for a game is in a fairly conventional seat on the balcony and requires turning your back on the suite, to the extent that it becomes just a glorified hot dog stand. And to delight in the suite's accoutrements, to wallow in them, necessarily pulls you away from the game. It just doesn't quite work.

You can stuff your face until the cows and pigs and all the other farm animals come home, you can kick back with your best pals, but a luxury suite is not a good place to watch a baseball game. If,

Diggin' the Dugout Club

The Dugout Club, which *USA Today* said in 2008 offered the best premium seat in baseball, might be another story. "Fastballs hiss and pop. Players argue with umpires. Teammates hug. All right in front of you," wrote the paper's David Leon Moore. "Being a member of the Dugout Club is sort like having a all-expenses-paid suite at the Ritz-Carlton." With seats closer to home plate than the pitcher's mound and waiters attending to your needs, this is serious all-purpose baseball pampering.

by some stroke of upside-down fate, a suite invite happens to be your only ticket to a game, then by all means grab it. If it's 100 degrees out in the bleachers, then don't think twice about cooling off in the suite's sweet shade. Otherwise, get yourself into the regular seats in the stands. It's not about being holier-than-thou. The stands are just better.

92 Free (But Expensive) Agency

Baseball's free agency era began with a Dodger. In December 1975, arbitrator Peter Seitz ruled that righthander Andy Messersmith, along with retired Montreal pitcher Dave McNally, no longer had contracts with their teams and could negotiate with any franchise. The decision overturned the major leagues' interpretation of the reserve clause, which the executives felt entitled teams to renew player contracts in perpetuity, even though the language of the contracts stated that teams could do this for one year after the player's last contract had been signed. Ironically, as players union leader

Marvin Miller wrote in *A Whole Different Ball Game*, Messersmith's contract dispute with the Dodgers originated with his desire for a no-trade clause that would help ensure he remained a Dodger. Instead, baseball's owners and commissioner Bowie Kuhn bet that Seitz would uphold the sport's longtime precedent that gave them the power to refuse Messersmith's request—and lost. In March 1976, the owners ended their attempts to appeal the decision, and there was no looking back. Free agency was here to stay.

Though fans had to bid farewell to some of their favorites sooner than they might have liked, everyone ultimately came to agree that the unilateral binding of players to teams, like puppies to their masters, was unfair, and subsequent history quickly proved that free agency would not ruin the game as baseball's leadership had insisted. However, it's no understatement to say that the Dodgers themselves have had mixed success in the free agent market, at best.

The Dodgers' first foray into free agency was belated and modest. They signed relief pitcher Terry Forster in November 1977, and he turned in a 1.93 ERA (182 ERA+) the following year, before faltering in subsequent seasons. Two years later, the Dodgers grew bolder—and the results scarred them for nearly a decade. Coming off their first losing season in 11 years, Los Angeles shelled out for free agent pitchers Dave Goltz and Don Stanhouse in November 1979. Goltz had been one of the AL's most consistent pitchers of the 1970s, posting six consecutive above-average seasons, while Stanhouse had been a top reliever for the AL champion Baltimore Orioles. Had either retained their value, the Dodgers no doubt would have taken the NL West instead of losing in a playoff game, but both pitchers were almost hopelessly ineffective.

Between then and the end of the 1987 season, as mainstays like Steve Garvey played out their contracts, the Dodgers' most noteworthy free agent signing was outfielder Terry Whitfield, plucked

Holdout

For all the decades before the reserve clause was overturned, baseball players had no leverage in salary negotiations except an appeal for goodwill—and the option of quitting the major leagues entirely. In January 1966, after a season in which they had combined for a 2.39 ERA and 592 strikeouts over 644 innings, Sandy Koufax and Don Drysdale took their chances, banding together in the hopes of obtaining contracts guaranteeing each roughly $166,000 a year for the next three seasons. The Dodgers, not surprisingly, offered Drysdale and Koufax only slight raises from their 1965 salaries of $80,000 and $85,000, according to Steve Delsohn in *True Blue*.

So the Dodgers reported to Vero Beach for spring training without their two star pitchers (along with Maury Wills, who was holding out separately for a raise from $60,000 to $100,000). Wills settled, but the pitchers took their holdout to the end of spring training. While public sentiment worked against them in those pre-free agent days, Koufax and Drysdale lined up enough outside work—from book deals to movie appearances—to keep from having to cave in completely. On March 30, two weeks before the regular season began, they agreed to one-year contracts: approximately $125,000 for Koufax and $110,000 for Drysdale. It wasn't a complete success, but the 50 percent raises, give or take, were enough for people to take note.

Drysdale ended up having the worst season of his career to that point (a 3.42 ERA doesn't sound bad, but his ERA+ was 96), while Koufax was extraordinary: 1.73 ERA (190 ERA+). Of course, Koufax pitched through such tremendous pain that he ended up retiring at the end of the season. However, one still wonders what might have happened had the Dodgers been willing to give him three years. Would they have lost money on the deal, or would they have kept the superhuman lefty for longer?

to be a platoon partner of Candy Maldonado in 1984 (and ending up another disappointment). But in the winter of 1987–88, the first since Fred Claire replaced Al Campanis as general manager, the Dodgers dove back in.

Had Claire's efforts stopped with Mike Davis, coming off three straight solid seasons with Oakland, and Don Sutton, who returned to his original team at age 43, the Dodgers might have considered handing their finances over to a blind trust. In '88, Davis had two home runs in the regular season and an EQA of .208, while Sutton ended his Hall of Fame career in August after a struggle with a sprained elbow. But Claire made one other signing of note: a player who, like Messersmith, had been freed by an arbitrator, in response to owners colluding to drive down salaries earlier in the decade. His name was Kirk Gibson, and he came to have a bit of a memorable year, thanks in part to a single, well-timed walk by Davis in the ninth inning of Game 1 of the World Series.

Given the team's postseason record since 1988, it's no surprise that no Dodgers free agent signing since Gibson has met with that kind of success, but there have still been some nifty ones. Brett Butler had EQAs near or above .300, sparking the Dodgers of the early 1990s. In February 1995, the Dodgers again broke new ground by acquiring the rights to Hideo Nomo, who came over from Japan to become NL Rookie of the Year with a 150 ERA+ and 236 strikeouts in 191⅓ innings.

Under new general manager Kevin Malone in 1998, the Dodgers got downright brash, signing pitcher Kevin Brown to a record seven-year, $105 million deal. Though Brown was sometimes injured, he was also sometimes spectacular, and in the end doesn't even belong in the conversation for the most disastrous free agent signing of the post-Gibson era. In the 2008 season, the Dodgers found themselves paying an injured Jason Schmidt $12 million in the middle year of his three-year, $47 million contract, at the same time they were laying out the first $14.1 million of Andruw Jones' two-year, $36.2 million sinkhole. Despite entering the year with 368 career home runs at the age of 30, Jones completely lost his batting eye, struggling to a 34 OPS+, the worst by a Dodger in 97 years.

The only playoff game won by a Dodger between 1989 and 2007 was a shutout in 2004 against St. Louis by Jose Lima, who had signed that year for relative pennies—and then departed just in time to collapse in 2005. Sometimes in the free agent era, the big splash has paid off for the Dodgers, but just as often it seems, a little has gone a long way.

93 The McCourt Ownership

By 2003, News Corp. had achieved its goals of using the Dodgers as a lynchpin for its burgeoning Fox sports cable network, but the franchise, as business writer James Bates noted in the *Los Angeles Times,* was gushing red ink. "The Dodgers' $54.5-million deficit (in 2001) was baseball's biggest. The team hasn't turned a profit in nearly a decade. Despite higher attendance, a lower payroll and an improved on-field performance, the Dodgers this year expect to lose $41 million. That's $13 every time a fan walks through a turnstyle." Though this was all relative for a megacorporation with revenue in the billions, the forecast wasn't any more appealing for Fox than it was for the O'Malley family five years earlier. Dodgers fans, who hadn't seen a playoff appearance since the O'Malley days and knew full well that it wasn't a top priority, had had about all they could stand from News Corp. head Rupert Murdoch's ownership as well.

That year, Boston real estate magnate Frank McCourt reached an agreement to buy the team in October, but the initial excitement over a return to family ownership dissipated even before the papers were signed. General manager Dan Evans had lined up the free-agent acquisition of a Hall of Fame candidate in his prime, right fielder Vladimir Guerrero, but baseball commissioner Bud Selig discouraged the signing out of fear that the Dodgers would spend too excessively, and McCourt appeased him. Speculation also abounded that McCourt was only interested in buying the Dodgers as a means to owning the valuable Chavez Ravine territory, which he could then develop and/or flip for profit—that was how he made his money, after all. The terms of McCourt's highly leveraged purchase, which showed that he had borrowed about as much as the purchase price, did little to diminish the speculation.

As it turned out, McCourt and his wife, team president Jamie McCourt, committed to Dodger Stadium, instituting a series of annual renovations (some good, some less so, but all well-intended) that essentially guaranteed baseball would be played there for years and years to come. Further, McCourt repeatedly voiced a commitment to bringing a World Series title back to Los Angeles, asserting that the city deserved no less. He raised the player payroll to unprecedented levels.

But the McCourt era has been even more tumultuous than the News Corp./Fox age. McCourt cleaned house almost like an obsessive housekeeper. Within McCourt's first month, Evans was told he had to interview for his own job (not surprisingly, he was replaced), setting the tone for widespread turnover within the organization. Employees up and down the ladder were fired, even as the team reached the NL playoffs in McCourt's first year. In 2005, when the Dodgers fell to their worst season in 13 years, McCourt approved second-year GM Paul DePodesta's firing of manager Jim Tracy and then, in the same month, the firing of DePodesta himself. Ned Colletti became the team's third general manager in three years. Grady Little replaced Jim Tracy as manager—and two years later, Little was replaced in clumsy "Did he quit? Was he fired?" fashion by Joe Torre.

Boston real estate magnate Frank McCourt and his wife, team president Jamie McCourt (pictured with Tommy Lasorda), proved they were committed to Dodger Stadium by instituting a series of annual renovations that guarantees baseball would be played there for years to come.

McCourt's relationship with the fans has been similarly chaotic, because in the name of building up the product and, to his credit, making the Dodgers profitable again, no owner in Dodgers history has ever been so aggressive in increasing the cost of attending a Dodgers game, on all fronts: tickets, parking, food, and concessions.

The fast-forged pattern of desire and impatience has left many a Dodgers fan bewildered over what to expect from the McCourts. In the end, they might well find the right formula for success or they might not, though it certainly won't be for lack of trying. Their goals are clear, but whether they have the proper temperament and lucidity to achieve them remains to be seen.

94 Boom Goes Boomer

In grainy, staccato footage from the 1970s, one can still picture a yellow-capped meteor, Dave Parker of the Pirates, roaring toward the sturdy but vulnerable form of Dodgers catcher Steve Yeager at home plate.

Yeager had shown signs of hitting promise at the start of the decade, but had settled into a role as a stalwart defensive catcher by the prime of his career, a supporting player to the renowned Garvey-Lopes-Cey-Russell infield and Reggie Smith-Dusty Baker bejeweled outfield. Yeager rarely drew attention for his performance, except on those occasions when people questioned whether his meager offensive contributions were sufficient.

And then, every so often, someone or something would all but put Yeager's life in jeopardy, and the appreciation would register.

The most bizarre incident came in September 1976. During a Monday Night Baseball telecast, waiting in the on-deck circle as Bill Russell fouled off a pitch, Yeager suddenly crumpled to the ground. It wasn't the ball that hit him; it was a shard from Russell's broken bat, piercing an area near his esophagus. News reports placed his life in jeopardy.

Yeager recovered after emergency surgery and was back on the field inside of three weeks, even though the Dodgers had been eliminated from the pennant chase by then. In fact, to allow him to hasten his return, Yeager and trainer Bill Buhler devised a plastic flap that would hang from his catcher's mask, to protect Yeager's throat from a foul tip at what was now his most vulnerable spot. (Buhler later patented the device, which became standard issue for major league catchers.)

The Throw

The ultimate defensive play in Brooklyn Dodgers history—the biggest play in the biggest situation—was probably Sandy Amoros' catch in Game 7 of the 1955 World Series. It was the antidote to Mickey Owen and a litany of Dodgers failings, an indispensable moment preserving the Dodgers' first World Series victory.

The Los Angeles version also takes place in the outfield during a World Series, but the context only detracts from it. It came during a game the Dodgers lost, in a Series they lost. Nevertheless, if you saw it, you could never forget it, and if you didn't see it, you need to know about it.

In the opening game of the '74 World Series, Oakland led the Dodgers, 2–1, in the top of the eighth inning. Bert Campaneris singled, and Billy North sacrificed him to second base. A throwing error by Ron Cey on a Sal Bando grounder allowed Campaneris to score, with Bando going all the way around to third. Reggie Jackson, the next batter, hit a fly ball to center fielder Jimmy Wynn.

Except Wynn didn't catch it. Seemingly out of nowhere, Joe Ferguson, a catcher who sometimes dabbled in right field, rumbled in front of Wynn, intercepted the ball like a defensive back, took one step and fired a laser beam to home plate. A stunned Bando was tagged out at home by catcher Steve Yeager, thrilling the crowd and inspiring the Dodgers to a rousing victory.

Well, maybe not that last part. Some good deeds go unrewarded.

Though he was able to put the unique trauma of that incident behind him, Yeager (who decades later would barely escape with his life following a car accident) continued to suffer a series of body blows at home plate, hardly limited to but ably represented by the Parker collision on August 24, 1977. The footage shows the 6', 190-pound Yeager in a crouch—the throw was in plenty of time—bracing for the punishment from the 6'5", 230-pound Pirate All-Star. Upon impact, Yeager seems to explode like a landmine, then raises an arm with ball in hand like Wile E. Coyote after a canyon fall, before collapsing.

"I don't remember holding the ball up. I can remember only spots and stars," Yeager told Ross Newhan of the *Los Angeles Times* in a barely audible voice while laid out on the trainer's table after the game, surrounded by ice. "That guy...he should be a tight end for the Rams."

"I've seen a lot of catchers hit hard, hit violently," Smith added, "but never before have I seen one hit by a runaway truck."

Though Mike Scioscia inherited the role as premier plate-blocker in the 1980s, there's no denying who set the standard for the Dodgers as the last line of defense.

95 May Your Son Be a Magnificently Named Son

In the Dodgers Name Hall of Fame, in the team's Sobriquet Field of Dreams, pitcher Sweetbreads Bailey can taste victory, while Welcome Gaston ingratiates himself in the bullpen alongside Pembroke Finlayson, with Pea Ridge Day eyeing the soup and Kaiser Wilhelm itching to take the throne. The designations are dizzying for Dazzy Vance, who is starting tomorrow's lidlifter, followed by Van Lingle Mungo in the nightcap (Preacher Roe or Schoolboy Rowe are ready to step in if either needs saving), and Brickyard Kennedy is throwing on Sunday. Good ol' Still Bill Hill might get the call to bulk up the staff if he can be disturbed, otherwise Cletus Elwood "Boots" Poffenberger will arrive, hopefully not made for walking. And all the while, the fans clamor for Cannonball Crane, clap for Chappie McFarland, and wonder about Mysterious Walker.

Wee Willie Keeler leads off and roams the outfield of course, flanked by Hunkey Hines and Overton Tremper. Jigger Statz replaces Rip Repulski as the fourth outfielder; Lemmie Miller is the speedster off the bench. Spider Jorgensen spins a web at the hot corner, edging out sentimental choices Frenchy Bordagaray and Cookie Lavagetto, and Snooks Dowd surprises at second, thrilled to turn a double play with monumental legend Pee Wee Reese. Oyster Burns backs up Pee Wee but can also play the other infield spots in a pinch, if Possum Whitted isn't the sleeper choice to step in and neither Bunny Fabrique nor Rabbit Maranville have the hops. (Simmy Murch gets left in the lurch, Stuffy Stewart gets you-know-what, and Packy Rogers—born Stanley Frank Hazinski—packs it in.)

Who else will go behind the dish besides stout Farmer Steelman? Deacon McGuire raises his authoritative hand, volunteering for part of the doubleheader.

The rest bide their time—you know the story, "Wait 'til next year!" Lady Baldwin, Win Ballou, and Buzz Boyle. Buster Burrell, Kid Carsey, and Moose Clabaugh. Watty Clark, Hub Collins, and Fats Dantonio. Wheezer Dell, Cozy Dolan, and Ox Eckhardt. Tex Erwin, Hod Ford, and Greek George. Lafayette Henion, Newt Kimball, Hub Knolls, and Candy LaChance. All feel they've earned their spot, but they'll wait their turn—alphabetically if need be, so dedicated are they to the cause.

Meanwhile, the beat writers keep their eye on the head-to-head battles: Patsy and Wild Bill Donovan, Broadway and Germany Smith, Jumbo and Rowdy Elliott, the Babes Dahlgren, Herman and Phelps, the Rubes Bressler, Marquard and Walker, and the closest call of all, Red Downey and Red Downs.

The Moniker Miracles have added few members in recent years, though Matt "The Bison" Kemp, "Weird Game" James Loney, "Golden God" Russell Martin, and His Royal Thighness Chad Billingsley are at least making it interesting. Vin Scully let the world know that Delwyn Young goes by Pee Wee at home, and there's nothing wrong with a proper homage.

But a challenge awaits the expectant Dodgers fan, a task at hand for the expanding clan. Have a child, take him to the park, play catch and set up the tee, drill him in the fundamentals and let him enjoy himself. But by all means, don't forget to give him a name we can savor, a name to stand the test of time. Give us another Boom-Boom Beck or Bones Ely, or at least another Buck Marrow. The Dodgers have a wondrous history in the scorecard as well as on the field—help them return to the glory days.

96 Evil

An unlimited buffet at a baseball game? Are the Dodgers trying to kill us? Or just make a killing? After all, the All You Can Eat Pavilion that took over Dodger Stadium's right-field bleachers in 2007 is no cheap ticket. You have to pack it away to make it worth your while, and then double-down if you're covering for any kids you bring. (Your best bet to out-eat your dollars is to get enough people together to book a group discount.)

On the other hand, even if you eat it on the financial side compared to what you would spend on regular left-field bleacher tickets and food, you'll walk away with few regrets of the non-gastrointestinal kind. It doesn't matter if the bleachers are filled to capacity; there's almost no waiting for Dodger Dogs, nachos, peanuts, popcorn, and soft drinks. Inhale, fill yourself up, exhale, fill yourself up again. You have an ample window, beginning 90 minutes before game time and ending two hours after the first pitch, to engage engorgement.

Marching and Chowder Society

It was a classic Vin-ism—before pointing out some player's accomplishment, he would preface by saying, "For members of the So-and-So Marching and Chowder Society ..." This has prompted many a Dodgers fan to wonder, "Where the heck did this phrase come from?"

This might not be the last word on the subject, but it's a pretty good yarn even so.

In 1868, according to New England historian John McDonald, a man named Eldridge T. Hooper founded the Cherryfield Chowder Society in Cherryfield, Maine. "The organization's early meetings were in the old Cherryfield Town Hall," McDonald wrote, "where Hooper and a small band of charter members would show up with their fixins and make themselves a huge pan of chowder and then serve it."

As time passed, the society grew in both size and ambition. Unsatisfied by a multitude of different chowder recipes, the members decided to add marching to their raison d'etre.

Though in their wildest dreams, the good people of Cherryfield could not have imagined their group being adapted to honor Jose Vizcaino's 10th sacrifice bunt of the year, it's unlikely they would have objected as long as the steaming bowls of chowder kept coming.

This being Dodger Stadium, the view from the behind the outfield and your food tray is resplendent. You might risk coherence if you find yourself in an unshaded seat on a blistering summer's day, but in cooler temperatures the pavilion could hardly be more pleasant. The upside of beer being excluded from the All You Can Eat price is that it helps keep a well-fed lid on most potential rowdies (if that means you, my apologies). And yet everyone's jovial, at least when the team is winning.

Culinary caveats: The pavilion's Dodger Dogs aren't grilled, there's no other main course, and the somewhat meager dessert options, like the beer, cost extra. And watch out for low-hanging

The All You Can Eat Pavilion that took over Dodger Stadium's right-field bleachers in 2007 is no cheap ticket, but the upside is that there's almost no waiting for Dodger Dogs.

beams supporting the bleachers—one misstep by anyone over six feet tall could brain you like a fastball to the ol' melon. Safer suppering can be found in the baseline box clubs, where the Dodgers have extended the all-you-can-eat option beyond the hoi polloi—but that's a whole other kettle of hot dogs.

97 Join the Online Dodgers Community

Weirdness alert: Some of my best friends are strangers I've never met in person.

The Internet isn't a night at the ballpark. It isn't the local bar, for worse though sometimes for better. It isn't the sidelines at a Saturday morning softball game, or a Sunday afternoon barbecue with friends, or a chat on the phone with your kid or your old man.

The online world is broader than all that and more antiseptic and yes, sometimes angrier, requiring responsibility. It's also, if you navigate it with the same kind of simple common sense that tells you not to swing at a ball in the dirt, one of the most rewarding ways to expand your enjoyment of the Dodgers: right in your home (or on your cellphone and someday no doubt implanted inside your brain.) In order to have the best and most current understanding of Dodgers news and analysis, the Internet should be your bench coach.

It's not just the speed and frequency of updates that online sources provide. There's the access to a wide range of information at sites like the popular Dodgers.com (the Dodgers were early adopters of the Internet, and the depth of their offerings reflects that) and the richly historical Walteromalley.com. There's also the exposure to a wide range of ideas about every aspect of the Dodgers, and you can pick and choose what's important to you. Blogs and message boards, like everything else in life, come in a whole spectrum of quality and style, and it's easy enough to find one that suits you like a good teammate and enriches you like that magic batting tip you've always needed. You don't need to abandon any Old School principles or sentimental values to expand your Dodgers allegiance online. At the same time, there's nothing to be gained from assuming you know everything there is to know about the team—or that the other guy or gal does. Fans have so much to contribute to the Dodgers universe, and you should be a part of that.

Truly, there are friends to be made in the online Dodgers world. You may never see them in person, but they are real. And like those chums you meet at the ballpark, they can take you on a conversation that goes beyond baseball into some really funny or meaningful places. By all means, use all the caution you need when socializing on the Internet and especially if taking those relationships offline. But the days of living life as a Dodgers fan offline—those are horse-and-buggy days.

98 World Series Drought, Part 1

The afterglow of a magical 1988 hung over Los Angeles into the year's winter months, but baseball fans are notoriously greedy. It was the team's first World Series title in seven years, only the second since 1965. How long would it be before they did it again?

Longer than anyone would have imagined. Long enough that before another title came, the franchise that wrote the book *The Dodger Way to Play Baseball* would lose its way.

Despite bolstering the infield before the 1989 season by trading for future Hall of Fame first baseman Eddie Murray and finding Yankee stalwart Willie Randolph to replace Steve Sax at second base, the Dodgers couldn't withstand the continued health problems of '88 NL MVP Kirk Gibson (who was limited to 292 plate appearances) and fell to 77–83 and fourth place in the NL West. To illustrate the difference between the two seasons, 1988 Cy Young award winner Orel Hershiser posted the same ERA+ of 148, but his won-lost record fell from 23–8 to 15–15.

Hershiser's workload caught up with him the following April, as he went out with the shoulder injury that would sideline him for

KKKKKKKKKKKKKKKKKK

Sandy Koufax shares the Dodgers record for strikeouts in a game—and not just with himself. Koufax fanned 18 San Francisco Giants on August 31, 1959 (Koufax needing to score the winning run in the bottom of the ninth on a Wally Moon home run) and then matched that performance by striking out 18 Cubs at Wrigley Field on April 24, 1962.

But on June 4, 1990, a lanky 22-year-old righthander from the Dominican Republic matched Koufax. Ramon Martinez shut out the Atlanta Braves on three hits while recording 18 of the first 24 outs by strikeout. Martinez couldn't break the team record, but in the post-Koufax era, the Dodgers have not seen a more dominating performance by one of their pitchers.

Martinez threw more than 120 pitches over a dozen times in 1990 and even crossed 130 and 140 pitches multiple times. His career peaked that season, offering at least one cautionary tale for those who suggest pitch counts—especially at a young age—don't mean anything.

nearly 14 months. And at the outset of the 1990s, the series of poor Dodgers drafts caught up with Los Angeles, which increasingly had to look outside the organization (Kal Daniels, Hubie Brooks, Juan Samuel) for help. Mike Scioscia was the only homegrown Dodger in 1990 to get more than 160 plate appearances. Murray led the major leagues in batting average, and 22-year-old Ramon Martinez added a 2.92 ERA (126 ERA+) and 223 strikeouts in 234⅓ innings, but the Dodgers settled for 86 wins and a second-place finish in the NL West.

In a bid to put themselves over the top, the Dodgers again sought external help, bringing Darryl Strawberry back to his hometown before the 1991 season, along with centerfielder Brett Butler. Both made huge contributions—Strawberry had 28 homers and an EQA of .312—but the Dodgers were sandbagged by the rise of the

Atlanta Braves from last to first in the division. Though they resided in first place from May 14 until the final weekend of the season, the Dodgers lost two games at San Francisco while the Braves were defeating Houston to deprive Los Angeles of a postseason spot.

From 93 wins in 1991 came the 99-loss disaster of 1992, in which the offense, young and old, faltered in almost every way imaginable. But despite the well-chronicled, crushing trade of Pedro Martinez for Delino DeShields after that season, an infusion of young talent raised hopes of an imminent return to the World Series. Eric Karros, Mike Piazza, Raul Mondesi, Hideo Nomo, and Todd Hollandsworth gave the Dodgers five Rookies of the Year in a row. The Dodgers were swept in first-round playoff series in both 1995 and 1996, and Tommy Lasorda had given away to Bill Russell as manager after suffering a heart attack, but expectations were raised. Surely they were on the right track.

However, the 1997 Dodgers never recovered from a devastating 12-inning loss at Candlestick Park that knocked them out of first place with eight games remaining in the season. The following year, after the O'Malley family sold the team, the trade of Mike Piazza and Todd Zeile for Gary Sheffield, Bobby Bonilla, Charles Johnson, longtime Dodgers nemesis Jim Eisenreich, and a minor leaguer left the Dodgers in neutral: 19–21 before the trade, 64–58 after. Though the Dodgers had the third-best record in the majors (behind Atlanta and Oakland) from 1988–1997 and had gone to the playoffs more years than any team except the Braves, 10 years had passed since the team's last victory in a postseason game. Impatience dominated the Dodgers' next decade.

99 World Series Drought, Part 2

It gets worse before it gets better.

Shortly after the Dodgers' new owners went over Fred Claire's head to make the Mike Piazza trade in 1998, they replaced Claire with Tommy Lasorda as Dodgers general manager on an interim basis. (At the same time, Glenn Hoffman replaced Bill Russell as manager). Then, during the offseason, the search for a permanent general manager led to Montreal Expos GM Kevin Malone. As shocking as the Piazza trade had been, nothing shattered the dignity with which the Dodgers had been known to operate more than Malone proclaiming upon his arrival, "There's a new sheriff in town." Malone brought in Davey Johnson, who had averaged 93 victories a year (during full seasons) in more than a decade of managing, to replace Hoffman before the 1999 season, but still Malone's team went 77–85.

Though the Dodgers won 85 games or more from 2000 through 2003, they could not break the grass ceiling, extending their streak without a postseason appearance to seven years. Dave Wallace and then Dan Evans replaced Malone, who put the finishing touches on his embattled tenure by getting in a fight with a Padres fan in San Diego. Jim Tracy, a Dodgers coach under Johnson, replaced his boss. But the team that once seemed a player away from winning the World Series became the team that was a man short of simply making the playoffs.

Amid 15 years of frustration and another ownership change, the Dodgers added even more tempest to their teapot by hiring Paul DePodesta as Dodgers' general manager shortly before the

2004 season. DePodesta was a bright, softspoken, 32-year-old ex-Harvard football player who had worked his way up baseball's front office ladder, but he arrived in a climate filled with suspicion. Not only was the Dodgers' new owner, Frank McCourt, struggling to convince Los Angeles that his intentions with the franchise were sincere, but DePodesta was a prominent figure in a recent book by Michael Lewis, *Moneyball*, that had caused a major stir in baseball circles by ostensibly promoting statistical analysis at the expense of scouting. At least, that's what the book was about if you talked to people like broadcaster Joe Morgan, the Hall of Famer who critiqued the book without even reading it. In truth, the main point of *Moneyball* was to suggest that it was a fine idea to look for undervalued players—a contention it would be difficult for anyone to find fault with—and that more accurate stats were one way to help achieve that, because traditional baseball methods could sometimes be deceiving. But so defensive was the baseball establishment, including the media, about its Old School values, that anyone associated with *Moneyball* was considered a rebel with a nefarious cause. DePodesta was on the defensive, particularly with widely read *Los Angeles Times* columnists Bill Plaschke and T.J. Simers, from the moment he arrived.

The Dodgers won the 2004 NL West title, thanks in no small part to DePodesta acquisitions like Jeff Weaver, Milton Bradley, and Steve Finley that built upon the core Evans left behind, but along the way, DePodesta gambled what little peace he had in Los Angeles on the very thing everyone had seemed to want—a deal that would push the Dodgers past mere division-title status into the World Series elite. He sent starting catcher Paul Lo Duca, a beloved figure in Los Angeles for his late-blooming rise to success, to Florida with outfielder Juan Encarnacion and reliever Guillermo Mota, in exchange for starting pitcher Brad Penny, first baseman Hee Seop Choi, and minor leaguer Bill Murphy.

Foul, Foul, Foul, Foul, Foul, Foul, Foul, Foul, Foul, Foul, Foul, Foul, Foul, Foul

On the night of May 12, 2004, they started counting foul balls on the Dodger Stadium left-field scoreboard, because shortstop Alex Cora couldn't stop hitting them. Batting in the bottom of the seventh against Chicago Cubs righty Matt Clement with a runner on and the Dodgers leading by a slim 2–0 margin, Cora took the first three pitches, two for balls.

He then proceeded to foul off the next 14 Clement pitches, sending the Dodger Stadium crowd into increasingly rapturous states of bliss, even though no tangible baseball play had transpired. Cheers of "Let's go, Cora" rose from all parts of the ballpark.

It was nothing, and it was epic.

"It was tough," Cora told The Associated Press. "He was throwing good pitches. When they put it on the scoreboard, that put me under a little bit of pressure. I had to stand back and regroup."

Finally, on the 18th pitch of the at-bat …a fair ball, a long fly ball, going to right field...going...gone!

It wasn't October, it wasn't the ninth inning, but it was beyond unbelievable—unscripted genius.

The outcry was like nothing Los Angeles had seen since the Piazza trade six years earlier. Most Dodgers fans were livid, and only a minority saw the trade for what it was—the exchange of three players entering the downside of their careers for three on the upside. When the 26-year-old Penny, a potential difference maker in a playoff series, was injured in his second start with the Dodgers, DePodesta was pushed further out onto the plank. The only thing that could save him in Los Angeles was victory.

For a while, that's what he got, as the Dodgers (behind Jose Lima) finally managed to win a playoff game for the first time since Orel Hershiser was shutting down the A's. But the following season, a series of injuries crippled a team that DePodesta was trying to rebuild on the fly (in a manner that manager Tracy was openly rebelling against), and the Dodgers lost 91 games, their most since 1992. Adding further anger to the angst was a clubhouse clash between Bradley and Jeff Kent that led DePodesta's antagonists to conclude he had lost control of the organization. In October 2005, barely 20 months into his tenure, DePodesta was fired, accused (ironically, if you like) of undervaluing the things that matter, things like chemistry and character, even though Dodgers teams before and after him had notoriously struggled in those very areas.

The PR-conscious McCourt replaced DePodesta with a former PR man, San Francisco assistant general manager Ned Colletti, who brought a more traditional approach to general management. In the 2006–2007 seasons, Colletti was handed an increased payroll and the best set of Dodgers prospects in three decades, but the pattern remained the same as it ever was: quick playoff exits alternating with an absence from the playoffs entirely. Witness to a sequence of trades and signings fraught with bad luck and/or foresight (Jason Schmidt, Juan Pierre, and Esteban Loaiza form just part of the list), numerous Dodgers fans continued tearing their hair out through their team caps.

From the 1903 debut of the World Series through 1946, the Dodgers won NL pennants all of three times, none of them followed by a victory in the Fall Classic. In the next 42 seasons, they won 15 NL pennants and six World Series. The team has known famine as well as feast, and with the expansion of major league baseball to 30 teams, it shouldn't surprise anyone that the race up Everest only became harsher. Yet when you consider that a team with the Dodgers' resources won fewer postseason games from 1989–2007 than all but Montreal/Washington, Texas, Tampa Bay, Kansas City, and Milwaukee, it also shouldn't surprise anyone that Dodgers fans entered 2008 very much on edge.

100 Read old first-hand stories

Let me tell you something that I've learned while writing this book—that is, something I already knew that was reawakened in me. You can read all the Dodgers books in the world; you can collect the DVDs and search for highlights on the Internet. But there hasn't been a time in researching an event in Dodgers history that I haven't experienced sheer pleasure in reading a first-hand account in the archives of a newspaper or magazine.

It's not just being taken back to the moment in time, though that's a big part of it. It's that invariably, little jewels emerge that otherwise are lost to history and memory. On-point descriptions of the circumstances leading up to the big moment. Great postgame quotes, fleshing out what happened, that went straight into journalist tape recorders or notebooks. And then there's the pleasure of seeing—more often than you might think—a journalist rise to the occasion and spin a phrase that makes you feel more a part of the action than a film or video clip ever could.

The Los Angeles Public Library offers free computer access to the *Los Angeles Times* historical archives—with some years available on your home computer at lapl.org—and microfilm of other local papers, such as the *Los Angeles Herald-Examiner* and the *Los Angeles Daily News* in its various incarnations. You can even check out the *San Diego Union*, which covered the Dodgers regularly for the franchise's first 10 years. From your home, you can also find juicy pieces from the archives of *Sports Illustrated* (si.com/vault) and *The Sporting News* (paperofrecord.com).

For newspaper stories covering the Brooklyn days, the *New York Times* website offers free access to articles that are at least 75 years old, with *NYT* subscribers able to get any article in the archives for free, up to 100 per month. And for the old, old stuff, the Brooklyn Public Library (BrooklynPublicLibrary.org/eagle) is a gateway to the archives of the *Brooklyn Eagle* from the late 1800s up to 1902—with possibly more to come in the future. Other magazines, such as *The New Yorker*, have tremendous stories in their archives worth pursuing and perusing, though these can come at a cost.

The point is, a book like this is only the beginning. If there's something to know about the Dodgers, it's never been easier or more rewarding to go exploring.

Acknowledgments

I came to this project knowing a lot about the Dodgers, but I knew I also had a lot more to learn. Without a safety net, I wouldn't have dreamed of writing a book about even one thing Dodgers fans should know and do. Alex Belth, Eric Enders, and Bob Timmermann, each exceptional baseball writers in their own right, reviewed drafts and offered important corrections and suggestions, not to mention much valued encouragement. The same is true of longtime Dodgers insiders Brent Shyer and Robert Schweppe. Also, if ever I had a question, Fred Claire, Carl Erskine, Mark Langill, Rich Lederer, and Josh Rawitch did not hesitate to help me. You could say the same for Peter O'Malley, who of course deserves special mention for honoring me with his foreword.

The readers of *Dodger Thoughts* form, quite simply, an unsurpassed online community. They're funny, thoughtful, insightful —occasionally brazen, but basically a dream group of people. Many members had suggestions for this book and particularly valuable support for me. Though I can't mention them all, there are a few I would like to single out: David Ambrose, Molly Knight, Martin Leadman, Craig Minami, Stan Opdyke, Sam Sokol, and Eric Stephen.

On a research level, Baseball-Reference.com and *Baseball Prospectus* were invaluable, as were the various archives I consulted. There are a lot of people behind the scenes involved in maintaining those resources, and I just want them to know I appreciate them.

For making it possible for me to write this book in the first place, I'd like to thank Michael Emmerich and Adam Motin of Triumph Books, as well as Jeff Gerecke and Ed Stackler, who provided critical guidance. But also, I'd like to acknowledge those who helped raise my profile as a baseball writer through the years, from my many friends and colleagues when I started out as a professional sportswriter, to those who had faith in me years later when I resumed writing about baseball as an amateur. In particular, I want to express appreciation to Jacob Luft, who hired me to write for SportsIllustrated.com.

Finally, to my friends, who not only have been supportive of my efforts but understanding about how bad I've been at staying touch with them while being hunkered down in front of the computer—thanks. And my family—I'd mention you in every chapter if I could. Of course, I'd tell the kids 100 things to know and do if I thought they'd listen.

Thanks, finally, to the Dodgers, who provided me with the thrills and memories to inspire this book. If I couldn't be Vin Scully, writing about the Dodgers is the next best thing.

Bibliography

Books

Allen, Maury. *Brooklyn Remembered: The 1955 Days of the Dodgers.* Champaign: Sports Publishing 2005.

Barber, Red. *1947—When All Hell Broke Loose in Baseball.* Garden City: Doubleday 1982.

Barber, Red and Robert Creamer. *Rhubarb in the Catbird Seat.* Lincoln: Bison (University of Nebraska) 1997.

Claire, Fred. *My 30 Years in Dodger Blue.* Champaign: Sports Publishing 2004.

D'Agostino, Dennis and Bonnie Crosby. *Through a Blue Lens: The Brooklyn Dodgers Photographs of Barney Stein.* Chicago: Triumph 2007.

Delsohn, Steve. *True Blue.* New York: HarperCollins 2001.

Edwards, Bob. *Fridays with Red: A Radio Friendship.* New York: Simon & Schuster 1993.

Eig, Jonathan. *Opening Day: The Story of Jackie Robinson's First Season.* New York: Simon & Schuster 2007.

Erskine, Carl. *Tales from the Dodger Dugout.* Champaign: Sports Publishing 2001.

Fussman, Cal. *After Jackie: Pride, Prejudice and Baseball's Forgotten Heroes.* New York: ESPN Books 2007.

Garvey, Steve (Ken Gurnick, Candace Garvey contributors). *My Bat Boy Days: Lessons I Learned from the Boys of Summer.* New York: Scribner 2008.

Gleeman, Aaron and Dave Studenmund (ed.). *The Hardball Times Baseball Annual 2006.* Skokie: ACTA 2005.

Green, Daniel S. *The Perfect Pitch: The Biography of Roger Owens, The Famous Peanut Man at Dodger Stadium.* Tamarac: Lumina 2003

Honig, Donald. *The Man in the Dugout.* Chicago: Follett 1977.

James, Bill. *The Bill James Baseball Abstract 1982*. New York: Ballantine 1982.

James, Bill. *The Bill James Baseball Abstract 1985*. New York: Ballantine 1985.

James, Bill. *The Bill James Baseball Abstract 1986*. New York: Ballantine 1982.

James, Bill. *The Bill James Guide to Baseball Managers.* New York: Scribner 1997.

James, Bill. *The Bill James Historical Baseball Abstract.* New York: Villard 1985.

James, Bill. *The New Bill James Historical Baseball Abstract.* New York: The Free Press 2001.

James, Bill. *The Politics of Glory.* New York: Macmillan 1994.

James, Bill and Rob Neyer. *The Neyer/James Guide to Pitchers.* New York: Simon and Schuster 2004.

Jareck, Joe, Josh Rawitch et al. Los Angeles Dodgers, *2008 Los Angeles Dodgers Information Guide*. Los Angeles: Los Angeles Dodgers 2008.

Jordan, Pat. *The Best Sports Writing of Pat Jordan.* New York: Persea 2008.

Kahn, Roger. *The Boys of Summer.* New York: Harper & Row 1971.

Langill, Mark. *Dodger Stadium.* Charleston: Arcadia 2004.

Langill, Mark. *Dodgertown*. Charleston: Arcadia 2004.

Langill, Mark. *Los Angeles Dodgers.* Charleston: Arcadia 2004.

Lasorda, Tommy and David Fisher, *The Artful Dodger.* New York: Arbor 1985.

Leavy, Jane. *Sandy Koufax: A Lefty's Legacy.* New York: HarperCollins 2002.

Lowenfish, Lee. *Branch Rickey: Baseball's Ferocious Gentleman.* Lincoln: University of Nebraska 2007.

Maraniss, David. *Clemente: The Passion and Grace of Baseball's Last Hero.* New York: Simon & Schuster 2006.

McNeil, William. *The Dodgers Encyclopedia.* Sports Publishing LLC, 2000.

Miller, Marvin. *A Whole Different Ball Game.* New York: Birch Lane 1991.

Neyer, Rob. *Rob Neyer's Big Book of Baseball Legends.* New York: Fireside 2008.

Rampersad, Arnold. *Jackie Robinson: A Biography.* New York: Knopf 1997.

Ruck, Rob. *The Tropic of Baseball: Baseball in the Dominican Republic.* Lincoln: Bison (University of Nebraska) 1999.

Shapiro, Michael. *The Last Good Season: Brooklyn, the Dodgers, and Their Final Pennant Race Together.* New York: Doubleday 2003.

Stout, Glenn and Richard A. Johnson. *The Dodgers.* New York: Houghton Mifflin 2004.

Sullivan, Neil J. *The Dodgers Move West.* New York: Oxford 1987.

Tygiel, Jules. *Past Time: Baseball as History.* New York: Oxford 2001.

Wolpin, Stewart. *Bums No More! The Championship Season of the 1955 Brooklyn Dodgers.* New York: St. Martin 1995.

Articles, Documents and Presentations

City of Los Angeles Resolution, May 11, 1959.

Smith, Dave. "Play By Play Analysis of the 1951 National League Pennant Race," 2001.

Timmermann, Bob. "Presentation on the History of Dodger Stadium," 2008.

Magazines

Irish America Magazine (Kelly Candaele)

Sport (Al Stump)

Sports Illustrated (Tom C. Brody, Robert W. Creamer, Gerald Holland, Larry Keith, Herman Weiskopf)

News Services

The Associated Press (Ted Smith)

United Press International (Jim Cour, Milton Richman)

Newspapers

Beverly Hills Times (Bill Stout)

Brooklyn Eagle

Los Angeles Daily News (Matt McHale)

Los Angeles Examiner (Vincent X. Flaherty)

Los Angeles Mirror-News

Los Angeles Times (James Bates, Dwight Chapin, Jerry Crowe, Mike DiGiovanna, Ron Fimrite, Frank Finch, Earl Gutskey, Dan Hafner, John Hall, Randy Harvey, Mark Heisler, Maryann Hudson, Mike Littwin, Sam McManis, Jim Murray, Ross Newhan, Bob Oates, Scott Ostler, Charles Perry, Bill Plaschke, Jeff Prugh, Howard Rosenberg, Keith Thursby, Sid Ziff, Paul Zimmermann)

New York Daily News (Dick Young)

New York Times (Dave Anderson, Murray Chass, Rick Lyman)

San Francisco Chronicle (Ray Ratto)

The Saturday Evening Post (W.C. Heinz)

The Sporting News (Harold C. Burr, Tommy Holmes, Joe Vila)

Village Voice (Gersh Kuntzman)

Wall Street Journal (Joshua Prager)

Websites

19th Century Baseball (19cbaseball.com)

Ballparks (ballparks.com)

The Baseball Biography Project (Society of American Baseball Research: Eric Enders, John Saccoman, Stew Thornley: bioproj.sabr.org)

Baseball-Reference.com

Baseball Analysts (Rich Lederer: baseballanalysts.com)
BaseballLibrary.com
Baseball Prospectus (baseballprospectus.com)
Blue Heaven (Ernest Reyes: dodgersblueheaven.blogspot.com)
Dodger Thoughts (Jon Weisman: dodgerthoughts.com)
The Futility Infielder (Jay Jaffe: futilityinfielder.com)
The Griddle (Bob Timmermann: griddle.baseballtoaster.com)
The Hardball Times (Chris Jaffe and Steve Treder: thehardball-times.com)
Los Angeles Dodger Adult Baseball Camp (ladabc.com)
National Baseball Hall of Fame and Museum (baseballhalloffame.org)
The Official Site of the Los Angeles Dodgers (Dodgers.com)
The Official Site of Major League Baseball (Ben Platt: mlb.com)
National High Five Day (nationalhighfiveday.com)
Bob Baker's Newsthinking (newsthinking.com)
Philippe's (philippes.com)
The Sport Gallery (thesportgallery.com)
Walter O'Malley: The Official Website (Robert Schweppe, Brent Shyer: walteromalley.com)
WGUC 90.9 FM (wguc.org)

TV/DVD/Film

Mechner, Jordan (writer and director). *Chavez Ravine: A Los Angeles Story*. PBS/JAM Flicks 2004.
Los Angeles Dodgers Vintage World Series Films. Major League Baseball Productions 2006.
Johnson, Dorothy M. (short story), James Warner Bellah and Willis Goldbeck (screenplay). *The Man Who Shot Liberty Valence*. Paramount 1962.
Nightline (ABC)